HOW TO DIRECT A PLAY

BRAHAM MURRAY

HOW TO DIRECT A PLAY

A MASTERCLASS IN COMEDY TRAGEDY FARCE SHAKESPEARE NEW PLAYS OPERA MUSICALS

OBERON BOOKS
LONDON

WWW.OBERONBOOKS.COM

First published in 2011 by Oberon Books Ltd
521 Caledonian Road, London N7 9RH
Tel: +44 (0) 20 7607 3637 / Fax: +44 (0) 20 7607 3629
e-mail: info@oberonbooks.com
www.oberonbooks.com

Cover design by James Illman

Printed and bound by CPI Group (UK) Ltd, Croydon, CR0 4YY.

CONTENTS

WARNING

I have just re-read what I have written and some of it seems so very complicated, so I thought I would warn you not to be worried about it. A director either has the knack or he doesn't, and a great deal of what he does he does instinctively; besides that, a lot of what he does involves common sense. I actually found writing this book made me more aware of myself as a director in a good way. It made it easier to marry the passion with the desire to be as helpful as possible to the actors and the creative team. So, I hope, it will be with you. Each of you will automatically know parts of what I am pointing to in the book but there will be parts you aren't aware of, and that is where I hope to be helpful. In other words, don't be intimidated but enjoy, enjoy!

For brevity and simplicity, I have used 'he', but the reader should assume that 'she' applies equally throughout.

MOST OF THEM GET IN YOUR WAY

The extraordinary thing about directors, those gods of the theatre, is that they didn't exist before the middle of the nineteenth century. There have, of course, always been actors, mostly there have been writers, but not directors. We know that in the Greek Theatre there was a chorus master, but no director. In the Elizabethan Theatre there is no record of a director. Presumably there was a stage manager to make sure the actors came to rehearsal. Probably the playwright was primary in the rehearsal process and maybe the theatre manager, but there was no director.

The director seems to have appeared in Europe as the theatre became more complex technically in matters of sound, lighting and scenery. Someone was required to coordinate these new disciplines, and to do that job he had to have an overall view of the play that was being performed. Until then, the actor or actor-manager had been at the centre of the production but now an outside eye was required to create a satisfying artistic whole.

So the director came into being, making up the job as he went along, gradually becoming more and more powerful and ultimately getting to be the visionary, psychologist, academic, interpreter, leader and megalomaniac that he is today. He chooses the play, casts it, supervises the designers (scenery, costumes, lights, sound, movement, music, fights) and is the final authority for the actors.

If this is extraordinary so is the fact that, until recently, he has been totally untrained and has probably never seen another director at work. Yet he is working with highly trained artists and technicians who he controls.

There is no one way of directing. In fact there are as many ways of

directing as there are directors. What then is the point of writing a book about directing? People who say that someone can be taught how to direct are talking nonsense. Directors can be helped to develop their talent: that is what I am trying to do in this book. Although there is no one way of directing, there is a pattern to all productions no matter who the director is. The same problems and challenges occur for everyone. One thing this book can do is to alert would-be directors to these problems and challenges and suggest ways of dealing with them. These will happen whether you have two weeks, five weeks or six months to rehearse, whether you are directing classics, new plays, comedies, tragedies or musicals, whether you are in-the-round, on the proscenium, in a studio space or a thousand-seater auditorium. These different circumstances have their own special challenges (which I will also deal with) but they also share a good deal in common.

This book is written by me so it will naturally reflect what I have learnt in nearly forty-five years as a professional director. It will only be about text-based theatre. I will give what I think is good advice but that advice is meant to be a stimulus not a prescription. I will take you through all the stages of pre-production, rehearsals and after the show has opened. You will have to decide if it is good advice but, if you reject it, at least it will stimulate you to find your own path. You may well start off your career as someone's assistant and watching other directors direct can be very helpful but beware. My first professional job was as an assistant to a very successful director, John Dexter at the Royal Court. He was an authoritarian who cowed his cast into submission. He was also brilliant at the physical staging of the production, the *mise en place*. He was the only director I had seen at work and I thought that was how you did it, you shouted and bullied until you got what you wanted. I imitated him in my first productions until I realized it wasn't what fitted in with my personality and didn't get wonderful performances from the actors. I have written this book not as a manual, which I believe to be impossible.

Recently a distinguished actor who was working with me for the first time said, 'You make it so easy.' When I asked him wasn't that the point,

he replied, 'Most of them get in your way!' Since finally it is the actor who stands in front of the audience and is the primary transmitter of the text, one of the main themes of this book is not only how to prevent the onerous job of directing, which requires stamina, concentration and a twenty-five hour day, from getting in the way but also about giving the actor the confidence to use his creative faculties to their fullest extent.

The first time I directed (at school), I was so frightened of the actors not carrying out my vision that I erected a booth at the side of the stage and shouted instructions to the actors during the performance like a football manager. It has been a long journey finding what I believe to be the right balance a director needs to fulfil what is finally a collective act of creation.

WHY DO YOU DO IT?

The director is an artist, not a creative artist like a writer but an artist nonetheless, an interpretive one, like a conductor. Like any artist, much of his process will remain unconscious to himself, but the more he can understand what it is that drives him, the better he is able to manage the process because, unlike a writer or composer, most of his work is done in collaboration.

As I will repeatedly say, 'fear' is bound to be part of his process and he may not even be aware of that! His greatest fear stems from the fact that he does not know where his creativity comes from and his creativity is the most important part of his armoury. There is no real answer to this conundrum. Creativity cannot be taught but it can be stimulated by the people you are collaborating with and by surrendering to the text. Faced with a difficult scene I will hand over the problem to my unconscious before I go to sleep and often I will wake up with the creative solution in my head. Finally you have to trust yourself which is the most difficult thing to do. If you do you sometimes find miraculously that the right thoughts and words come out of you, things that have never consciously occurred to you. I have often felt that someone else is directing the play.

One night in March 1959 set me in motion as a director when I was sixteen years old. It took me years to understand the significance of it but it is worth recounting.

I had wanted to be an actor since about the age of ten. Why? Simply because I enjoyed doing it. As I grew older, I saw more and more theatre and acted more and more at school till I became the leading actor there. Then on that night in March, I sat in the gods at the Lyric Hammersmith and watched Michael Elliott's extraordinary production of Ibsen's *Brand* with Patrick McGoohan in the title role. I identified with Brand totally.

13

I admired his single-mindedness, his passion, his lack of compromise, his vision of perfection and his raw will. Never mind that years later I realized that he was a defective and dangerous fanatic, on that night I felt that I was not alone in the world, that there were people who understood me and that I too should be strong and fight for what I believed in. A night in the theatre changed me, in the hackneyed phrase: 'It made a difference.' From that moment, I too wanted to make a difference.

The obvious way, since I was an actor, was to play Brand at school which I did disastrously. There was a moment in rehearsal when we were doing the scene when the villagers turn on Brand and stone him so that he flees up into the mountains to meet his death. The villagers weren't that good, and I knew that I could not play the scene unless they were galvanized. I took over rehearsals and propelled them into action. At that moment I was filled with an adrenalin-fuelled ecstasy. I was in charge, I was in control, people were doing what I wanted them to do and I was expressing myself totally. I felt fulfilled.

There in those two experiences of *Brand* were what I believe to be the two main strands of what has driven me as a director. I wanted to make a difference and I wanted to experience that ecstasy. The one desire is relatively selfless, the other ego bound but you can't realize the first without the second.

I believe that theatre is of immense importance. People gather as a community at a theatrical performance in communion with the actors. From the three-week festivals in Greece, when from dawn to dusk each day the whole population, from rulers to slaves, watched four plays, through the Elizabethan experience, to the riots caused by Ibsen or O'Casey, great theatre has stirred the profoundest emotions in the audience. At its best it sends them out of the theatre enlightened and strengthened. To present a piece of theatre is to wield immense power over an audience, a power that can be used for the positive or the negative. For the purposes of this book, I am assuming that a director wants to 'make a difference' for the good.

But the director is a megalomaniac. Does that sound extreme? He chooses the play, he casts the actors, he chooses the creative team and he is the final arbiter of everything they do. By the time the actors arrive, the show is designed and fundamentally they have to fit in with the decisions that have been taken. Throughout the rehearsals he is the sole judge of what the cast do. That is megalomania. It is important he recognizes it because then he can mitigate the negative results it can bring about, most importantly by opening himself to change and improvement. He has a vision and he wants everyone to realize it. This can lead directors to ridiculous excesses. There's even one director who never let the actors say their lines out loud until the dress rehearsal. She gave them their moves and as they moved spoke their lines out loud for them. On the other hand, there was one very successful director who would sit in rehearsal reading a newspaper until the actors, in panic, began to rehearse themselves, then he would leap into action and use what they were doing and pull everything together at the eleventh hour. In between lays every shade of manipulation from bullying to flattery out of sheer terror.

You are projecting the production out of yourself. The more conscious you are of this, the more you can guard against its negative effects. As a young director I did a production of *A Midsummer's Night Dream* which became a howl of despair at love, rather than the sublime comedy that Shakespeare wrote. Why? Because I was desperately unhappy at the break-up of my marriage. I believed I was doing a brilliant and original production. Actually I was destroying the play, but if anyone had told me that while I was rehearsing, I would not have believed them.

The more you understand these drives, the more you can guard against them. The more you know yourself, the richer director you become. There are directors who direct a script merely to show themselves off, to see what they can do with it. These directors can be very successful but only for a while. They use up the well of their inspiration without replenishing it. Their productions are destructive acts; they are done despite the author.

What I have written may seem like generalities but they are actually the starting point. I now intend to take you through the steps of putting on a production to illustrate practically what I mean. They are lessons learned after forty-five years of making mistakes!

PRE-REHEARSAL

<u>Choosing a play</u>

This is more complicated than it sounds. I've been lucky in that I've been an Artistic Director since 1965, so I've never in that time had to do a play I actively didn't want to do, but when you're starting out as a director, or going through an out-of-work patch, you will be offered plays that you had not thought of doing and you will be inclined to accept, whatever they are.

The best scenario is straightforward. You have a play you are desperate to do. You feel at one with the author. The play is about something you care for passionately; you may even have a vision of how to do it. Even here, beware! You should be sure that you can cast it. It's no good committing to do *King Lear* if you haven't got an actor to play it.

I did *Hamlet* because I met and worked with Robert Lindsay. You might want to do *Hamlet* in the abstract but unless you find an actor who is your Hamlet, the one that speaks with the voice you can hear in your head, and unless you are sure he is developed enough emotionally and technically, there is no point in doing it. I did *Othello* because I met Paterson Joseph, I did *Antony & Cleopatra* because I met Josette Bushell-Mingo. I wanted to do those plays but I knew that there were few actors who could bring off those parts the way I envisaged them.

Most plays don't work like that. Usually you know that you will be able to cast the plays you want to do because the leading roles are not so special and particular. It doesn't mean to say that the casting is not so important but just that there are the actors who can play the parts.

One step down is choosing a play because your company or another one needs to complete a season and asks you to come up with, say, a comedy. It is remarkable how few directors have a comedy as a first choice.

Further down the ladder is when you are offered a play you have no interest in, or even actively dislike, but you can't afford to turn down.

The complication is that you may be wrong about the play you want to do and equally wrong about the play you're not interested in.

I was wrong to do *A Midsummer's Night Dream* when I did because I was not in the right psychological state to direct it. Years later Tom Courtenay asked me to direct Molière's *The Miser*. I read it and had no interest in it at all. I did it because of my admiration for Tom. It was a huge success. I agreed to do *The Black Mikado* in the West End in 1975 because I was out of work and needed the money. I had no initial interest in it. It was a long-running hit and certainly one of the best shows I have ever done. I agreed to another musical, *Fire Angel*, based on *The Merchant of Venice*, because I was out of work and needed the money. It was a massive flop. I actively disliked the rock *Othello, Catch My Soul* but people still say it was one of the best musicals they have ever seen.

How do you deal with this mystery? Sitting round a table after several bottles of wine, the creative team of a musical I did, *Dr Heart*, asked what in life gave you the most intense pleasure. We all expected everyone to say 'sex'. Actually what each one said was the moment of creativity which seemed to come from somewhere else. For a director it is when you are in rehearsal and you suddenly find yourself saying something quite brilliant which you had never thought of before and that takes hold of the rehearsal room.

There are no rules about what plays are going to connect with your unconscious processes and release that creativity. Sometimes plays come and search you out, sometimes you find them. Sometimes a play you have never been attracted to seems to rewrite itself and become of pressing importance. For years I never wanted to do *Hamlet*. I thought it a silly play about a ditherer who dies through dithering. One day I picked it up again and found that Shakespeare had rewritten it into a thing of genius. The play hadn't changed of course. I had.

There is no easy way through this maze, but as you make your choices and have your successes and failures, you will begin to find your way

more surely. Certainly always try to do the plays you are passionate about. If you are wrong, if you are too close to the material to realize it properly, then you will learn. Making mistakes is inevitable, and crucial if you are to learn. When you dislike a play make sure it is not something in yourself that is censoring your reaction. It could be this is the very play you were meant to do.

Having thoroughly muddled you, I'm now going to assume that you've chosen your play and that it is a good choice and try and point you in the right direction during the pre-rehearsal process.

<u>Choosing the team</u>

The process of putting on a play is what makes theatre so extraordinarily wonderful. A group of people of different talents, all experts in their particular fields, coming together to create something much greater than any of them could do alone, and that includes the director. The forming of that group is critical. Harold Prince, the great director of musicals, said that the secret was not to have a group of stars but a real team who shared a sense of purpose and controlled their egos to work together towards a common end. He was talking about writers and composers but the same goes for the creative team of any production. If you're running a company it goes for the stage management, the workshop, the wardrobe, for any of the countless people without whom the production could not happen.

The most important relationship you have is with your designer. You will note that most directors have their favourite designer who they work with on a regular basis. A production is going to have to nourish the audience visually and it is the designer who will provide that nourishment. You need to find someone whose approach to theatre chimes with yours, someone who wants to express the centre of the play visually rather than using it as a pretext for displaying their own talent.

Each production demands a different way of working, even with the same designer. Sometimes you will know exactly how you want a production designed and your designer will be working to a strict brief;

sometimes even though you know and love the play, you haven't a clue how to express it externally, or your designer has an immediate reaction on reading it and that is what happens on stage. Sometimes both of you know that the process will be deeply collaborative and take some time to evolve into the final design. Most of my working life I have worked with two designers, Johanna Bryant and Simon Higlett. You gradually build up a trust and a shared language. Your designer is an artist, just as you are. Even when you think you know what you want, listen to them.

I decided to direct *The Tempest*. I chose Johanna Bryant to design it. Neither of us had a clue initially what it should look like. Every production of *The Tempest* is completely different from each other, for the island is a magic island. Step one was to discuss the play together as much as possible. One character sees the island as lush, the other as barren: what does that mean? What does Ariel look like? What does Caliban look like? The mysteries are endless. I talked about the play as being an inner journey so that the characters were different parts of Prospero's psyche and he goes to the island, a symbol of introversion, to come to terms with them. What did that mean? How on earth could we explain that?

Then one day Johanna had the solution. The floor and the walls were all mirror. The characters were reflected again and again. Miranda came from a cave whose entrance was a huge shell, an obvious feminine symbol, Caliban from behind a very male jutting out rock. I don't know where she dreamt this from but there it was; a wondrous solution. Everything else followed. It was easy to refine the detail together.

Go and see designers' work. Find the ones who seem to work in a style you like, meet them and find out if you really want to work with them on a deep level. Also remember that certain designers suit certain plays. The process is much like casting. If you're doing a musical you probably need something more flamboyant and extrovert than if you're doing Chekhov.

The lighting designer is the next important appointment. For some plays they are as important as the designer. Your designer probably has

someone they are used to working with and provided you get on with that person it's best to go with their choice.

I did a new play by Edna O'Brien called *Haunted*. It is the most difficult play I have ever had to have designed for the Royal Exchange because it was written for the proscenium and it absolutely requires a door, an actual door. *Haunted* is like *The Glass Menagerie*: a memory play. An old man looks back on his marriage and how he became infatuated with a young woman and as a result wrecked the lives of both women and, indeed, himself.

I knew immediately that I wanted the same designer, Simon Higlett, who had done *The Glass Menagerie* and Jo Town, the same lighting designer, not because I wanted them to do the same thing again but because I knew they would be sensitive to the requirements of the play and would automatically be able to make the lateral jump from the proscenium to the round. Indeed they did and, when it came, the solution was simple. If you had to have a door it had to be see-through, and it followed that the whole set was glass (perspex). This in turn led to exciting possibilities of projection both from above and below the stage floor. I had cast the team well!

In some plays the nourishment of the audience aurally is vital; that is the job of the sound designer. Beyond that there may be fight directors, vocal coaches, movement directors and so on and so on.

It's your job to find this team, to inspire them initially with your vision and release them to add to that vision with their own creative expertise. It is important to keep all of them in close contact with the evolving design. When the design is shown in its various stages, make sure they are there; they will interact and help each other. The closer they are, the easier it will be to make productions homogeneous.

Casting

Cast a play right and seventy-five percent at least of the job is done. Cast it wrong and the play will never work as it should.

The actor may have lost power to the director over the last one

hundred and fifty years, but they remain the most important person in the production. They are the one person you cannot do without. Even the writer is finally expendable; the actor can, and sometimes has, improvised a script. I am thinking particularly about *commedia dell'arte*.

At the birth of theatre, the actor was the High Priest performing and transmitting the mysteries of their religion to the congregation. That is still their role. The writer speaks directly through them to the audience. The truly great moments in the theatre happen through acting. You can have great sets, striking lighting, wonderful music etc but it is only when the actor reaches into the hearts of the audience and makes them as one that the theatre truly performs its function.

The problem of casting is that it is not enough to find the best actors you can, but the best actors for the parts. The greatest actor cannot play everything. The crudest example is beauty. If you are casting a part which is constantly referred to as being beautiful, you cannot cast an actress who cannot seem beautiful. Take it one step further. If you want your Ophelia to have spiritual purity it is no good casting an actress who is obviously sexually experienced. That purity cannot be acted; it has to be there for free. That does not mean that the actress needs to be actually pure. The great Jean Forbes-Robertson who played, amongst other roles, Mary Rose, was actually a rough-trade addict, famously sleeping with someone just before she went on stage. On stage she radiated a transcendent spiritual beauty. It was her quality for free. When Olivier and Gielgud, alternated the roles of Romeo and Mercutio, Olivier, the earthed sexy actor, was a great Romeo and a lousy Mercutio. Gielgud, the spiritual one, was an equally great Mercutio but couldn't make Romeo remotely believable.

Your job is to know your play backwards, identify the essence of each character and find the right good actor to play it. Sounds easy? Beware of how you can trip yourself up. There is a great danger in endowing an actor who you find sexually attractive with qualities he or she doesn't have, for obvious reasons. More complicated is the fact that the actor may embody what you fancy, but not what the audience does. The other

related complication is that there is almost always in a production a character that you identify with. This identification used to be for me entirely unconscious. It led to awful mistakes. One very good director I know was casting Romeo and having great difficulty. He asked me to come to his final auditions. I sat through actor after actor who just didn't seem right. Sometimes I couldn't even work out why the actor had been recalled at all. Suddenly an actor walked in who made the hairs on the back of my neck tingle. The director didn't want to cast him. I was stunned. Slowly I realized that this actor looked rather like him and he couldn't imagine himself as Romeo. It was a decision born out of his own sense of physical inferiority. I persuaded him to cast him. The actor was a huge success and is now something of a star.

As with choosing the right play, the more you know yourself the less likely you are to make a mistake.

Auditions

Some parts you cast with people you already know, either through working with them or having seen their work; the rest you cast through auditions.

If you've ever been with an actor the night before an audition you will know how nerve-wracking it is for them. They have probably been out of work for a while, or they desperately want the part they are auditioning for. Friends will send good luck cards, even presents, because, for many, just to get an audition for a good company is a breakthrough. They are going to put themselves on show to a perfect stranger who has complete power over them.

You want the actor to be at their best so you must do your best to put them at ease, to communicate your enthusiasm for the project and to make them feel special. It's up to you whether you want them to stand up and do a speech or whether you want them to read from the play with you or the casting director. Then you're in the minefield.

Some actors do very good auditions but then are stuck when in rehearsal, while some excellent actors are appalling auditioners. How do

you sense if an actor will be a good company member or a difficult prima donna? In a young actor, can you see beyond the particular philosophy their drama school has taught them, to what they really are?

What kind of actor are you really interested in? Different directors and companies are looking for different types of actor. One famous actor defined two categories: the 'head' actor and the 'heart' actor. The 'head' actor is the Olivier brand: technically brilliant, charismatic, with the ability to mesmerize and thrill an audience but, and this is crucial, never to move them. The 'heart' actor is the one who moves the audience to tears, who makes them share the character's emotions. If you are a 'heart' director, and I hope you are, beware being seduced by brilliance that you know will delight an audience, it may not help you realize your proper ambition.

By that I mean if you want to move your audience like a piece of music does, you have to have an actor who reaches into their hearts and, if necessary, disturbs them. This is a very special gift and many actors deliberately cultivate a more superficial style.

The right casting director is invaluable in this process. Just as with your creative team you need someone who understands and has sympathy with your approach. Although you may want to cast from people you know, your casting director will have a far greater knowledge of available actors, particularly the younger ones just out of, or coming out of, drama schools. A good casting director will make your casting richer.

My process is to chat to the actor first, let them talk about the highlights of their CV, make them feel I care, which I do. Then talk about the play, have them read or do a speech, give them direction and generally try to make them forget it's an audition, or if not forget it, at least enjoy it.

Before the recall day, when the best come back, I try to talk to them on the phone about their audition and what I would like them to work on. This can have spectacular results, especially with younger actors. Also I really like them to read with each other. Terribly important if you're casting lovers because the chemistry that is needed is elusive.

At the end of the audition, if you like the actor but don't think they are right for the part, you might even say so, or get the casting director to tell the agent. The feeling of rejection for an actor is terrible and it's difficult to explain that they are not being rejected as an actor but because they are not the right casting.

It is a nerve-wracking experience for both sides and my tips may not work for you, but develop your own, because you need them to be good, as much as they do.

<u>Working on the script</u>

You're designing the show, you're casting and of course you're working on the text. Everybody develops their own method of doing this. When I started and was directing up to ten productions a year, I winged most of them, particularly the comedies, except when I was faced with Shakespeare or the equivalent. Now I have my particular way which I will outline, while emphasizing again that you will find yours.

You ingest the play, make it part of your being, know it inside out, discover the author's technique, all the time becoming more and more aware of the clues they are giving you until you become clear as to what your task is to realize what they have written. If it's a period play, you research the period; discover the particular values of the time, and how they differ from today. You'll also have to make sure you understand the language and you might have to consider cuts for sense and to lose the dead wood that intervening centuries have made antipathetic to a modern audience.

You will, of course, make notes as ideas occur to you about character, interpretation, the rhythm and music of the piece and the visual ideas that you dream up. 'Dream up' – important because, once again, your unconscious mind will throw up ideas that seem like a free gift.

When I started directing I read with total fascination and admiration Stanislavski's books. He suggested a method of preparation based on 'objectives'. Anything a character says has a dynamic objective designed to achieve something in another character. If a character says 'Good

Morning', what are they trying to bring about? They maybe want to make someone feel welcomed, they maybe want to say, 'Keep your distance, I've got a hangover', they maybe want to frighten, to seduce and so on. Each objective creates a beat, and each beat ends and a new one begins when a character's objective changes. Scenes or Acts are divided in turn into movements which have an overriding objective that includes so many beats. Each Act has overriding objectives for each character and the entire play has a super-objective for each character. I'll give concrete examples later because it sounds forbiddingly technical. In fact, what it does is to force you into a deep examination of the play and it gives every moment of the play a dynamism.

I'm going to give you an example of what I mean by talking you through the first scene of Tennessee Williams's *The Glass Menagerie*. I'm using this play because I've just directed it at the Royal Exchange with Brenda Blethyn, so it is particularly fresh in my mind.

SCENE ONE

Movement A

TOM enters, dressed as a merchant sailor, and strolls across to the fire escape. There he stops and lights a cigarette. He addresses the audience.

TOM: Yes, I have tricks in my pocket, I have things up my sleeve. But I am the opposite of a stage magician. He gives you illusion that has the appearance of truth. I give you truth in the pleasant disguise of illusion. To begin with, I turn back time. I reverse it to that quaint period, the thirties, when the huge middle class of America was matriculating in a school for the blind. Their eyes had failed them, or they had failed their eyes, and so they were having their fingers pressed forcibly down on the fiery Braille alphabet of a dissolving economy.

In Spain there was revolution. Here there was only shouting and confusion.

In Spain there was Guernica. Here there were disturbances of labour, sometimes pretty violent, in otherwise peaceful cities such as Chicago, Cleveland, Saint Louis...this is the social background of the play.

(Music begins to play.)

The play is memory. Being a memory play, it is dimly lighted, it is sentimental, it is not realistic. In memory everything seems to happen to music. That explains the fiddle in the wings.

I am the narrator of the play, and also a character in it. The other characters are my mother, Amanda, my sister, Laura, and a gentleman caller who appears in the final scenes. He is the most realistic character in the play, being an emissary from a world of reality that we were somehow set apart from. But since I have a poet's weakness for symbols, I am using this character also as a symbol; he is the long-delayed but always expected something that we live for.

There is a fifth character in the play who doesn't appear except in this larger-than-life-size photograph over the mantel. This is our father who left us a long time ago. He was a telephone man who fell in love with long distances; he gave up his job with the telephone company and skipped the light fantastic out of town...

The last we heard of him was a picture postcard from Mazatlan, on the Pacific coast of Mexico, containing a message of two words: 'Hello-Goodbye!' and no address.

I think the rest of the play will explain itself...

Movement B

(AMANDA's voice becomes audible through the portieres.)

(Legend on screen: 'Ou sont les neiges.')

(TOM divides the portieres and enters the dining room. AMANDA and LAURA are seated at a drop-leaf table. Eating is indicated by gestures without food or utensils. AMANDA faces the audience. TOM and LAURA are seated in profile. The interior has lit up softly and through the scrim we see AMANDA and LAURA seated at the table.)

27

AMANDA: *(Calling)* Tom?

TOM: Yes, Mother.

AMANDA: We can't say grace until you come to the table!

TOM: Coming, Mother. *(He bows slightly and withdraws, reappearing a few moments later in his place at the table.)*

AMANDA: *(To her son)* Honey, don't push with your fingers. If you have to push with something, the thing to push with is a crust of bread. And chew – chew! Animals have secretions in their stomachs which enable them to digest food without mastication, but human beings are supposed to chew their food before they swallow it down. Eat food leisurely, son, and really enjoy it. A well-cooked meal has lots of delicate flavours that have to be held in the mouth for appreciation. So chew your food and give your salivary glands a chance to function!

(TOM deliberately lays his imaginary fork down and pushes his chair back from the table.)

TOM: I haven't enjoyed one bite of this dinner because of your constant directions on how to eat it. It's you that make me rush through meals with your hawklike attention to every bite I take. Sickening – spoils my appetite – all this discussion of – animals' secretion – salivary glands – mastication!

AMANDA: *(Lightly)* Temperament like a Metropolitan star!

(TOM rises and walks toward the living room.)

You're not excused from the table.

TOM: I'm getting a cigarette.

AMANDA: You smoke too much.

(LAURA rises.)

LAURA: I'll bring in the blanc mange.

(TOM remains standing with his cigarette by the portieres.)

AMANDA: *(Rising)* No, sister, no, sister – you be the lady this time and I'll be the darky.

LAURA: I'm already up.

AMANDA: Resume your seat, little sister — I want you to stay fresh and pretty — for gentlemen callers!

LAURA: *(Sitting down)* I'm not expecting any gentlemen callers.

AMANDA: *(Crossing out to the kitchenette, airily)* Sometimes they come when they are least expected! Why, I remember one Sunday afternoon in Blue Mountain —

(She enters the kitchenette.)

TOM: I know what's coming!

LAURA: Yes. But let her tell it.

TOM: Again?

LAURA: She loves to tell it.

(AMANDA returns with a bowl of dessert.)

AMANDA: One Sunday afternoon in Blue Mountain — your mother received — seventeen! — gentlemen callers! Why, sometimes there weren't chairs enough to accommodate them all. We had to send the nigger over to bring in folding chairs from the parish house.

TOM: *(Remaining at the portieres)* How did you entertain those gentlemen callers?

AMANDA: I understood the art of conversation!

TOM: I bet you could talk.

AMANDA: Girls in those days knew how to talk, I can tell you.

TOM: Yes?

(Image on screen: Amanda as a girl on a porch, greeting callers.)

AMANDA: They knew how to entertain their gentlemen callers. It wasn't enough for a girl to be possessed of a pretty face and a graceful figure — although I wasn't slighted in either respect. She also needed to have a nimble wit and a tongue to meet all occasions.

TOM: What did you talk about?

AMANDA: Things of importance going on in the world! Never anything coarse or common or vulgar.

(She addresses TOM as though he were seated in the vacant chair at the table though he remains by the portieres. He plays this scene as though reading from a script.)

My callers were gentlemen – all! Among my callers were some of the most prominent young planters of the Mississippi Delta – planters and sons of planters!

(TOM motions for music and a spot of light on AMANDA. Her eyes lift, her face glows, her voice becomes rich and elegiac.)

(Screen legend: 'Ou sont les neiges d'antan?'.)

There was young Champ Laughlin who later became vice-president of the Delta Planters Bank. Hadley Stevenson who was drowned in Moon Lake and left his widow one hundred and fifty thousand in Government bonds. There were the Cutrere brothers, Wesley and Bates. Bates was one of my bright particular beaux! He got in a quarrel with that wild Wainwright boy. They shot it out on the floor of Moon Lake Casino. Bates was shot through the stomach. Died in the ambulance on his way to Memphis. His widow was also well provided-for, came into eight or ten thousand acres, that's all. She married him on the rebound – never loved her – carried my picture on him the night he died! And there was that boy that every girl in the Delta had set her cap for! That beautiful, brilliant young Fitzhugh boy from Greene County!

TOM: What did he leave his widow?

AMANDA: He never married! Gracious, you talk as though all of my old admirers had turned up their toes to the daisies!

TOM: Isn't this the first you've mentioned that still survives?

AMANDA: That Fitzhugh boy went North and made a fortune – came to be known as the Wolf of Wall Street! He had the Midas touch, whatever he touched turned to gold! And I could have been Mrs. Duncan J. Fitzhugh, mind you! But – I picked your father!

LAURA: *(Rising)* Mother, let me clear the table.

AMANDA: No, dear, you go in front and study your typewriter chart. Or practise your shorthand a little. Stay fresh and pretty! – It's almost time for our gentlemen callers to start arriving. *(She flounces girlishly toward the kitchenette.)* How many do you suppose we're going to entertain this afternoon?

(TOM throws down the paper and jumps up with a groan.)

LAURA: *(Alone in the dining room)* I don't believe we're going to receive any, Mother.

AMANDA: *(Reappearing, airily.)* What? No one – not one? You must be
            joking!

*(LAURA nervously echoes her laugh. She slips in a fugitive manner through the
half-open portieres and draws them gently behind her. A shaft of very clear light is
thrown on her face against the faded tapestry of the curtains. Faintly the music of
'The Glass Menagerie' is heard as she continues, lightly.)*

            Not one gentleman caller? It can't be true! There must be a
            flood, there must have been a tornado!

LAURA: There isn't a flood, it's not a tornado, Mother. I'm just not
            popular like you were in Blue Mountain…

*(TOM utters another groan. LAURA glances at him with a faint, apologetic smile.
Her voice catches a little.)*

LAURA: Mother's afraid I'm going to be an old maid.

(The scene dims out with the 'Glass Menagerie' music.)

The scene divides pretty obviously into two movements. Movement
A is Tom's soliloquy, and Movement B is the family meal.

What are the 'given circumstances' that colour Tom's soliloquy? He
tells us a great deal of the 'given circumstances' that we need to play
Movement B, but what is the tone of Movement A? To find that, you
have to read the whole play and see what state he is in at the end. You
will see that the play is an expiation of his guilt for having left his mother
and especially his sister Laura. The last soliloquy of the play tells us that
she was, and is, the most important relationship in his life, 'Oh, Laura,
Laura, I tried to leave you behind me, but I am more faithful than I
intended to be!' So we know that this Tom, who is older than the Tom
who appears in the main body of the play, is a man in torment and this
will inform how he plays the opening.

Tom gives us most of the 'given circumstances' for Movement B.
America in turmoil and depression and a one-parent family that we can
see from the set and costume is struggling to make ends meet. Before I
leave the opening, I should point out that it also tells you how to direct
the play, or at least the style. Williams, who was clearly fed up with the
naturalistic theatre of his time, gives elaborate directions about the use of

projections and captions of music to create a different kind of experience. At the same time, he has so many different rooms it's a mystery as to how you fit them in, especially in the round where I directed it. The clue is that it is a 'memory play' and that Tom is the narrator/stage manager. The set is not naturalistic, you need the pieces of furniture that Tom remembers without room divisions. Sound and light can be exaggerated, as in memory. The first speech packs in an awful lot of information.

Movement B requires you to decide at what point the family is in in relation to each other. By the end of the play the family will have split up, maybe forever, so the undercurrents, the subtext of this scene, will reflect this. It has thirteen beats and I'm going to go through them. Some objectives will seem banal and some you won't agree with. It doesn't matter; it's the process that counts.

(AMANDA's voice becomes audible through the portieres.)

(Legend on screen: 'Ou sont les neiges.')

(TOM divides the portieres and enters the dining room. AMANDA and LAURA are seated at a drop-leaf table. Eating is indicated by gestures without food or utensils. AMANDA faces the audience. TOM and LAURA are seated in profile. The interior has lit up softly and through the scrim we see AMANDA and LAURA seated at the table.)

AMANDA:	*(Calling.)* Tom?
TOM:	Yes, Mother.
AMANDA:	We can't say grace until you come to the table!
TOM:	Coming, Mother. *(He bows slightly and withdraws, reappearing a few moments later in his place at the table.)*

Beat 1

Amanda's objective is to make Tom come to the table. The family eating together is important to her. The old values of her early life in the Deep South. Tom's objective is to stay out. His obstacle is his love for his mother and more his desire not to upset his sister. Every mealtime is a trial for all of them.

AMANDA:	*(To her son.)* Honey, don't push with your fingers. If you have to push with something, the thing to push with is a crust of bread. And chew – chew! Animals have secretions in

their stomachs which enable them to digest food without mastication, but human beings are supposed to chew their food before they swallow it down. Eat food leisurely, son, and really enjoy it. A well-cooked meal has lots of delicate flavours that have to be held in the mouth for appreciation. So chew your food and give your salivary glands a chance to function!

(TOM deliberately lays his imaginary fork down and pushes his chair back from the table.)

TOM: I haven't enjoyed one bite of this dinner because of your constant directions on how to eat it. It's you that make me rush through meals with your hawklike attention to every bite I take. Sickening – spoils my appetite – all this discussion of – animals' secretion – salivary glands – mastication!

Beat 2

Amanda's objective: to make Tom healthy. It is very important that everything Amanda does, however apparently annoying, has an objective of caring for her family.
Tom's objective is to make her stop. By the end of the play he will have gone. How near is he to cracking? This scene has been played so many times.

AMANDA: *(Lightly.)* Temperament like a Metropolitan star!

Beat 3

Amanda's objective: to make Tom lighten up.
(TOM rises and walks toward the living room.)

You're not excused from the table.

Beat 4

Tom's objective: to get out of the room.
Amanda's is to stop him.

TOM: I'm getting a cigarette.

AMANDA: You smoke too much.

Beat 5

Tom's objective is to smoke. The drug relieves his pain.

Amanda's objective is to stop him. Genuine anxiety.

(LAURA rises.)

LAURA: I'll bring in the blanc mange.

(TOM remains standing with his cigarette by the portieres.)

AMANDA: *(Rising.)* No, sister, no, sister – you be the lady this time and I'll be the darky.

LAURA: I'm already up.

Beat 6

Laura's objective is to get out of the room. This is unbearable to her.

Amanda's is to stop her. If the family breaks up now, what does the rest of the evening hold?

AMANDA: Resume your seat, little sister – I want you to stay fresh and pretty – for gentlemen callers!

LAURA: *(Sitting down.)* I'm not expecting any gentlemen callers.

AMANDA: *(Crossing out to the kitchenette, airily.)* Sometimes they come when they are least expected!

Beat 7

Amanda's objective is to make Laura prepare herself to be the enticing bait she wants her to be. It may be a crazy fantasy but Amanda has to believe it. It would solve part of their poverty-stricken existence.

Laura's objective is to break her mother's fantasy. She is guilt-ridden at not being able to be what Amanda wants her to be.

Why, I remember one Sunday afternoon in Blue Mountain –

(She enters the kitchenette.)

Beat 8

Amanda's objective: to escape into the past.

TOM: I know what's coming!

LAURA: Yes. But let her tell it.

TOM: Again?

LAURA: She loves to tell it.

Beat 9

Tom's objective is to get Laura to allow him to stop her.
Laura's is to make him indulge Amanda. This best illustrates the closeness of
brother and sister.

(AMANDA returns with a bowl of dessert.)

AMANDA: One Sunday afternoon in Blue Mountain – your mother
              received – seventeen! – gentlemen callers! Why, sometimes
              there weren't chairs enough to accommodate them all. We
              had to send the nigger over to bring in folding chairs from
              the parish house.

TOM: *(Remaining at the portieres.)* How did you entertain those
              gentlemen callers?

AMANDA: I understood the art of conversation!

TOM: I bet you could talk.

AMANDA: Girls in those days knew how to talk, I can tell you.

TOM: Yes?

(Image on screen: Amanda as a girl on a porch, greeting callers.)

AMANDA: They knew how to entertain their gentlemen callers. It
              wasn't enough for a girl to be possessed of a pretty face
              and a graceful figure – although I wasn't slighted in either
              respect. She also needed to have a nimble wit and a tongue
              to meet all occasions.

TOM: What did you talk about?

AMANDA: Things of importance going on in the world! Never anything
              coarse or common or vulgar.

*(She addresses TOM as though he were seated in the vacant chair at the table
though he remains by the portieres. He plays this scene as though reading from a
script.)*

              My callers were gentlemen – all! Among my callers were
              some of the most prominent young planters of the
              Mississippi Delta – planters and sons of planters!

(TOM motions for music and a spot of light on AMANDA. Her eyes lift, her face glows, her voice becomes rich and elegiac.)

(Screen legend: 'Ou sont les neiges d'antan?'.)

	There was young Champ Laughlin who later became vice-president of the Delta Planters Bank. Hadley Stevenson who was drowned in Moon Lake and left his widow one hundred and fifty thousand in Government bonds. There were the Cutrere brothers, Wesley and Bates. Bates was one of my bright particular beaux! He got in a quarrel with that wild Wainwright boy. They shot it out on the floor of Moon Lake Casino. Bates was shot through the stomach. Died in the ambulance on his way to Memphis. His widow was also well provided-for, came into eight or ten thousand acres, that's all. She married him on the rebound – never loved her – carried my picture on him the night he died! And there was that boy that every girl in the Delta had set her cap for! That beautiful, brilliant young Fitzhugh boy from Greene County!
TOM:	What did he leave his widow?
AMANDA:	He never married! Gracious, you talk as though all of my old admirers had turned up their toes to the daisies!
TOM:	Isn't this the first you've mentioned that still survives?
AMANDA:	That Fitzhugh boy went North and made a fortune – came to be known as the Wolf of Wall Street! He had the Midas touch, whatever he touched turned to gold! And I could have been Mrs. Duncan J. Fitzhugh, mind you! But – I picked your father!

Beat 10

Amanda's objective is to evoke her past happiness. The objective fails at, 'I picked your father!'

Tom's is to help. He does this for Laura. It's a long beat.

LAURA:	*(Rising.)* Mother, let me clear the table.
AMANDA:	No, dear, you go in front and study your typewriter chart. Or practise your shorthand a little.

Beat 11

Laura's objective is to stop her mother. The father's desertion is unbearable.

Amanda's is to make her study. It is the other solution.

> Stay fresh and pretty! – It's almost time for our gentlemen callers to start arriving. *(She flounces girlishly toward the kitchenette.)* How many do you suppose we're going to entertain this afternoon?

(TOM throws down the paper and jumps up with a groan.)

LAURA: *(Alone in the dining room.)* I don't believe we're going to receive any, Mother.

AMANDA: *(Reappearing, airily.)* What? No one – not one? You must be joking!

(LAURA nervously echoes her laugh. She slips in a fugitive manner through the half-open portieres and draws them gently behind her. A shaft of very clear light is thrown on her face against the faded tapestry of the curtains. Faintly the music of 'The Glass Menagerie' is heard as she continues, lightly.)

> Not one gentleman caller? It can't be true! There must be a flood, there must have been a tornado!

LAURA: There isn't a flood, it's not a tornado, Mother. I'm just not popular like you were in Blue Mountain…

(TOM utters another groan.)

Beat 12

Amanda's objective is to make Laura believe in the possibility of a gentleman caller.
Tom's is to stop her. He can't restrain the groan.
Laura's is also to stop her mother creating the fantasy. It is very painful to her.
(LAURA glances at him with a faint, apologetic smile. Her voice catches a little.)

LAURA: Mother's afraid I'm going to be an old maid.

(The scene dims out with the 'Glass Menagerie' music.)

Beat 13

Laura's objective: to be forgiven.

Movement B's objectives are: Amanda wants to have a happy family

evening; Laura wants to avoid pain, and Tom wants to please his mother and sister (the obstacle being the anger rising in him).

When I first started working on the play, I was always longing to get on to the later, more overtly dramatic, scenes. When I broke it down like this, I realized what a dramatic, emotion-packed scene it is, albeit mostly in subtext. It sets up the play perfectly.

I used only to apply this approach sparingly. I used it only for plays by O'Neill, Chekhov, Ibsen etc but gradually over the years I came to realize that every play benefited from it, be it farce, comedy, tragedy, modern or classical. Every play must have a real base, from *Hamlet* to *Charley's Aunt*. The more there is at stake for each character, the funnier or the more tragic the performance will be.

There is an awful tradition of playing comedy or farce in this country where the actors are aware of being funny. In period comedy, like Wilde or Sheridan, there is a fake style which makes them into creatures that bear no resemblance to ourselves or anyone we know. Every good play works because its reality is recognizable to the audience; we are moved because we identify with the play or we laugh at ourselves for the same reason.

Recently I directed *The Importance of Being Earnest*, and found preparing it impossible because it was unique and perfect, and because it had more well-known lines than any play in the English language. I didn't know how to get into it or what I could possibly do to make it really live. Then I decided to apply the Stanislavski principle to the text. What was revealed to me was Wilde's most subversive play about a society which did its best to kill off 'love' and how that love triumphs. Each so-called epigram had a purpose and a serious intent for the character. The result was a very fresh and funny production which attracted a remarkably young audience. Now there isn't a play I don't apply this discipline to. It always reveals truths that I know no other way of finding. It is also a very good way in the early stages of rehearsal of getting the actors to dig deep into their parts very quickly. More of that later.

THE IMPORTANCE OF BEING EARNEST

Oscar Wilde

Section taken from ACT I

ALGERNON: How are you, my dear Ernest? What brings you up to town?

JACK: Oh, pleasure, pleasure! What else should bring one anywhere?

Beat 1

Algernon's objective is to make Jack feel at home.
Jack's objective is to get the upper hand. Algernon always makes him feel slightly inferior.

Eating as usual, I see, Algy!

ALGERNON: *(Stiffly.)* I believe it is customary in good society to take some slight refreshment at five o'clock.

Beat 2

Jack's objective is to make Algernon feel in the wrong.
Algernon's to defend himself.

Where have you been since last Thursday?

JACK: *(Sitting down on the sofa.)* In the country.

Beat 3

Algernon's objective is to find out where Jack has been.
Jack's objective is to tell him.

ALGERNON: What on earth do you do there?

JACK: *(Pulling off his gloves.)* When one is in town one amuses oneself. When one is in the country one amuses other people. It is excessively boring.

Beat 4

Algernon's objective is to find out about Jack in the country.
Jack's objective is to fob him off, as this life is secret.

ALGERNON: And who are the people you amuse?

JACK: *(Airily.)* Oh, neighbours, neighbours.

ALGERNON: Got nice neighbours in your part of Shropshire?

JACK: Perfectly horrid! Never speak to one of them.

ALGERNON: How immensely you must amuse them! *(Goes over and takes sandwich.)* By the way, Shropshire is your county, is it not?

JACK: Eh? Shropshire? Yes, of course.

Beat 5

Algernon's objective is to push Jack further.
Jack's to continue to fob him off.

Hallo! Why all these cups? Why cucumber sandwiches? Why such reckless extravagance in one so young? Who is coming to tea?

ALGERNON: Oh! merely Aunt Augusta and Gwendolen.

Beat 6

Jack's objective is to find out what is going on and to change the subject. Algernon's is to provoke Jack. He knows the effect the news will have. Jack is in love.

JACK: How perfectly delightful!

ALGERNON: Yes, that is all very well; but I am afraid Aunt Augusta won't quite approve of your being here.

JACK: May I ask why?

ALGERNON: My dear fellow, the way you flirt with Gwendolen is perfectly disgraceful. It is almost as bad as the way Gwendolen flirts with you.

Beat 7

Jack's objective is to anticipate the joy.
Algernon's to put him down.

JACK: I am in love with Gwendolen. I have come up to town
           expressly to propose to her.

ALGERNON: I thought you had come up for pleasure? – I call that
           business.

Beat 8

Jack's objective is to have Algernon sympathize with him.

Algernon's to douse him.

JACK: How utterly unromantic you are!

ALGERNON: I really don't see anything romantic in proposing. It is very
           romantic to be in love. But there is nothing romantic about
           a definite proposal. Why, one may be accepted. One usually
           is, I believe. Then the excitement is all over. The very essence
           of romance is uncertainty. If ever I get married, I'll certainly
           try to forget the fact.

Beat 9

Jack's objective is to make him feel inadequate.

Algernon's to bring him to his senses. Algernon will have cause to rue his
remarks. These discussions are serious.

JACK: I have no doubt about that, dear Algy. The Divorce Court
           was specially invented for people whose memories are so
           curiously constituted.

ALGERNON: Oh! there is no use speculating on that subject. Divorces are
           made in heaven –

Beat 10

Jack's objective is to put him down.

Algernon's to outsmart him.

           *(JACK puts out his hand to take a sandwich. ALGERNON at once
           interferes.)* Please don't touch the cucumber sandwiches.
           They are ordered especially for Aunt Augusta. *(Takes one and
           eats it.)*

JACK: Well, you have been eating them all the time.

ALGERNON: That is quite a different matter. She is my aunt.

Beat 11

Algernon's objective is to stop Jack eating the sandwiches.
Jack's to persuade him.

> *(Takes plate from below.)* Have some bread and butter. The bread and butter is for Gwendolen. Gwendolen is devoted to bread and butter.

JACK: *(Advancing to table and helping himself.)* And very good bread and butter it is too.

Beat 12

Algernon's objective is to divert Jack to the bread and butter.
Jack's to eat the bread and butter because of Gwendolen.

ALGERNON: Well, my dear fellow, you need not eat as if you were going to eat it all.

Beat 13

Algernon's objective is to stop Jack eating it all.

> You behave as if you were married to her already. You are not married to her already, and I don't think you ever will be.

JACK: Why on earth do you say that?

ALGERNON: Well, in the first place, girls never marry the men they flirt with. Girls don't think it right.

JACK: Oh, that is nonsense!

ALGERNON: It isn't. It is a great truth. It accounts for the extraordinary number of bachelors that one sees all over the place.

Beat 14

Algernon's objective is to prepare Jack for the worst.
Jack's to find out why. This is a stunner.

> In the second place, I don't give my consent.

JACK: Your consent!

ALGERNON: My dear fellow, Gwendolen is my first cousin. And before I allow you to marry her, you will have to clear up the whole question of Cecily. *(Rings bell.)*

JACK: Cecily! What on earth do you mean? What do you mean, Algy, by Cecily? I don't know anyone of the name of Cecily.

Beat 15

Algernon's objective is to soften Jack up.
Jack's to bluff his way out. The obstacle being, it knocks him for six.
Enter LANE

Alongside this is Stanislavski's 'given circumstances'. Before you can even begin to break the play into objectives, you must pinpoint where in the lives of the characters the play begins. You must decide how they have lived their lives up to this point. In a good play all that information will be contained in the text somewhere.

Moves

How far do you pre-block the play? In other words how far do you predetermine where the actors are placed on stage in relation to one another and when and to where they move. Finally these decisions are crucial because they communicate to the audience the characters' relationships to one another. Watch people in real life, do they keep their distance, invade another space, signal attraction, disinterest, or antagonism? Where the actors are placed tells the story. Again there is no easy answer. In theory, blocking is best done with the actors in rehearsal, when they know enough about what they are doing to feel their moves, rather than have them imposed upon them. In practice, unless you are doing a small cast play like *The Glass Menagerie*, you won't have time to wait.

While you are working with your designer, you will inevitably have forming in your mind how you're going to move the play. You will be making sure that the ground-plans enable you to stage the play. Is the furniture in the right place? Will the entrances and exits work (especially important in farce)?

If the play is an epic, a Shakespeare or any multi-scene play, you will have to go much further. Making sure the play flows smoothly from

location to location, marshalling your troops so that one set of actors takes over from another, means your pre-blocking becomes more detailed. If you have a large cast then you will have to pre-conceive the scenes for two reasons. The first is to stop them bumping into each other, the second is to make the correct stage picture to tell the story. Stanislavski said that your blocking should be such that if a sheet of glass came down between the stage and the audience, they should still be able to tell what is going on. I can think of plenty of modern plays where that would be impossible but it's a good thing to have in the back of your mind.

Blocking

Every director will block differently according to their visual sense but there are some obvious guidelines. You need to know, whatever the shape of the stage, where the power points are. On the proscenium, as the old actor managers will tell you, up stage centre (USC) is the most powerful position. Some directors subscribe to the circle of power. Draw a semi-circle from down stage right (DSR) to down stage left (DSL). Any position on the semi-circle is powerful. On the proscenium blocking is anti-natural, whereas in the round actors can stand in natural relations to each other, not having to move like crabs or cheat their faces out front. In the round the centre is, of course, a power point but so is the side of the stage looking inwards. More of the audience can see you than if you are in the centre. On a thrust stage the upstage point of the thrust is again obviously powerful but then so are the DSL and DSR points looking up to USC. You then decide the order of importance of each character and place them accordingly. Tricky if you're doing the final scene of *Lear* for example.

Much depends on what kind of a visual director you are. Some people are best at working out the scenes at home with the model of the set moving little figures around. Others can't do that. They need to wait until they have the actors in the space and then they have a natural sense of how to place them. A combination of the two seems to me to be ideal. You go into rehearsal with a plan which you are happy to adjust, even radically, as you rehearse.

<u>Fear</u>

You have chosen the play because you believe that what the author wants to express is important to you, and you want to bring it to life and communicate it to an audience. You have analyzed the text, you have researched the material. You have worked closely with your designer, your choreographer, your composer, your fight director etc., so that each facet of the production is working in harmony with each other. You have cast the play so that you believe you have married each actor with the part, and that you have created a group that will work well and creatively with each other.

In a sense this is the easy part. This is all theory. You have the perfect production in your head. Now you are approaching the moment when you actually have to bring it alive. However excited you are, however much you are longing to start, you need to realize that somewhere inside of you there is also a great 'fear'. It is how you deal with this 'fear' that will crucially affect how you direct. There is a scene in a movie directed by Vincente Minnelli, called *Two Weeks in Another Town,* when Edward G. Robinson, playing a movie director about to shoot a new film, wakes up in bed screaming after nightmares. His wife asks him what the matter is. The matter is that, although he is a seasoned director with many, many movies under his belt, he doesn't know when he starts the shoot whether he will have the right inspiration, whether he'll say the right things, whether anything will come out of his mouth. On top of this, the director will be worrying whether he's cast it right, had it designed right and so on and so on.

This fear will recur right up to opening night. You must learn to acknowledge its presence and you will get to know its habits more and more intimately. If you are not conscious of it, it can turn you into a tyrant, as some directors are, and it can turn off the tap of creativity, making you seek easy options instead of adventuring. I'll have a lot more to say about fear because you're not the only one who will have it. Your actors will as well!

Preparing for the actors

You've now reached the transitional moment. Until now you have been totally in control of everything and the production is imaginatively in your head in considerable detail. Tomorrow is the first rehearsal and all that is about to change. The actors are coming!

In some sense the actors are in thrall to the director because he has the overall concept, he has supervised the designing of their clothes and, if called for, even wigs. They are there to make actual his vision.

There are many kinds of director, as I have said, from the bullies who believe actors are there to do as they are told, to the directors who are great conceptually but are hopeless in a rehearsal room. I've never been the latter, I hope, but I've certainly been the former. If you start directing at school or university you are almost bound to tell the actors what to do and they'll probably be grateful; they are untrained amateurs. The moment you start working with good actors, you realize that they are capable within the bounds of the production of giving performances far richer and more vivid than you have imagined.

Therefore it is good to have discussed with your leading actors the production that is in your mind before rehearsals start, or even before you finally cast them. For example, when Brenda Blethyn agreed to do *The Glass Menagerie* it was crucial to both of us to agree how Amanda Wingfield was to be approached. It was my feeling that the part was often miscast as a sort of Blanche DuBois; a faded southern belle who had become an appalling mother. We both agreed that however annoying and overbearing Amanda was, it sprung out of a deep love for her children and the courage she needed to protect them from the poverty that faced them because of their father running off. Now suppose I had simply asked Brenda to play the part, she had agreed, and it had become clear at the beginning of rehearsal that she had a different view of the character and we were at loggerheads.

It is as well to talk to as many of your actors in this way as you can. Again on *The Glass Menagerie* everyone came to the first rehearsal knowing how the production was to be rehearsed, partly because it had

been discussed in the audition process.

The director also needs to prepare himself psychologically for this transitional moment. He has to be prepared when he walks into the rehearsal room to be open to everything, besides letting go the basic reason why he is doing the play.

This is much harder than it might sound because of our old friend 'fear'. You will constantly want the reassurance that things are going well, and since the actors are starting from scratch they will be working at a different rhythm from you and that can easily panic you into not allowing their creative processes to take their time. You'll learn how to cope with this over a period of time. It took me years. That is why the casting process is so important, and why over the years you will gather around you a group of actors who you enjoy working with and trust. It gives you firm ground from which to start rehearsal.

THE REHEARSAL PERIOD

I'm going to assume a four-week rehearsal period, and then some previews before the opening night. Every play makes different demands, so this is a rough guide only.

The first rehearsal

Few actors realize how frightening the first day of rehearsals is for the director, and indeed the director mustn't show that fear; excitement, yes, but not fear. Fear and excitement is there in abundance for everyone.

For the actors this is the first day in a new school. Many of them won't know what to expect. Will they get on with their fellow cast members? Is there a star who they are in awe of? What will the director be like? What decisions, especially about costumes, have been taken? Will they be up to the job? Will they be ready in a month's time? etc. etc. If they are working away from home, somewhere like the Royal Exchange, it will be first day at boarding school. They'll be living away from their support system, mainly in digs. Will they be happy enough to cope over the three months or so that they'll be away?

It is important to make that first day as reassuring as you can. At the Royal Exchange, the Green Room ladies have seen the photos of the actors and memorized their names so that they feel at home immediately. The Company are issued with a welcome pack containing a massive amount of information about how the Theatre works, how the city works, where to eat, where to drink, even where to exercise. The stage management bend over backwards to make everyone feel important.

The Company then assemble in the rehearsal room and the director introduces them all, and makes his speech about the play, why he is doing it, and how he is going to work. Get this speech right and you will have bought the benefit of the doubt from the actors for at least a week. Your

speech can inspire them, can give them confidence and make them feel that they are the crucial element in an important project. I try to make sure that when I outline the structure and content of the play I mention every part, or group of parts, however small, so that no one is left out.

Then between them the director and designer introduce the actors to the set and costumes. In a complex show it is important that the actors have a vision of how the production will work. The stage management should take photos of the model so that they can be referred to by the actors later.

The showing of the costumes can be a tricky moment. With a contemporary play you can emphasize that the drawings are open to change, but on a big Shakespeare, or equivalent, there won't be room for that because the clothes will have an overall concept, a colour scheme or style which has to be maintained. For instance, if you are doing *Antony and Cleopatra,* the designer will have made major decisions as to how the Romans and Egyptians are to be differentiated and made vivid. The actors will have to accept that, and you must help them do so.

All of this will take the best part of the morning and the actors will, most likely or not, feel overwhelmed by the amount of information they have been bombarded with, but if you have done your job well they will be excited by it all. You will be feeling relieved if your speech has gone well and that particular apprehension will have been placated. Now comes an even more frightening moment for everyone: the read-through.

The read-through

Some directors dispense with the read-through as being, at best without value, at worst destructive, because work has not yet begun properly, so how can it be helpful? I disagree. It is the first time the cast will have heard the text out loud. It's the first step to their possession of the production.

I emphasize that this is not a test because they have already got their parts, it is not a radio broadcast, it should be a relaxed way of testing out your thoughts and beginning to get to know your fellow actors.

I think for the director it is the single most terrifying moment, apart from the first audience, because as they start to read, none of them are saying the lines as you imagined it! A terrible panic can well-up inside of you. How am I going to get this production ready in four weeks?! Even now, primed though I am to deal with this panic, I still cannot wholly control it.

However, if you can get over that and concentrate on your actors, you will begin to get an immediate sense of where the bonuses and the problems are going to be. More than that, you are hearing the play for the first time and, even at this stage, it can start to confirm your plans or start to adjust them.

One actress said to me after a particularly happy production of *The Beaux Stratagem*, 'Of course, we all knew it was going to be good after the read-through.' When I queried that, she said, 'Oh, you always do!' I don't know if I believe that. It's a terrifying thought that the outcome is already determined at that moment.

Whatever you feel, and if you've cast the play well you should be happy, make them believe that you're delighted. Your job during rehearsals is to build their confidence until their inhibitions and fears disappear, and that starts here. If you have worked with your leading actors before rehearsals as I've suggested, their reading is likely to boost everyone's spirits too.

After the first day is over and everyone's tension slackens, I recommend company drinks so that everyone has a chance to properly meet everyone else in a relaxed atmosphere; maybe even a meal together if they are away from home. Tomorrow the real work starts, but you might have taken some big steps towards the outcome during the first day.

Improvisation

I can only tell you what I feel about improvisation and people will certainly disagree with me! When I started out I used it a lot but gradually my use of it diminished and now I use it very sparingly. Looking back I think I used it a great deal because I thought it was fun and smart but

as I worked with more and more experienced actors I cut down its use.

I now feel you should only use it when you are really stuck on a scene and need to come at it some other way to break the block. If you are working with experienced actors of the right sort they may not need it at all. Too often it is used as a substitute for the real work. Anyway there are very good improvisers who can't act and many good actors who can't improvise – so there is a big casting trap there.

It can be a very useful tool to break down barriers between actors who have to play intimate love scenes for example. In Chekhov, improvisation based on the subtext and indeed emotion recollection exercises can be invaluable. But it should only be used if necessary. When I first did *Uncle Vanya* years ago I used this to good effect to make the cast feel the stultifying boredom of life on Serebryakov's estate and to experience overtly the pessimistic subtext which then had to be suppressed. Years' later doing the same play on Broadway I simply didn't have to use it, the actors were perfectly capable of imagining it and subsuming it into their performances.

Improvisation is much used in drama schools, and quite rightly so, as it can teach students to open up their creative faculties, but directors should beware. I have seen it too often used to actually avoid the real process. Some directors will improvise for the precious first week of rehearsal and spend too little time on the actual text which will actually do the work for them.

Overview of rehearsals

My way of rehearsing has the aim of making the actors as confident as possible, as quickly as possible. Ideally, I believe that the final week of rehearsals should have a run-through every day so that the production has become theirs before the production weekend, which can be a disruptive and destructive time if it interrupts the actors' process at the wrong moment. For the sake of neatness I'll go through the process week by week, but in fact each phase of the process can be quicker, or slower, depending on the play. In a major Shakespeare, which should have a

minimum of five weeks' rehearsal, you might not get to a run-through so early, with a farce you will, and it is imperative you do.

<u>Week one</u>

Some directors spend at least the first week sitting round the table with the actors discussing text. Some directors, incomprehensibly to me, spend much of the early period playing games with medicine balls and the like, to create a team spirit, while some directors start by blocking the play first and actually running chunks together from the beginning. My way is an amalgam of the first and third.

I have prepared the script à la Stanislavsky, as I have described. I take the text movement by movement and get the actors to read it first. Then I take them through the beats, giving them my objectives all the whilst emphasizing that they are not holy writ. They are merely my preparatory work which should neither inhibit the actors so that they feel their decisions have been taken away from them, nor lull them into a sense of false security. 'Oh, he's done it all, I don't have to bother.' All the objectives can be changed as the actor gets to know what he is doing. What you should do is drop the actor as deep as possible into the play but not take away his process. Then I get the actors to read the movement again so that they can try out what has been discussed and hopefully give them a basis to proceed from.

I do believe that if you leave it there and don't get the movement on its feet, it creates uneasiness in the cast, so I do move it roughly. This also helps the actors learn their lines because the physical association of the words is helpful to them.

More and more, actors are learning their lines before rehearsal, especially if they are playing a huge part like Iago, or if they are at an age when learning lines has become a challenge. The danger of learning lines too early is that you become set in your vocal patterns before the text has been examined as a body. The ideal for me is that the actor knows the text intimately without actually learning it, and has, of course, thought about it and if necessary researched about it. Then the second time we go

through the play, I like the company to be off the book because the real creative phase cannot satisfactorily take place till the scripts are down.

This phase can take a very long time; the average length for me is ten days and the director will get very tired of his own voice. If it works – that is, if you have done your preparation well – it sinks the anchor deep into the play and gives the actors plenty to dream about and begin to create in relation to it, or even against it.

I warn you this is a very tiring phase for the director. You are pumping energy out from ten in the morning till six at night (or later if you are doing three sessions), and for most of the time you are getting very little back; indeed you shouldn't expect to. The actors are taking it all in; they won't necessarily give you much back.

As you get to the end of the play you may find a reluctance in yourself to go into quite so much detail. This is because the last act of a play, Shakespeare especially, is difficult to rehearse till you are at a much more advanced stage; then the last act can become relatively easy because you know your characters so well.

Second week phase

The actors are off the book, they have been dreaming their parts, they are ready to start flexing their muscles and trying things out. The structure is the same. You go through each movement. The actors run it first to give them a chance to try out how well they've learnt their lines and to experiment. Then you take the movement to bits and work slowly through it. Besides being pleased with what is going well, you will also begin to see where you will need to adjust, or radically change things. You will see which scenes are going to be difficult and which seem to play themselves. You will also get to realize which actors are sailing, which are not, and which are going to be difficult.

This is where the director/psychologist comes in. Every actor has a different psyche and needs different treatment from you. Everything stems from insecurity. The 'star' may be wary of another actor's talent, two people may rub each other up the wrong way, one actor will want to

take up what's called 'director time' to boost their own ego, another will be so timid they won't ask for help or risk themselves at all. The quicker you can overcome these problems and bind the company together, the better. The real truth is that the better the other actors are, the more the worried ones are going to thrive. Once they begin to feed off each other, their fears will begin to dispel.

When you've worked the movement again, you get them to run it once more so that you and they can measure the progress. At the end of the first phase you should make sure that each actor leaves each movement saying, 'I've got enough to go away and think about.' Then at the end of the second phase each actor should be saying, 'I have a real idea of this scene, and know it's going to work.' The first phase has been planting the seed, the second phase is watering.

Do not expect too much too quickly. Inside yourself you will want reassurance as quickly as possible that the production is going to work. The danger is that you will push your actors too hard so that they will be acting to please you and not because they are making their roles firmly part of them. You will, with experience, get to know how much to expect at every phase. That will help you hold your nerve. You can't make a flower grow faster than is natural and if you try to pull it up out of the ground before it is grown, you will destroy it. I have known directors (I'm sure I've done it myself) inhibit actors and even turn them against the director by off-loading their anxiety on them. It can create a sour atmosphere in rehearsals because the actor feels inadequate and resentful and in that state nothing truly creative takes place. The bully directors, the sergeant-major directors, all fall into that trap.

You will be aware at the end of phase two, as will the actors that you are halfway through the rehearsal process. Suddenly the first audience is not so far away. You need to ensure that the actors feel that everything is on schedule.

You need to ensure if you're doing a *Hamlet* or a *Peer Gynt* that your leading actor is quite far on in his process as he should be if you have worked with him before rehearsal. He has a mountain to climb and

he will need to feel that it is within his reach. At the same time, you have to ensure that the smaller parts are not neglected. There is nothing better than seeing a real ensemble playing on stage, which to me means selfless acting with star performances, and this will only be achieved if the smaller roles are played by actors who feel you think they are important.

You are coming now to the third week, the week so many people tell you is when the crises occur and the production can feel as if it's falling apart. It shouldn't be like that.

<u>Third week phase</u>

This is the phase when the flower begins to bud. The actors are now growing in confidence (they absolutely know their lines) and are stretching themselves emotionally. They have confidence in each other and the crucial scenes are beginning to have a real life. In this phase, I again take the play movement by movement, run it, work and run it, but this time I put the play together in bigger chunks. The movements are run together, and the scenes and then the acts. If there is time, I even run the two halves. The actors slowly get used to the full scheme of the play.

It is important to emphasize that the rehearsal period is <u>only</u> halfway through. Finished performances are not required but at the end of each rehearsal the actors should be saying, 'I know this is going to work. This is the right way.' If there are sections which you still haven't cracked then this is the moment to concentrate on them till you have. The actors will be giving you more and more which you must be alert to and use.

This is also the phase to start thinking about the tempo of the playing. During the initial stages of rehearsal pace is secondary. There is no point in going faster unless you are secure in the stepping stones. Sometimes, as an a exercise, you can tell the actors to play a scene cueing fast because it can give them a clue as to how the scene has been constructed and even make it easier for them, but in general it's wrong to fluster them by demanding a technical speeding-up until they are ready.

It is difficult to generalise about speed. Farce eventually goes at breakneck speed; in Shakespeare you pause at your peril unless he has

signalled a pause in the verse. My rule is this: it is better to have the audience slightly behind you, running to keep up rather than having them jogging alongside you or even in front of you. This means they are being pulled along by the story, eager to know what happens next. This applies to all plays. It does not mean you go as fast as you can, but as fast as you can while giving the full emotional weight to each moment.

Cueing is often the key. Unless there is a good reason not to, come in bang on cue. That does not mean speaking fast. On the contrary, fast cueing enables you to take the time you need to speak the lines.

Actors naturally tend to pause before they speak. They complain that they need time to think before they utter. This is not true of life. In life we are ready to speak immediately. We think while we listen to the other person and for the most part come in on cue! We already understand the point the other person is making long before they actually come to a halt.

You have to judge when to tighten the playing. In a farce, you'd be mad not to be starting to do it during the third week. At speed you'll find new gags and you'll find that some you've invented won't work. On the other hand if you're doing *Long Day's Journey into Night,* you may want to wait until much later, even to the previews, before making a judgement about pace.

Plays like that are so psychologically complex and demand such extremes of different emotions throughout every scene that to tighten before the actors are ready is to ensure that the end result will be inadequate. I recently directed *True Love Lies*, a new play by Brad Fraser. It was a particularly happy experience with a cast, none of whom I had worked with before. Brad writes in short scenes and each one has a distinct emotional contrast but always at high pressure. This play about the break up of a family leading to divorce and desperation in the children leading to one of them determined to shoot to kill the person he thinks has precipitated the crisis, is particularly demanding. Such was the trust between the actors and myself that they were able to say right up to the production week, 'we know eventually we have to cue fast (that's the way Brad writes) but we're not quite there with such and such a scene, please

don't make us do that yet'. However for the most part the actors cueing on time and handing the baton on at the end of a line by inflecting up, rather than down, makes life easier for everyone.

At the end of the week, I like to do a stagger-through of the whole play. This is helpful for the director and the actors. The director can see clearly where the production stands. They can see the whole shape. They will have a clear idea of the pacing of the play and they will know what remains to be done. The actors will be having a first go at what, at that point, seems a marathon. The leading parts need this information to keep the growing process.

Although notes should be given at this stage, they should be general. Detailed notes will come later and can distract from the broad lessons that are being learnt.

It is very important after this run/stagger-through that the actors have a full opportunity to express where they think they are and voice their problems still to be solved. They should be able to do this at all times, but to do it collectively at this point can be very valuable.

Fourth week phase

As I've said the ideal is to have a run-through every day which will allow the performances to grow naturally. You still have half of each day to do working notes based on the previous run. This is not rigid. If your first stagger-through has thrown up lots of problems then it's pointless running again until they have been addressed.

It is still important not to expect too much too quickly. By the last Friday or Saturday the show should be in good shape but until then there is still a journey to be made.

After the shock of the stagger-through it will take several run-throughs for the actors to gain confidence and to stop regarding the play as a marathon. Also after each working notes session it is probable that the next run will be a remembering what has been rehearsed run and not as good as you are hoping it to be. Same advice: don't panic. Don't try and make the flower grow by pulling it upwards!

About halfway through the week I try to do a stopping run which will probably take two or three sessions. That is, working through the play and stopping when the actors, or you, find something they're still not happy with. With the pressure of a full run off, it is surprising how much extra detail can be sorted out. It is easy for any of you to have not bothered to face some things that have been worrying, either because you don't want to cause trouble, or because you've taken a subconscious decision that it will somehow sort itself out.

You will find it very difficult to concentrate on every run-through and your judgement may be clouded by your mood. If you're tired, you may find the run-through boring or stale for example. It is important to be aware of your moods and always ask the actors how they think it has gone.

You are bound to have one or two runs that don't go well. There is often one that suddenly seems flat, rather like a mid-week matinée six months into a run. This is often because the actors stop playing their parts as if they don't know what is coming next. A bad run-through can be an extremely helpful run-through because it's the best lesson in what not to do. The creating of each moment so that it is fresh, so that when something happens to the character it is a real shock, is what makes a play electric to an audience. They, and the character, are experiencing it at the same time. The same is true of the truth of the emotion. If the actor is experiencing the emotion then the audience will, even if the emotion is not being expressed externally. Eventually the actor should be able to express the emotion as easily as they speak their lines, but it is all too easy at the run-through stage to stop working at the emotional truth.

The note sessions are important. They should now be very detailed but not too long. The actors will be tired and if you hammer away for too long you can destroy their morale. However critical, the notes should be positive. There is a way of giving the most negative of notes so that the actor feels they are being helped. Again, let the actors bring up things, let them play their full part.

In this phase too the strain you are going through will be intensified. This week your creative team and the people in the company, dressers, sound and light operators who will be working the show will be coming to see the run-through. You will be working with your designers after rehearsals. Your designers will be reacting to what they see and advising you that you are not using the set properly! Your lighting designer will want an exhaustive briefing cue by cue about what you want, and your sound designer will probably be feeding sound into the run-through. This is the twenty-five hour day, eight day week.

You will be tired. If you're like me, you won't have found it easy to sleep throughout the four weeks; the play will be going round and round in your head, even in your dreams. You will be feeling vulnerable. Your megalomania (!) has made you the lone arbiter for an awful lot of people and you don't often know how good the production is or if it's going to work. The brilliant director, Michael Elliott, said to me when I was in a blue funk on one production, 'If you don't believe in it, nobody will.' He was right, and that is what you have to do. It's not easy. I remember on several of my best productions, I had no idea in the last week if they were working or not. I knew that rehearsals had been positive, so I just had to have faith. The problem is there were productions which I did have faith with because they were good, but it turned out they weren't! Michael's advice was good. Whatever the pressure, whatever the fear, you mustn't let your nerve crack.

As a balance to this, sometimes you have a string of undeniably good run-throughs and you can know that a standard has been reached which will not vary greatly. You and the cast may think there has been a disastrous run-through, but actually it will be only slightly below the norm. This rule is important to remember as you approach production week. If you've had it right, it should come back again despite the ups and downs of this most extraordinary week.

The technical rehearsal

This is the exciting moment when all the aspects of the production come together. There are two main purposes of the technical rehearsal; the first is to enable your creative team and technical operators to do their work, and the second is to guide your actors to the use of the set and costumes. Technical rehearsals can be long and arduous; you have to keep everyone happy, which is no small task.

I'm assuming for this description that the play you are doing is highly complicated. Your Deputy Stage Manager (DSM) is crucial to the smooth running of the technical. It is as well to have a cueing meeting with the lighting and sound designer the day before the technical. The DSM then marks in their book where the cues are, which prepares them and saves a lot of time during the technical.

On a big show you should try to have a lighting and a sound session before the actors join. You will make adjustments later, but at least you will know that you are all starting from the same point.

There will be dozens of people at the technical: wardrobe, make-up, wigs, props, workshops, all seeing their work realized for the first time. You must give everyone time to do what they have to. Don't leave anything until it is solved. Because you want everything to run smoothly there will be a tendency to say to yourself, 'I'm sure that will be all right.' Don't! It will save time later. You will be keeping up a constant dialogue with your designers because sound levels and lighting always change when the actors are actually there.

The greatest challenge is for the actors. After a month of intimate rehearsals in their own clothes they are suddenly having to come to terms with their costumes – especially if it is a period play – the lights, which may require changes of blocking, the use of the set, which may have many different levels which can't be reproduced during rehearsals, the big production effects which may even involve flying them, and quick changes. This is why it is so important to get the production as solid as possible by the end of the preceding week. The actors' process is going to be violently interrupted, and if they are shaky going into the technical

that can be dangerous. What you are hoping is that the contrary will happen and that the design elements will complement what you have rehearsed and the whole show will take a big step forward.

Prepare them for the technical by saying that they must stop if they need to and not feel guilty! If they are worried about their costumes, and some will be, to tell you quietly, so that you can deal with the problem. The whole technical team will be tired, so be tactful; keep the problem initially between you and them so that no one need get unnecessarily upset. The designers will be as tense as anyone else.

However, you may have to upset people. Parts of the set may have to be changed, or even cut, a costume may have to be remade or even reconceived. The people who have made the sets or costumes may be disappointed and frustrated, the designers may be furious, but it is your job to create the whole and you mustn't back off. Technicals can get very nasty if the director clearly panics, but if you appear calm and they know you are serious and working for the whole, you will get it all to happen.

The three other crucial people besides the DSM, who you must also ensure have the proper time to practise complicated sequences, are the production manager, the stage manager, and the company manager. The production and company manager work behind the scenes, making sure that all the departments have the right back-up and have a schedule to make the adjustments that are arising from the technical. During this period the theatre is in use twenty-four hours a day because things like finishing the painting, or re-hanging flying pieces can only take place after the actors have finished. The stage manager will drive the technical forward liaising between you, the DSM, and the actors, making sure everyone knows what is happening next, or what is being gone back on. It all sounds complicated and daunting but if you have the right attitude it can be the most thrilling experience.

The first dress rehearsal

It is obvious that after all this exhausting and exhaustive work, the first dress rehearsal may be awful. It is unlikely that the actors will be able

to concentrate fully on their acting; they will be naturally preoccupied with getting used to all the new elements. Warn them that that is the case, and warn yourself. They will believe you but it might not stop you from going into a complete panic as you sit there and watch all the work apparently disappearing, leaving you with a flat empty performance! You now have to wait until the second dress rehearsal, if you have time for one, or even the first preview or public dress rehearsal, and hope it will all come back. If the production is solid, and the design complements it, it will. Like the helpful bad run-through, the bad dress rehearsal will automatically tell the actors what not to do. Above all, just tell the actors it was what you warned them of, it was what you expected and everything will be all right. Sleep well!

After the dress rehearsal you will also be giving technical notes, as will the designers. It's only when you see the show run straight through that you can really see how the lighting and sound work, and if the set in a complex production is doing what is required of it. Everyone will be very tired but they, and you, are on the last lap and it's your enthusiasm that will keep them going.

First preview

The final piece of the jigsaw is about to be put in place: the audience. The audience will tell you whether you are on the right track, or not. For that reason, I find the first preview more frightening than the opening night. For one thing, you can get drunk on opening night; you can't on the first preview.

I link the first preview to opening night. Opening night is often poor because the actors are inevitably distracted by the thought of the critics. It makes them slightly sit outside of themselves and that weakens the performance. First preview is therefore good practice for opening night. As on opening night, the cast will have massive adrenaline pumping through them, and the job is to get them to use that adrenaline to do the real job of living their characters' lives moment by moment, and not to allow themselves to be distracted in the wrong way by the fact that

there is an audience out there. Things are bound to go wrong on the first preview, their job is to go on telling the story and the audience will be won over.

The first preview will set your agenda for the rest of the pre-opening period. You will finally know if the pacing is right and, if it is a comedy, you will see where the laughs come and where they do not. So will the actors. Some productions get off to such a good start that there is not much work left to be done. In that case, don't fret, just let the actors rest, but you will usually find that they like to meet at some point, maybe just to warm up by running some scenes. You may find there is a lot of work to be done. Get it clear in your own mind and do it. It is surprising at this stage how fast you can work if you are all on the same wavelength. If there is a great deal of work to be done, don't go at it all at once but, like a sculptor, chip away at it over a period of days until it comes right.

It sometimes happens that the first preview doesn't work and you are convinced you have a disaster on your hands. This is a terrible moment but you can't give in to it. I can remember two awful times when it happened, one was an adaptation of Russell Hoban's great work, *Riddley Walker*, when the audience scarcely applauded at the curtain call, and the other was the Pinero comedy, *The Cabinet Minister*, where the audience hardly laughed at all. I completely panicked internally but told the cast it would be all right tomorrow. To my astonishment, it was. In both cases something clicked into place. It's the Michael Elliott rule. You have to go on believing. I'll deal with what happens if it's a real flop later.

You are nearly there; you just have to get your cast and yourself through the opening night.

Opening night

The atmosphere in the theatre will be electric. First night presents, first night cards, everything, and everyone, in a stage of high excitement. The problem is how to help the cast to use the adrenaline positively. There are two major complications that make it even more difficult than the first preview. The first thing is the nature of the audience. They will

not be normal. Some of them will be there to see you fail, and some of them will be there to help make you succeed. There will be invited VIPs from both the profession and sometimes local dignitaries. They may well not react like the preview audience. Especially in a comedy, you may find them strangely muted, especially in the beginning. All you can do is to warn your cast and tell them to keep to the job and not be thrown.

The second thing is the critics. At the Exchange for example, besides the half dozen or so national critics, there are at least twenty-five other critics from local newspapers, local radio etc, etc. They get two tickets each, so you've got a significant proportion of the audience who are even more atypical. By definition, critics cannot react normally to a show because part of their minds is on what they are going to write, some of them almost immediately after the performance has come down. Even the action of taking notes means that their concentration is being constantly broken. This is the nature of their job and nothing can be done about that.

They are also the people that the cast are most aware of. Tomorrow, or over the next few days, what these people are going to say about them in print to thousands of readers is going to have an affect on their careers and most certainly their egos. There is no knowing how they will react. Years ago I did a rock musical of *Othello* called *Catch My Soul*, which I was convinced was going to be roasted and read with grateful incredulity a set of sensational reviews that could have been written by my mother. By the same token, you can be totally delighted by what you have achieved, buoyed up by the positive response of the preview audience, and find yourself slated by the press.

What I say to the cast, and I think it is true and helpful, is that there are several hundred people in the audience on opening night whose only chance to see the production it is: do it for them.

That closing speech you give to the cast can be almost as important as the speech on the first day of rehearsal because it can steady their nerves and give them a formula to get them through the performance.

I know how difficult this is for the actors. Last time I directed in New York, Broadway producers, trying to lessen the fears of opening night, declared that the critics could come to any of the last ten previews and that opening night would just be an ordinary performance with no critics involved. The result was terrific tension for ten performances instead of one, and even worse, on the opening night, because everyone knew that the reviews were written, especially in the all-powerful *New York Times*; no one could concentrate because the fate of the production was already decided.

Some directors cannot watch their opening night, and indeed it is a temptation, because for the first time since the whole process started, the mighty director has no power whatsoever. It is all in the hands of the actors. I always watch, I think it would drive me mad not to. If you do, my simple advice is try to get drunk if you can! The trouble is, it is amazing just how much you can drink without it having the slightest effect because your adrenaline burns it all up!

The rest of the run

The reviews will have a big effect on the cast. Even if they don't read them, and many don't, they will certainly know what they are like by osmosis. A bad review can have an awful affect on an actor's confidence, and a good one can make them very self-conscious. Do not think therefore that your job is over.

Some directors oversee their productions throughout the run, even every night in some cases. Most directors, myself included, find it very difficult to see their production ever again. You spend so much willpower getting the show on and believing in it, that after it has opened it is rather like a love affair that has cooled. In spite of this, you should check up on it regularly. The actors don't want you there all the time, it can be inhibiting and prevent them really making the show their own, but they do appreciate you giving notes every so often.

I generally leave the production alone for a week or so to let it play in. Once the opening night is over, a barrier comes down in the cast and

they begin to relax, to discover and to expand. If the production has been planted and watered properly, this is a very positive development. Two weeks into a run, the production should have matured way beyond the first performance. The cast will now be playing the audience like a finely tuned instrument, especially if the production is a success.

The first time you see the show after opening night can be a very unnerving experience because you are seeing it objectively for the first time. Sometimes all you can see is what is not right, and that can be very depressing. Warn yourself against this because it may make you overreact negatively and cause you to disturb the cast.

Generally speaking you should be able to keep the production in trim by giving notes but there will be times when your new objectivity can be productive and you will want to make some adjustments because you can see more clearly. All in all, the cast, if it has been a happy experience, will suddenly feel parentless when you go, so be a good parent, let them grow-up but be there from time to time to give advice.

Finally, it's all relatively easy if you have a success; it's pretty horrible if it's a flop. You have to judge for yourself how much it is good to be around. It may be that you make matters worse for the cast. For my own part, I would say this. In the long run your failures, and you will have them, are crucial for your development as a director. It's your failures that teach you, not your successes. Eventually you will come to understand what you did wrong. You may need the help of someone you trust and respect to put you on the path to understanding but once you are on it, you will find yourself strengthened for the future. It can be very hard, and it can hurt, and it can be a long time before you will feel able to approach that kind of play again. Almost forty years after doing a poor production of *Antigone*, a production I thought was wonderful, until I saw it in front of an audience, I am now preparing to do another Greek play; it has taken that long to learn and gain confidence to take it on again. That is the wonder of our job, everything can be redeemed.

That then is a template, but of course every kind of show has its own special procedures. I'm going to deal with some of them.

MUSICALS

A director once said to me that directing musicals was like childbirth. If you remembered how difficult it was, you'd never do it again. He was right. Unfortunately it's a bit like a drug. If you bring it off, it's so rewarding you'll want to do it again. If you then have a flop, it'll simply make you want to do another one.

The first musical I ever directed was by Trevor Peacock and it was called *Erb*. I read the book, i.e. the script, I heard the music and I was delighted. I had done revue before and I had done plays with music like *The Hostage*, and I didn't foresee any special problems. How wrong I was!

Ideally, that is if you have seven or eight weeks rehearsal, the first thing you should do with the cast is to go through the script so that they know their characters well, so that when they're taught the songs they know what they are singing about and what the emotional attack should be. In practice, it happens the other way round. The music has to be learned and this will take at least a week. The music has to be learnt, not only for the obvious reason that the cast can't begin to work the songs until they are familiar with them, but also so that the choreographer can begin their work. The choreography takes up more time than everything, more time than you can possibly imagine; it means hours of rehearsal time each week. The big chorus numbers have to be conceived, executed, and drilled.

You will find yourself wondering when you are going to be able to rehearse the acting scenes. The answer is you're the boss and that's up to you. You are the scheduler and you have to have in your mind how long will be needed for all the disciplines to come to fruition. It seems that everything happens out of sync, and you won't be able to put the show together until very late in the process because you won't be able to

tell how a song or a routine is going to work until it is properly ready. Musicals don't grow like a play does. Dancers are forced and drilled. After you've done a couple of musicals, you will get used to this and become familiar with its rhythm.

That does not mean that you are doing nothing whilst all these learning processes are taking place. The production is your conception and during the pre-production phase you will have worked closely with your musical supervisor, who may be doing the orchestration, your musical director who is your conductor, and your choreographer, to make sure you are all sharing the same vision about what each moment of the show is trying to achieve.

During their rehearsals you keep an eye on what they are doing so that you can check them if they go in the wrong direction. If you don't do this properly, when the time comes to put the elements together, you could be in for a nasty shock and it may well be too late to correct. That is why West End shows often have a long out-of-town run or extensive previews.

Inevitably, you will have to pre-block most, if not all, of the show because there is no time to let the actors feel their way into the parts and then the moves. All in all you may feel more like a Regimental Sergeant Major, than a director.

To date, I have only done new musicals and they have the complication of having the composer, lyricist, and book writer there trying to make adjustments to the material as you go along, although the truth is, the big adjustments don't come till very late in the day.

The casting also has its own problems. Does the show need singers who can act, or actors who can sing? Does it need singing, dancing actors? What is the balance? People who do predominately musicals, however good they are, don't work like actors. They quite rightly tend to take shortcuts. When I did the André Previn, Johnny Mercer, Ronnie Harwood musical of J.B. Priestley's, *The Good Companions*, I didn't realize the difference, and cast a mixture of people working in radically different ways.

The rehearsals are tiring and frustrating and in no way as fulfilling as doing a straight play. You are playing a diplomatic, interventionist waiting-game. You are hoping that everything is going at the right speed and in the right way, but there is no way you can really tell.

You then come, usually very late on, to put the show together. You will begin to judge if the songs are correctly spaced, whether they are sufficiently varied in tempo and feel, and whether the choreography is working. Almost always choreographers make their routines too long initially, so they have to be cut down. The acting levels have to be at the right pitch, so that when a song finishes the acting doesn't seem too small and anti-climatic. 'Bigger, bigger' you will find yourself saying, in direct contradiction to what you would be doing in a drama. It is at this point that things can get very exciting if you glimpse that the complex machine is working. Now you are hurtling towards the production weekend. Before that, you have the first band call with the cast. This is usually a relief after weeks of rehearsal pianists, or tapes. It's your job now, with the composer, to judge the orchestration. A good orchestration will orchestrate the words, making life possible for the singers; a bad one will swamp the number. Is the orchestration right in tone for what each number needs to convey? This is tricky; there isn't much time to adjust. For that same musical, *Erb*, I had an orchestrator who did a superb job with a relatively small band in Manchester but when the show transferred to London with a big band, he over-orchestrated and lost the individuality that he had had before. I had to force big changes. That is your job; you have to make the whole homogeneous. No one else can do that.

The technical is massive because on top of everything, like a huge complicated set, you have to allow proper time and deal with the sound balance which can be make or break for the show. Beware the orchestra seating rehearsal; it always takes forever as the players argue about where in the pit they should be. Unlike the actors, the orchestra only do rehearsal periods of three hours and that can be maddening. I remember one show I did where in mid-song the orchestra stopped playing and trooped off.

More than any other theatrical genre you don't know what you've really got until you have your first audience. Then you will know very fast. I thought my biggest flop, *Fire Angel*, was a great show, and so did the producer Ray Cooney, until its first performance, and then I, I suspect along with everyone else, knew it was probably doomed. The rehearsal period in spite of all kinds of problems with the cast and indeed the choreographer (mostly my fault although I didn't realize it!) nevertheless seemed to be successful. So successful that Cooney offered to buy me out of my percentage for the then princely sum of £20,000 (1977). He had hardly given me a note during the final run-through stage. I turned the offer down because I was so confident. The great musical director Anthony Bowles told me we were about to change the face of British musicals. When the curtain went up in Wimbledon on our out-of-town try-out the reaction of the audience told me that there was too much that was horribly wrong. I saw it through their eyes and realized the gaping holes in the fabric of the show. I then had to slog through a horrendous fortnight of re-writing and re-rehearsals knowing in the pit of my stomach that nothing could save it. To my great relief I was sacked!

Hopefully that bit of experience won't happen very often. More usually you will immediately see what needs to be done, what numbers need to be cut and whether new numbers need to be written. This can be traumatic. A performer may find that his part has been cut to shreds and his one solo has gone. It's a hard business. Stories are legion about how *Old Man River* was only introduced into *Showboat* just before the Broadway opening after weeks of touring, or *Let The Punishment Fit The Crime* into the *Mikado*. *Guys and Dolls* had its book rewritten thirteen times before the director George Abbott – desperate – wrote the version which we know now.

The hard thing for the cast is that they will be rehearsing the new version of the show during the day and playing the old version at night. Rewrites in a musical can take ages because they involve re-orchestrating not only the songs, but the incidental music, the segues between scenes

and underscoring. It's a hair-raising time and people will be tired, and on edge.

You will be bombarded with questions from the beginning of the technical onwards. Advice I was given early on in my career was that the crucial thing was always to answer, even if you're not sure. If the director falters, then there is no one they can have confidence in.

You simply never know with a new musical if you have the right formula and whether you give birth to a flop or a hit, the work will be just as hard. Why then do we go on doing them when the ratio of hits to flops is so appalling?

It's because when you have a hit and you stand at the back of the auditorium and see the galvanic effect it has on the audience you experience an exhilaration which is unique. The song and the dance have always been the life force of society and when they catch fire in a musical it is like nothing else. I have had several hits but the one I remember most was the opening night of *The Black Mikado* at the Cambridge Theatre. It was as if audience, actors, and musicians had come together in one joyful whole. It was a celebration of life. That's why you do it, and that's why it is such a potent drug.

OPERA

I've only done three operas as I write this, Verdi's *Sicilian Vespers*, and two new operas by Tod Machover of Tolstoy's *Resurrection* and David Almond's magical novel, *Skellig*. I do not claim therefore to be an expert but I assume my experiences are much the same as any.

It is not the same as a musical. The main difference is that because an opera is entirely music, you are not in overall charge. The conductor is at least as important as you, if not more so. You are not responsible for the rhythm and tempi of the performance; he is. Whereas in a musical you set the agenda for how the singers deliver the music, here he does. Therefore the obvious point is be careful who you are going to work with because if you want to do a radical production of, say, *Cosi*, it is important that he is in sympathy with your approach and that you see the characters in the same way, otherwise you are in trouble from the start.

This also makes it seem like only half a job because in the theatre you orchestrate the production. The most difficult part of the job remaining is to get the singers to act and, when I say singers, I mean the chorus as well. I have been lucky, both in my singers, and in my conductors. The conductors have been eager to be properly involved in the pre-production and the singers have been eager to act well. But they are not actors and they don't have the actor's process, and they don't rehearse like actors.

They come to the first rehearsal knowing the score and of course ready to sing it flat out. This is in direct contrast to actors who slowly build up their knowledge of their part until they are ready to do it towards the end of the rehearsal process at full tilt. What you have to do then is to 'earth' them, give them the detail of their characters so that they can give their roles the reality the opera needs. This is not as difficult as it sounds because you are both working from the same basic material: the score.

You are underpinning what the performer is already doing.

There is also the question of how much flexibility you have in terms of placing so that the performers can see the conductor, and this goes with the physical limitation of what they can do and sing at the same time.

The opera of *Skellig* taught me something else. Normally you have little to do with the casting process; you are given a cast and you get on with it. This obviously has its difficulties because the casting will have been done entirely based on the artists' singing abilities.

On *Skellig*, I was allowed to be part of the casting process. Once again I had an exceptionally collaborative conductor, Garry Walker, and the hierarchical divisions disappeared. The result was it was very accurately cast from every perspective and that made the job so much easier, just as it does in the theatre. If you can manage it, try and create the same circumstances, it is so worth it.

My method has been to rehearse the libretto like a play and try and get the emotional content of the scene really clear before they sing it. This has worked quite well but sometimes falls flat on its face. In *Resurrection*, a great part of the action takes place in a prison camp in Siberia. Love blossoms in one of the large cells. I rehearsed the singers carefully so that they were as quiet as possible while the others slept. Excellent until they then sing the scene. Unless the other prisoners were deaf, the scene made no dramatic sense in the conventional manner. You just have to get used to that: no one else minds.

You also have to make sure that the singers stand and gesticulate like ordinary human beings rather than waving their arms about and standing like old-fashioned ham actors declaiming Shakespeare. Actually when you get them to do this they find it easier to sing because they are channelling their energy into the aria.

Trickiest of all is the chorus. If you are doing a very stylized production it is easier because it is a question of drilling but if you are doing a naturalistic one you will have to animate them by giving them specific characters and business. A hint here is that the chorus is very large so

find out who the best ones are and put them at the front. Rehearse them intensively and you will find that the others will work to improve, and if they don't, they are sufficiently hidden for it not to matter too much.

Also try and make the chorus feel part of the production. They are used to being treated as second-class citizens and they respond in kind. In Houston, I insisted on the chorus being present at the initial design presentation and director's speeches. This had never happened before. The result was they were very cooperative and since they understood my concept of the production I had something to refer to in rehearsals instead of treating them like cattle. They are very important to your production. It is worth the effort.

Your other weapon is your designer. You should be pictorially very bold so that the story is being told visually. More than any other genre you need a concept. If the concept is strong enough you can get away with fairly simple movement. What you have to remember is that the audience is there primarily to experience the music; your job is to enhance that experience, not to dominate it. That experience is very stylized and the opposite of naturalistic. You have to accept that but try to make it real; that is, truthful.

The other frustrating thing about rehearsals is that you are continually having time off for either singing rehearsals or for the singers to rest their voices. You may have thought that rehearsals for the theatre were gruelling and relentless; you'll begin to long for that kind of concentration.

The production week of *Skellig* went like this. On the Monday was the sitzprobe; that magical moment when the singers and the orchestra play together for the first time. Nice for the director to hear; but nothing for him to do. Tuesday and Wednesday were the technical days where there was of course only a pianist in the pit. Then on Thursday, there were two sessions on stage with the orchestra and the singers. This was the conductor's rehearsal: nothing for the director to do!! Friday there was a dress rehearsal; Saturday was off, and Sunday was a public dress rehearsal. The frustration I felt was awful and the see-saw of emotion very wearing. I became quite detached which was alarming because it

was opposite to what I usually felt. By opening night, I was genuinely calm because the show was set and had worked in front of an audience and, I realized, there could be much less variation than in a play. My job was effectively over. Of course, that is never true. You have to keep your concentration at full pitch despite everything, and you still have the job of helping company morale.

You will miss the cumulative excitement of the build-up to the technical/production week. At the Houston Grand Opera, where I did *Resurrection*, I realized with a huge orchestra of about sixty and a cast of eighty-five, I wasn't going to get any time with all of them together. It was simply too expensive. The technical was done with a single pianist and adjustments were done in the rehearsal room if you were lucky.

I learnt then, especially if you are a rookie opera director, the value of having a good assistant, preferably one who reads music. They will steer you through the pitfalls and will manage to communicate the changes you want the chorus to make, even if they have to stand in the wings during a performance and bellow at them through a megaphone.

What sustains you through all this, much more than a musical, is the music. You don't have to analyze the text; you lie back on a couch and let it invade you. Images come into your mind and you're filled with the inspiration that a genius can give you. Of course it's difficult with new operas. We didn't get the music for *Skellig* until the design process was over. The whole production had to be planned without the score. Luckily everything seemed complementary. I hope never to experience the opposite! In rehearsals it is the same; the music lifts you onto another plane and, sometimes, even though you should prepare your blocking very carefully, as for a musical, you won't get it right until you have the cast standing there and singing.

That is the final reward. We have all seen, far too often, dreadful productions of operas apparently stuck in some old-fashioned nineteenth-century Victorian tradition, but when a great singer, a great orchestra under a great conductor interpreting a great score, with good acting and staging all come together, it is a transcendent experience that is unique.

<u>Footnote</u>

You can actually be unable to sing in tune or read a score to direct musicals and opera. You might cause hilarity in your cast when you try to demonstrate how to deliver a song or aria, but you can still tell when someone else is a good singer, or not. You might not be able to read a score but you'll soon learn how to follow one, and that is all you need. Take it from me; I know!

NEW PLAYS

To direct the world première of a play is one of the great excitements of directing. You are going to be the first person to give life to the play. Therefore this is one of the most creative roles a director can play.

The challenge is that you are dealing with a living playwright and almost invariably this causes great difficulty. Every playwright thinks they have written a masterpiece and they have conceived in their heads how the production should be, especially in terms of how the characters are and how they should look. Since a primary creative artist's inspiration comes partly from their unconscious, this can mean that they don't, necessarily, understand their own play.

The first new play I ever directed I thought was a brilliant pastiche sending up *Waiting for Godot*. The playwright thought he had written an intensely serious original piece. The result was, after he had seen a run-through, that I had to ban him from the auditorium. That excellent playwright Ronald Harwood wrote a marvellous play, *Poison Pen*, insisted on directing himself, and missed the obvious theatrical device that he had written and censored the essentially bisexual nature of the material. He later acknowledged it. To get one of my favourite playwrights, Gerard McLarnon to change a comma, never mind a line, was an heroic and epic struggle. I found Rod Wooden backstage giving notes to the cast of *Your Home in the West* during the first preview. The major relationship I have with a playwright is with the Canadian, Brad Fraser. You never know if the process with him is a thing of joy, or a bloody battle. That's how it is. It is almost impossible for a playwright to let go of his conception but that is precisely the implication of writing for the theatre rather than being a novelist. You cannot control what the director and the cast is

going to do but you can have a bloody good try and, in extreme cases, you can denounce the production publicly, or even take out a court injunction to stop the production being shown.

Plays come to you in very different stages of completion. Sometimes you get the finished article; sometimes you are required to be a dramaturg and coax cuts and rewrites out of the writer. It doesn't matter if the writer is inexperienced, or an old hand; this can be very tricky.

There has over the past decade or so evolved a practice of workshopping new scripts before you produce them. I always viewed this with suspicion. I couldn't understand why, if for hundreds of years writers just wrote and their plays were produced, this was valuable. However some playwrights, like Brad Fraser, use workshops as part of their process and it is remarkable to watch his scripts evolving. The danger is that, if the director's advice is bad, ensuing drafts can actually get worse. I have seen this happen too often for comfort.

It is important to form the best relationship you can with your writer from the word go. It sounds obvious but in the case of the first play I mentioned, I was sent it, I read it, I liked it, I agreed to do it and the playwright was delighted. I never discussed it with him. It just didn't occur to me to do so.

Now I wouldn't dream of agreeing to do a play unless I was sure that the writer and I are in basic sympathy as to what the play is about. I like the writer to be at auditions, both so that I can better understand what they are after, and so that their view of who could play the part might broaden. If not, the writer might come to a run, like Brad did once, and be totally horrified because no one was how he imagined them.

Equally important is the design process for the same reason. The writer will have a strong idea of how the production should look. If he's Eugene O'Neill, the detailed description of what he wants, even down to the colour of a character's eyes, can be intimidating, to say the least. Tennessee Williams's directions of how to stage *The Glass Menagerie* are minutely itemized. You and your designer may disagree radically with the writer's vision. You will have to decide whether to try and win them

over as you go, or simply face them with a *fait accompli*, which it is too late for them to change.

As far as rehearsals go, I always ask the writer to be there as I go through the play for the first time. They can hear through the beats and objectives the main line of interpretation and they can contribute at that stage. I then ask them to go away until the run-through stage of the last week. There are two reasons for this. First, their continuing presence can be an inhibition in the rehearsal process and, second, they can get so close to the production that they can't be objective about it. If they come back for the last week they will have the objective eye that you need so much.

One crucial rule is that they never give notes to the actors without talking to you first. It is a disaster if there are two bosses giving contradictory orders; the actors become dispirited because they are being pulled in opposite directions and any sense of security or confidence is quickly eroded.

When it all works well, you and your cast will have realized the essence of the writer's work, and expanded it in ways that they never imagined consciously. This is hugely and immensely rewarding. When it doesn't work; it's horrible. My experiences have been mostly positive but I have heard of instances recently where well-known playwrights have been so obstinate, even when preview audiences have given them clear signals, that they will not cut or alter anything in their script. The result is that their play has received a critical mauling when there was a good play waiting to get out. It's like working with a difficult actor, you have to use all your resources of persuasion and diplomacy to make sure the full potential of the piece is realized. Which leads me to my last point.

What is certain is that the cast will be full of requests to change how their lines are written. This will start on day one. Tell them that you want them to stick with the play as written. If the playwright is any good (and if he isn't why are you doing the play?), he will mean what he has created. If after testing out the lines there are legitimate problems, then you can persuade the writer to make the changes. Rookie writers

can easily become overawed by the rehearsal process and particularly by older, experienced actors, and readily start to rewrite. This can lead to open day on the text. There probably will be things to be done and the playwrights themselves, when they hear the text out loud, may want to change lines but keep this part of the process tightly controlled, or you may find yourself in trouble.

FARCE

A lot of directors won't touch farce and if you don't have a sense of humour and a love of gags it's best to keep well away. It is very hard work and requires a lot of nerve but the sound of an audience rocking with laughter is one of the most rewarding sounds you have ever heard.

The essence of great farce is that it is only one step away from tragedy. If it didn't work itself out at the last moment then the leading characters' lives would fall apart. There are many great French farces, mostly by Feydeau, though I prefer Hennequin and Veber, and at least three English ones, *Charley's Aunt, See How They Run,* and *The Happiest Days of Your Life,* all of which I've done. I've also written two, a zany *Three Musketeers,* and a spoof *Dracula* called *Bats.* This is what I am writing about now rather than the American farces like *Arsenic and Old Lace,* or the Ben Travers oeuvre which is played entirely with eccentrics in a situation you don't believe in, in other words where there is nothing truly at stake.

Take *The Happiest Days of Your Life,* it's set just after the end of the Second World War in a boys' boarding school. By mistake, the Ministry of Education billets a girls' boarding school on them. The respective Headmaster and Headmistress, surrounded by their entrenched staff, battle for supremacy to protect their charges. What happens is that love blossoms between two young teachers, and doesn't between a predatory frustrated spinster and her terrified opposite number.

It is set at that moment when the old English Puritanism about sex and the cloistered nature of separately sexed education began to crumble. For some it was liberating, for others, those who found it safer to have nothing to do with the opposite sex, it was terrifying. The play is hilariously funny but is much funnier if it is produced with this serious undertone in mind.

When you analyse *Charley's Aunt* it has an extraordinary undertone. Kitty, Amy, Ela and Charley are all orphans and Jack's mother is dead. You can't play this overtly in the text but it makes their desire for love particularly intense. The men, Sir Francis, Jack, Charley and Fancourt Babberley, are all stricken with the British disease of shyness. The women make the running, albeit in Ela's case unwittingly. The play, which I believe is closely modelled on *The Importance of Being Earnest* is about love versus greed for money as Spettigue holds most of their fates in his hand. Most movingly, Lord Fancourt Babberley first of all finds himself being wooed for his/her money by elderly men and then falls in love with a girl who he can't woo because he's disguised as a woman. I had done this play twice in 1965 and 1972 with the incomparable Tom Courtenay but at that stage I hadn't realized the real rule about farce and, although the productions were successful, when I did it as a proper serious play in 2010, the result was not only moving but much funnier. In *See How They Run*, a German POW has escaped. He is armed and the lives of those who live in the vicarage are in danger. If the audience believe that the characters in the play believe in the situation, then the play is funny. If they don't, they aren't, or at least not as funny as they should be.

Casting farce is very hard. You need first-rate actors but if they don't have what I call 'the chuckle', then the farce won't work. What is 'the chuckle'? Difficult to describe but easy to spot. They are actors who are inherently funny and engage an audience's sympathy immediately. They must also enjoy the genre. A good serious actor, even one who is quite clever at business, will be like a lead-weight on the show if they haven't got the chuckle.

Your preparatory work and the first week of rehearsal will be different from any other genre. You will pre-block much more carefully and fully because positioning for the gags is crucial. Simple example: a character comes on stage, doesn't see another character on there, makes some terrible remarks about the person they don't see, then something happens that makes them turn and see the person. It requires the correct positioning and only you can see it.

In the first week of rehearsals, although you will have broken down the text in the usual way, it won't take long to go through the play. There is little complexity in farce and so you will be getting it on its feet pretty quickly to give the actors the feel of the production. Your aim is as usual to get them to the point when they are confident enough to start inventing business organic to their own characters.

The invention and trying out of business is singularly unfunny and serious. You'll find yourself saying something like, 'Why don't you walk across to the table, slip on that patch of water, fall off balance, crash into that table, grab the ruler which flips the rubber into the air and falls onto the head of the other teacher who is correcting prep.' The actor does it. You watch and say, 'No that isn't funny. Try it again, and this time the rubber lands in the inkpot and splashes the Master's corrections, he jumps up and backs into the Games Mistress who is practising her tennis swing and brings her racquet down over the Headmaster's head.' You watch again. 'Yes, that's funny, let's keep that.' So it goes on and by the time you get to the last week you and everyone else have probably lost faith that what you have invented is funny at all. There's no one in rehearsals to laugh and everything seems purely mechanical and the more you run it the less funny it seems.

I remember doing *The Miser* with Tom Courtenay and becoming convinced that we were producing the unfunniest show ever. I managed to rustle up a small audience of Friends of the Theatre to watch a late run-through, they screamed with laughter and my confidence was restored. You will get used to this but it is very nerve-wracking.

Enforced speed is of the essence. If ever there is a genre which requires the audience to be galloping to keep up with you, this is it. Pauses are out. It's sometimes necessary to tighten scenes in terms of cueing quite early on, as this both energizes the actors and gives them a glance of what the final result will be. If you go too slowly, the audience will see through the inevitable mechanical contrivances of the author. They mustn't have time to think. The only pauses should be for laughter. Even here, don't let the audience dominate you. Once each laugh has hit its peak and is

beginning to die, tell the actors to come in with their lines. Not only does this help the rhythm stay correct but it builds and builds until that great moment when the audience laughs so loudly and even applauds, so that you just have to wait.

Gags are, of course, mechanical but a good farceur will make them seem natural and therefore funnier. That old chestnut – the double-take – is hysterically funny if done for real in shock surprise. No gag should seem like a gag, and the actors should never seem to be asking the audience to laugh. Feydeau's advice was never to bother with laughs in the First Act but to draw the audience into the play so that they are involved in the story, all the whilst winding up the mechanism tighter and tighter and then letting it go, then the frenzy of what ensues will be totally believable. I don't fully subscribe to not bothering about laughs in Act One but he's right to emphasize involving the audience in the reality of the situation.

To get the right breakneck speed and the reality of the play, you will have to be a martinet and drill the cast because the pace is not real and will have to be imposed. Your pay off, and theirs, will come with the first audience and their laughter.

COMEDY

If you ask any director to make their wish-list of plays they want to direct, it is pretty certain that the list will include few, if any, comedies. Somehow we feel that it is in the tragedies, the great dramas, that are the most important parts of the theatre. Yet on the Greek vases you will find that Comedy and Tragedy are given equal prominence. At the Greek festivals each day ended with a Satyr play, a comedy.

In Tragedy, the audience undergoes catharsis born out of fear and pity; pity for the characters in the play, and fear for ourselves because, as we share their human faults, we risk ending up like the characters. In Comedy, we laugh at those very same characters. Being able to laugh at that which otherwise terrifies us, is one of the best things theatre can do for us.

As with farce, directors are often scared of doing comedies because they require a knack of invention and a sense of humour that cannot be taught. The famous quotation goes something like, 'Tragedy that's one thing, but Comedy, that's a serious business.'

That quote is crucial for the approach of a director to comedy. A good comedy is serious. It is about something serious. It takes a certain view of it and at the end things turn out well enough for there to be the possibility of a future for most of the characters. It provides a relief for the audience.

I'm briefly going to refer to two comedies that I have directed twice, once at the start of my career and once after about thirty years, to show you what I mean.

The first is *She Stoops to Conquer*. It was written much later than the Restoration but its style means that it belongs with Sheridan, Congreve and Farquhar. I first did it in 1969 for the 69 Theatre Company at

the suggestion of Casper Wrede. We had been to see a not very good production of it and he felt that Young Marlow would be an ideal part for Tom Courtenay. I thought it was a very funny play, so I agreed. I didn't analyse the play, I just did it. I could see what was funny but I didn't think to wonder why it was funny, I just did it. With Trevor Peacock as Tony Lumpkin and Juliet Mills as Kate, it was a great success. It went to the West End and ran to packed houses for its six month run.

When I came to do it again, I had by this time, as I mentioned before, come to the point of breaking every genre down into beats and objectives in order to sink the anchor as deep as possible into the heart of the play. This time, instead of just concentrating on the Young Marlow/Kate relationship and using Lumpkin and Mr and Mrs Hardcastle as figures of fun, I realized that the play was about a seriously dysfunctional family locked-up with itself miles away from civilization in the country.

Mr and Mrs Hardcastle are in their second disastrous marriage, they both have children who detest each other and Mr Hardcastle allows his wife to tyrannize over her ward, Constance. By the end of the play all the children are released from tyranny, two of them will marry and the third, Lumpkin, can lead the life he wants to and grow up. As in many great comedies, one character is left out in the cold, Mrs Hardcastle suffers the fate of Malvolio or Mrs Malaprop.

SHE STOOPS TO CONQUER

Oliver Goldsmith

Section taken from ACT I

SCENE - A Chamber in an old-fashioned House.

Enter MRS HARDCASTLE and MR HARDCASTLE.

MRS HARDCASTLE: I vow, Mr. Hardcastle, you're very particular. Is there a creature in the whole country but ourselves, that does not take a trip to town now and then, to rub off the rust a little?

> There's the two Miss Hoggs, and our neighbour Mrs. Grigsby, go to take a month's polishing every winter.

HARDCASTLE: Ay, and bring back vanity and affectation to last them the whole year.

Beat 1

Mrs Hardcastle's objective is to make Hardcastle change his mind. Hardcastle's is to make her stop.

> I wonder why London cannot keep its own fools at home! In my time, the follies of the town crept slowly among us, but now they travel faster than a stage-coach. Its fopperies come down not only as inside passengers, but in the very basket.

MRS HARDCASTLE: Ay, your times were fine times indeed; you have been telling us of them for many a long year. Here we live in an old rumbling mansion, that looks for all the world like an inn, but that we never see company. Our best visitors are old Mrs. Oddfish, the curate's wife, and little Cripplegate, the lame dancing-master; and all our entertainment your old stories of Prince Eugene and the Duke of Marlborough.

Beat 2

Hardcastle's objective is to make her feel ashamed. Mrs Hardcastle's is to make him feel ashamed.

> I hate such old-fashioned trumpery.

HARDCASTLE: And I love it. I love everything that's old: old friends, old times, old manners, old books, old wine;

Beat 3

Mrs Hardcastle's objective is to frighten him. Hardcastle's to frighten her.

> and I believe, Dorothy *(Taking her hand.)*, you'll own I have been pretty fond of an old wife.

MRS HARDCASTLE: Lord, Mr. Hardcastle, you're for ever at your Dorothys and your old wifes. You may be a Darby, but I'll be no Joan, I promise you. I'm not so old as you'd make me, by more than

one good year. Add twenty to twenty, and make money of that.

Beat 4

Hardcastle's objective is to make her feel better.

Mrs Hardcastle's to make him realize her worth.

HARDCASTLE: Let me see; twenty added to twenty makes just fifty and seven.

MRS HARDCASTLE: It's false, Mr. Hardcastle; I was but twenty when I was brought to bed of Tony, that I had by Mr. Lumpkin, my first husband; and he's not come to years of discretion yet.

Beat 5

Hardcastle's objective is to take her down a peg.

Mrs Hardcastle's to make him face the truth.

HARDCASTLE: Nor ever will, I dare answer for him. Ay, you have taught him   finely.

MRS HARDCASTLE: No matter. Tony Lumpkin has a good fortune. My son is not to live by his learning. I don't think a boy wants much learning to spend fifteen hundred a year.

Beat 6

Hardcastle's objective is to make her ashamed.

Mrs Hardcastle's to make him see sense.

HARDCASTLE: Learning, quotha! A mere composition of tricks and mischief.

MRS HARDCASTLE: Humour, my dear; nothing but humour. Come, Mr. Hardcastle, you must allow the boy a little humour.

HARDCASTLE: I'd sooner allow him a horse-pond. If burning the footmen's shoes, frightening the maids, and worrying the kittens be humour, he has it. It was but yesterday he fastened my wig to the back of my chair, and when I went to make a bow, I popt my bald head in Mrs.   Frizzle's face.

Beat 7

Hardcastle's objective is to make her apologize for her son.

Mrs Hardcastle's to soften him.

MRS HARDCASTLE: And am I to blame? The poor boy was always too sickly to do any good. A school would be his death. When he comes to be a little stronger, who knows what a year or two's Latin may do for him?

HARDCASTLE: Latin for him! A cat and fiddle. No, no; the alehouse and the stable are the only schools he'll ever go to.

Beat 8

Mrs Hardcastle's objective is to make him recant.
Hardcastle's to make her face the truth.

MRS HARDCASTLE: Well, we must not snub the poor boy now, for I believe we shan't have him long among us. Anybody that looks in his face may see he's consumptive.

HARDCASTLE: Ay, if growing too fat be one of the symptoms.

MRS HARDCASTLE: He coughs sometimes.

HARDCASTLE: Yes, when his liquor goes the wrong way.

MRS HARDCASTLE: I'm actually afraid of his lungs.

HARDCASTLE: And truly so am I; for he sometimes whoops like a speaking trumpet –

Beat 9

Mrs Hardcastle's objective is to evoke Hardcastle's pity.
Hardcastle's is to make her face the truth.

(*TONY hallooing behind the scenes.*) – O, there he goes – a very consumptive figure, truly.

Enter TONY, crossing the stage.

MRS HARDCASTLE: Tony, where are you going, my charmer? Won't you give papa and I a little of your company, lovee?

TONY: I'm in haste, mother; I cannot stay.

MRS HARDCASTLE: You shan't venture out this raw evening, my dear; you look most shockingly.

TONY: I can't stay, I tell you. The Three Pigeons expects me down every moment. There's some fun going forward.

Beat 10

Hardcastle's objective is make his point.

Mrs Hardcastle's is to make Tony stay.

Tony's objective is to go.
HARDCASTLE: Ay; the alehouse, the old place: I thought so.

MRS HARDCASTLE: A low, paltry set of fellows.

TONY: Not so low, neither. There's Dick Muggins the exciseman, Jack Slang the horse doctor, Little Aminadab that grinds the music box, and Tom Twist that spins the pewter platter.

Beat 11

Hardcastle's objective is to make her see his point.

Mrs Hardcastle's is to make him see the lowness of his friends.

Tony's objective is to defend his friends.

MRS HARDCASTLE: Pray, my dear, disappoint them for one night at least.

TONY: As for disappointing them, I should not so much mind; but I can't abide to disappoint myself.

MRS HARDCASTLE: *(Detaining him.)* You shan't go.

TONY: I will, I tell you.

MRS HARDCASTLE: I say you shan't.

TONY: We'll see which is strongest, you or I. *(Exit, hauling her out.)*

Beat 12

Mrs Hardcastle's objective is to stop him from going.

Tony's objective is to go.

HARDCASTLE: *(Solus.)* Ay, there goes a pair that only spoil each other. But is not the whole age in a combination to drive sense and discretion out of doors? There's my pretty darling Kate! The fashions of the times have almost infected her too. By living a year or two in town, she is as fond of gauze and French frippery as the best of them.

Beat 13

Hardcastle's objective is to relieve his feelings. To hold sway.

Movement

The Hardcastles : to dominate each other.

Tony : to get out of the house.

I have no doubt which was the best overall production. The second one gave life to a complete world so that every scene was filled with human detail. The audience was involved with the fates of everyone.

The same was true of *Loot*. I was fortunate to do the second production of *Loot* in 1966, the one that saved it from oblivion after its disastrous pre-West End tour came to a grinding halt. Michael Codron asked me if I would have a second try at it, and I did with Century Theatre in Manchester. Everything revolved around Inspector Truscott, brilliantly played by Julian Chagrin, and again it was a great success resulting in its international life.

When I came to do it again later, I realized that Orton was writing about a nuclear family. McLeavy and Fay are the parents, Hal and Dennis the children. The family is apparently middle-class, religious and decent like every family in their street. In fact, like every family in their street, says Joe, they are murdering, criminal, bisexual, greedy and rotten. It is Truscott, the denizen of the law but amoral, and more rotten than anyone that is the catalyst for the near break-up of the family. The result was once again more satisfying than the earlier production.

There were two reasons for the later successes. The first was that I took them seriously, but the second was that I had grown older and was now looking with closer interest at the older generation rather than just the younger one.

Wilde never wrote a play that wasn't serious. All his plays are attacks on the society he lived in, so he had to cloak the attack in comedy. Shakespeare's bisexual comedies that Charlotte Brontë was warned against reading for fear of being corrupted, the same, and Orton absolutely the same, he could never have written those plays unless they were comedies. There is the story of the first production of *Entertaining Mr Sloane* at the Habimah in Israel. After three weeks of rehearsal the Habimah asked the

original director of the London production, Patrick Dromgoole, to fly out and help them because they seemed to be getting nowhere with the play. He went, sat through a run-through. 'What are we doing wrong?' they asked. 'It's a comedy,' he replied. They hadn't realized and played straight, it was a repulsive, vicious play. If Coward's *Private Lives* is played with Strindbergian intensity it is darkly funny because the brilliance of the writing offsets the intensity of the battles between Elyot and Amanda.

So to rehearse the play you need a mixture of the straight play and the farce approach. Take as long as you need breaking the text down and letting the actors understand their complex characters. Then eventually you will have to speed things up, making sure as you do that you lose nothing of the complexity but going as fast as you can in relation to that.

One extra thing, when the play is properly wound-up and set loose don't forget that the plot itself will provide the laughs as it twists and turns and unravels. I was stumped by the horse-pond scene in *She Stoops to Conquer* the first time round. That is the scene where Lumpkin on the pretext of taking his mother and Constance to a stern aunt miles away, actually drives them round and round in circles finally dumping Mrs Hardcastle in the horse-pond. It was terminally unfunny in rehearsals. I tried every trick I knew but the scene remained stubbornly earthbound. I apologized to the cast before the first night and said we'd sort it out later. The play went well until I realized with a sick feeling that the scene was upon us. The scene started and to my total disbelief the audience roared with laughter right through it. The characters had been properly established and the audience wanted to enjoy Mrs Hardcastle's discomfiture, Lumpkin's revenge and Hardcastle's bewilderment.

'Comedy, now that's serious.'

SHAKESPEARE

S hakespeare, if not the greatest artist the world has ever known, is certainly the greatest playwright ever. I have done sixteen productions of his genius and they have been the most challenging and rewarding part of my career, over fifteen percent of my total output. I'm going to write about them because by doing so I will be able to show how a director evolves over the years and might be of help to directors approaching him for the first time.

The first thing to say and perhaps the most important is that Shakespeare was a man of the theatre. He was a theatre manager who oversaw the building of theatres, he ran companies, he was an actor and he was a playwright. Too many people, especially academics, forget this, and actors and directors become inhibited at the idea of acting or directing him. Remember they are finally just plays and the approach to them is the same as any other play. Like any other play they have their own particular problems. One is that they were written four hundred years ago and the other is that they were written in dramatic verse. As with any play from a different time you have to connect them to our time to bring them fully alive and as with any other play written in verse you have to know how to speak it. The third point, which can scarcely be called a problem, is that Shakespeare was a genius who had as profound an understanding of humanity as anyone who has ever lived. You will have to measure up with him but then you have to with the three Greeks, Aeschylus, Sophocles and Euripides, Ibsen, Strindberg and Chekhov. There is no special toolkit for directing Shakespeare.

My introduction to Shakespeare was at prep school when I was about eleven. I had an eccentric English teacher who was obsessed with *Macbeth*. My memory is that most lessons consisted of his reading the play

aloud, playing all the characters and creating in that classroom a world of witches, murder and madness. For my birthday present that year, I asked my surprised mother for a recording of *Macbeth* and was duly given two LPs of the recent Old Vic production starring Alec Guinness and Pamela Brown. This I listened to endlessly, poor parents, till I knew the text off by heart and all the intonation of the actors. I went to the Old Vic and Stratford as I grew up and saw I don't know how many productions, some awful but some like the ground-breaking Zeffirelli production of *Romeo and Juliet*, Bill Gaskill's mesmerising *Cymbeline* and, of course, Michael Elliott's *As You Like It* with Vanessa Redgrave, which remain in my mind to this day.

Then in 1965 at the very young age of twenty-two, John Harrison asked me to direct *The Winter's Tale* at the Birmingham Rep. I was at an age where nothing held terrors but I did know that I had better find out about verse speaking.

Some directors use specialist coaches to teach their casts how to speak the verse, presumably because they don't feel they can cope with it adequately, so surrounded is it with technical jargon and mumbo-jumbo. I believe it an important part of a director's weaponry and it is not nearly as forbidding as it seems. I have written about how I learnt about it in my autobiography, *The Worst It Can Be Is A Disaster*, and I'm reproducing that section here because I can't write it any better.

Neville Coghill agreed to give me a 'tutorial' on directing Shakespeare. Coghill was an Oxford don who was an authority on verse speaking and indeed directed the OUDS Major Shakespeare in Worcester Gardens every summer. His 'tutorial' in verse speaking was a revelation. He made me turn to Act V, Scene 3 where Paulina conjures the statue of Hermione to come to life:

Music, awake her; strike!

'Tis time; descend; be stone no more; approach;

Strike all that look upon with marvel. Come,

I'll fill your grave up: stir, nay, come away:

Bequeath to death your numbness; for from him

Dear life redeems you. You perceive she stirs:

He had already explained the break halfway through each line called the caesura, and end-stopping, which meant you also took a break at the end of every line, less when there was no punctuation, more where there was, now he told me to read. I rattled through the first line and a half. 'No, no, a semi-colon is a pause, a colon a bigger pause, a full stop a bigger pause. Leave in all the pauses.' I reread those lines with pauses and I realized what he meant. The statue doesn't come alive immediately. It takes so long, Paulina starts to doubt that it will. It is a being coming painfully and slowly back into the world after years of 'death'. Apply these rules to the whole play and you will see how Shakespeare gives his actors instruction as to how he wants it played. So look at it again:

Mus<u>ic</u>, aw<u>ake</u> her; str<u>ike</u>!

(A pause before *strike* as if she wants to make the moment magic.)

'Tis time; descend; be stone no more; approach;

(Then an open line with four marked pauses and cajoling words. By the end of the line, doubt has crept in.)

Strike all that look upon with marvel. Come,

(Third line has the caesura, the pause, just before the last word. She is losing her cool. Then *Come*, end of line.)

I'll fill your grave up: stir, nay, come away:

(Next line begins with an extraordinary image, *I'll fill your grave up*. That is something unthinkable. Then big pause with the colon in the caesura. Urgent second half of the line with short words, the first three monosyllables.)

Bequeath to death your numbness; for from him

(Say the next line up to the caesura out loud *Bequeath to death your numbness*, the brilliant simplicity of numbness. *For from him*, end of line. What? What?)

Dear life redeems you. You perceive she stirs:

(Beautiful first half of the line, *Dear life redeems you*. No wonder Hermione responds. Numbness is one way of dealing with life but *dear life redeems you*. Caesura with full stop. Hermione moves, *You perceive she stirs*.)

This is one of the great moments in Shakespeare but every second of all his plays should be looked at this way. No writer has ever given clearer instructions to his actors!

Coghill despised the Royal Shakespeare/Peter Hall Classics Illustrated verse speaking as boring and lifeless, almost as much as he despised what he called 'The Kottomites', the followers of Jan Kott, whose radical reinterpretation of Shakespeare, especially in Brook's *Lear*, was all the rage. The rest of the verse-speaking mystery, he believed, took care of itself, if you had a feel for the poetic value of the words. Even the question of the iambic pentameter, with its five stresses in each line, would take care of itself, if you observed the caesura, the end-stopping and the punctuation, because it would then come naturally to the actors, even as it did in Shakespeare's day. He was absolutely right. It takes about half an hour to teach a cast how to speak the verse so that it is more alive and resonant than I have ever seen on the Stratford stage.

I did that first Shakespeare production more or less unconsciously, that is to say, I had no overall concept of how it should be done, or indeed what it was about. I loved the story and I told it as best I could. Visually I let my designer do what she wanted which was based on the prevailing periodish approach. I did have the idea of framing it as if the audience was gazing into a fire and the play emerged from and eventually returned to the flames and this helped the fairytale feel of the play. I still have my production copy of the play and my notes tell me that I did understand the story very well but there was no conscious attempt to impose myself on it.

Apart from the verse speaking which worked immediately very well, I learned very basic lessons. The first is to understand the text. This sounds easy because there are plenty of erudite editions of the plays which discuss the more obscure passages but actually you have to be rigorous to understand every word because you may think you have but actually words have changed their meanings over the centuries and you will also be faced with different possible explanations of what they mean. I strongly recommend you buy a copy of C.T. Onions's *A Shakespeare*

Glossary which is more exhaustive, inspired and helpful than any single edition I have read.

The same Neville Coghill who taught me verse speaking also taught me that judicious emendations to help the audience understand the play are allowable. In *The Winter's Tale* when the Young Shepherd brings the baby, Perdita, to the Old Shepherd, the baby is referred to as 'sure, some scape'. Scape means bastard and Coghill suggested it was legitimate to change the word. At the same time he believed that in any Shakespeare play there will be dead wood that hinders the audience's appreciation and that cutting may be necessary. I'm sure he was right about both those things, although I didn't immediately act on the idea of cutting.

The production was a great success, I assume because the audience was wrapped up in the story which was simply told. My assumption was that I had cracked Shakespeare at my first attempt and a difficult late play at that. So as soon as I ran my first company, Century Theatre, later that year, I was determined to do *Macbeth*. I can remember very little about it except, just as with every Shakespeare I have ever done, I spent the entire rehearsal period in total ecstasy. You are plugged straight in to genius and it gives you an extraordinary energy.

The third production, *The Merchant of Venice*, was done in the same state. It was a conventional production done without real discussion in Elizabethan costume and set in, well, postcard Venice. These first three productions were very successful but they happened to be the three Shakespeares that I was to do again later and, it is the contrast between the productions, or even, in one case, the lack of contrast, that is of interest.

It was *The Merchant* that first made me conscious of what I was really doing as a director of any play, let alone Shakespeare. When I saw the production objectively for the first time, which you don't do until the first night is over, I realized that I was expressing myself in the production very powerfully. I am Jewish and clearly my emotional affinity with that side of the play was very apparent. Again Coghill had taught me that if Shakespeare says something through his characters, he means it. Thus

when Shylock is told that he must forfeit his possessions and become a Christian and says, 'I am content,' he means it. For me to ensure that he did mean it was a big thing and I didn't realize until I saw it. For the first time, I realized that just telling the story as clearly and simply as possible was not enough, there had to be creative interpretation so that the profound essence of the play could be communicated.

Romeo and Juliet with Tom Courtenay was my next, and my first, collaboration on Shakespeare with the designer Johanna Bryant, who has done almost all my subsequent Shakespeares. Later we would begin to develop a different approach but this production was not markedly different to what had gone before.

Then came *A Midsummer Night's Dream* with the same designer and there was a difference. It had begun to dawn on me that setting the plays in an Elizabethan period was actually putting up a barrier between the real power of the plays and the audience. The plays are profound, passionate, and often disturbing revelations about the great mysteries of our existence, yet the danger that I felt I, and other productions I had seen, were falling into was making them seem like museum pieces from a bygone age so that audiences could disassociate themselves from the characters. They felt they were nothing to do with them.

The *Dream* came at a time in my life when I was disillusioned with love, sex, marriage, the whole caboodle. To me the lovers in the forest, falling in and out of love for no rational reason, were nightmare creatures. The Fairies were literally nightmare creatures sporting multiple penises out of a Bosch nightmare. The play was set in modern Greece. For the first time I was trying to jolt the audience out of its comfortable relationship with a piece of classic theatre.

I learnt one important thing from this experience which predictably divided audiences and which I don't regard as a success, and that is that your job is to give life to your author and not to impose a view of the play which actually reduces its scope. It is not there for your personal therapy or fantasy. I reduced the *Dream* and it is quite fashionable for directors to indulge themselves in concept productions of Shakespeare that do precisely that. They are often quite, or very, successful but they are not

acts of creativity but of destruction. It was a step forward, although it felt like a defeat but a stumbling one.

I stumbled on. Next was *Much Ado About Nothing* (which I will come back to when I talk about how to handle difficult actors). I needed to make the war as real as possible because it seemed to me the play was about men coming back from the war and redirecting their testosterone at personal relationships. I plumped for setting it at the end of the Napoleonic Wars because it seemed to me the last moment before the relationship between men and women in England changed as the Victorian era arrived. It looked well enough and the production seemed to please but I still felt dissatisfied. Whenever I read a play by Shakespeare I was carried away by its wisdom, its richness, its poetry and its drama. Whenever I staged one it didn't seem to come near to what I had read on the page. I hadn't ever flopped in production but on my own terms I had never really brought one off. It took a nasty shock to create real movement.

Twelve years after its first production, I was to direct *The Winter's Tale* again at the Royal Exchange, in a production that was to do a major European tour on both sides of the Iron Curtain. I was very confident because I had done it so successfully before. I now knew the play very well and thought I understood it far more consciously than before. My speech at the first rehearsal was superb. I analysed the play as a clash of the Apollonian (Sicilia) and the Dionysiac (Bohemia). Leontes, like Pentheus in the *Bacchae*, was in denial of his animal side. What is repressed finally rises up and explodes poisoning all around it. The child, Perdita, is abandoned on the wild shore (which of course doesn't exist) of Bohemia. There she meets Polixenes's son who believes her to be a shepherdess, and they fall in love. Finally the plot sorts itself out and they marry, thus joining the Apollonian and Dionysiac, and causing the rebirth of the supposedly dead Hermione. The speech went on for about an hour and everyone was in raptures.

The next day I woke up with the mumps and the doctor told me it would take weeks to go and there was no possibility of being able to rehearse the play. Now I had long ago become wise to the fact, and

so should you, that I was prone to getting ill in rehearsal. I knew this was the frightened voice inside me, the coward saying if you're ill you don't have to do the show and you'll never be found out. I realized that the speech may have delighted the company but it had terrified me. To the doctor's astonishment the mumps disappeared and I went back to rehearsal the next day.

I was right to have been terrified for what I had failed to do was to reinvent my approach to the play. I had simply tried to recreate the twelve-year-old production. This meant that although I understood it better, I was bringing nothing new to it. I had subconsciously briefed the designer to do what I had done with another designer a decade before and, if nothing else, styles of expression are constantly evolving, and this production was stuck in the past. It again was not a flop but I was bitterly disappointed.

The first lesson I learned was never do a play for the second time unless you have a very good reason. Either you did it badly the first time, or your attitude to it has changed and you have seen more in it and therefore have more to say than before.

The big lesson was that I hadn't truly realized the profundity of the challenge of doing Shakespeare. I tried to crystallize the dilemma. The plays were written in the sixteenth/seventeenth century. Wherever they were set, Greece, Italy, Spain, Cyprus, Ancient Britain, Medieval Denmark, contemporary Windsor, they were about England at that moment, Elizabethan England. They were played in virtually no set and always in contemporary costume. Shakespeare was speaking directly to his countrymen and they knew it and wanted to hear.

Four centuries later, the plays were still the greatest plays about the human condition and urgently needing to be done. I had done a production of *Much Ado About Nothing* written in the sixteenth century, set it in the nineteenth century in order to speak to an audience in the late twentieth century. I had found a way of doing the play but had I actually built a strong enough bridge to span the centuries? How did you build that bridge? Was it possible at all? I knew that if there was any point

in going on, and I couldn't bear the idea that there wasn't, I would have to be far more radical and a little bit braver.

Measure for Measure was the turning point, not the absolute realization, but the turning point. I felt I knew the main theme of the play, the meditation on power through Angelo (the abuse) and the Duke (neglect) and about sexuality and repression. Again following Coghill's dictum, the final union of the Duke and Isabella at the end had to mark the end of an extraordinary journey for both of them and had to be made to ring true.

Measure for Measure is called a problem play and the main problem is the Duke. Who is he, and what is he? It was when I was reading the speech, 'Be absolute for death' that lightning struck. I recognized it, I knew I had seen it somewhere else before but I couldn't remember where. Then it came back to me. It is practically an exact quote from *The Tibetan Book of the Dead*. I decided then and there that the Duke should be disguised as a Buddhist monk. He wouldn't have to lurk behind a cowl, which usually makes life very difficult for the actor because you can't see his face, he would simply as the Duke have an elaborate wig and then in character shave his head. It would be a completely convincing disguise and it would make the audience listen to his every word.

I set the production in modern times changing the name of Vienna to 'The City'. That was not particularly original but it was absolutely apposite and the strange monk proved to be the guide into its lower depths. Making him come from another culture threw the problems of the City into sharp relief. The settings by Johanna Bryant were very simple and always contained one dominating image rather like an unfolding dream.

I am not saying the production was a complete success but it had a musicality and an excitement which I had not achieved before. The audience were stimulated into a live relationship to the text and the way of approach did not seem to diminish or constrict the play, it just brought it up fresh. The actors seemed to be released by the context and

the context thrust them forward to the audience rather than swamping them.

Having achieved this, which as you can imagine I was very excited by, I knew I would never slip backwards even though I might get things mightily wrong. Then came the production where everything came together for the first time.

Jonathan Miller once said that one day you would be working with an actor and you would suddenly realize that you had met your Hamlet. You could hear him speak the lines and you'd know you had to do the play. I met Robert Lindsay.

I worked with him regularly over a two-year period and I asked and he agreed to play Hamlet. There were two major matters that we had to be at one over, how to cut the play and when to set it.

If you did the whole of *Hamlet* the audience would be sitting there for four and an half hours. Anyway, what is the whole of *Hamlet*? Is it the *Hamlet* of the Folio, or the good Quarto? What of the bad Quarto, which seems to have a much better scene order and must have been based on a prompt copy? I realized that you made your own *Hamlet* choosing from all the available texts and cutting to shape the whole. Jan Kott in *Shakepeare Our Contemporary* tells how in the police state that was Poland, his *Hamlet* focussed on the political, murder in the night, the spies like Rosencranz and Guildenstern, and so on. I decided my *Hamlet* was to be the opposite. I saw it as essentially a family play, the father, a mother, and a son in one family, a father, daughter and a son in the other. Based on this premise I cut ruthlessly. The political side was axed, even Fortinbras. It seemed to me that the end of the play with the kingdom being ruled by someone called Strong in Arms was not what would work for the audience. The text was pared down to run just under three hours. This was exciting work; almost detective work. Should it be 'this sullied flesh' or 'solid flesh'? Almost every word had alternatives which completely altered the feel of the speeches. I did adopt the bad Quarto scene sequence which I still think places 'To be or not to be' in a much better context.

That was the easy task; the nightmare was how and where to set it. I knew I wasn't going to do it Elizabethan and I couldn't see the point of setting it in any other century so it seemed that modern dress was the only option. The problem was it didn't seem right. It foundered on the King. There was no equivalent except perhaps the Shah of Persia and he didn't seem to be a potent image. All-powerful kings no longer existed. I reached the point where there seemed no way of setting it in any period. Suddenly I realized that would be the answer. Don't set it at any time, set it in a rehearsal room with the actors in rehearsal clothes.

There was no set, just a bare stage and the actors set around the stage, stayed on the whole time and got up to act. The rehearsal clothes were evolved during the rehearsals to underpin the character they were playing. You couldn't, for example, have Ophelia wearing a plunging neckline at the beginning of the play. The play was lit in open white by four North Lights. There were no cues. The props were essentially rehearsal props. The only exception to this style was the Players scene which was costumed and lit like a conventional RSC production.

It worked. The first scene, as it would have been at the Globe, was brightly lit. The actors had to act the dark and the cold. In a second the audience were involved. They were being asked to use their imaginations and they were compelled to listen to the words.

The scene between Hamlet and his father, the Ghost, is the best example. Usually this scene is layered with special effects so that one scarcely listens to its content. Here, Philip Madoc just stood up in his cashmere sweater and Hamlet acted you're my father and you're a ghost. The scene is a father/son scene where the father burdens the son with the invocation of revenge. It is an intimate, passionate scene and is the spur to Hamlet's behaviour for the rest of the play. This style of presentation brought out the full content.

The result was a success beyond our wildest dreams. The production played for eight weeks in Manchester, six weeks touring the country and three weeks at the Barbican, and there was never an empty seat. In Manchester, people queued from four in the morning to get the seats that

were sold on the day, and groupies came again and again. Teachers wrote to say what a breakthrough the production had made in their efforts to introduce their pupils to Shakespeare. The audience was packed with young people.

Of course the vital element in all this was Lindsay's phenomenal performance; he had a way of talking to the audience direct in the soliloquies so that he was talking personally to them and more importantly for them. However, I'm sure it was the removal of the usual clutter that enabled him to be so released and I'm sure it was the imaginative involvement of the audience that gave the evening its power.

There it was, for the first time I could say that I had brought off a Shakespeare, and what a Shakespeare, perhaps the most famous one of all. Now I knew how to do his plays.

No I didn't. I immediately walked into my own trap. My next production of Shakespeare was my second one of *The Merchant of Venice*. I cared passionately about the play, about the treatment of Jews and the effect it had on them, about the clash of the Old and New Testaments and the importance of the Fifth Act which was about the difficulty of love and which had to be the climax of the play, although Shylock doesn't appear in it. I had the great Norwegian actor, Espen Skjønberg in it, and I had Harriet Walter as Portia. Indeed it was a very good production but not in the way I insisted on it being staged.

It was modern dress and that worked well enough and the design was minimalist which also worked well enough but I insisted on the actors sitting round the stage again, this time wearing green dressing-gowns which they took off when they got up to act. The idea being by making it a play within a play it would have the same effect on the audience's relationship to the actors as in *Hamlet*. That was rubbish and it simply seemed like a slightly bewildering device. The green dressing-gowns are still around, used by the actors backstage to protect their costumes. I wish the Company would get rid of them. They still invoke chuckles for those who remember where they came from. The lesson is simple. There

is no one way to do Shakespeare, unless you want to constrict him. Each production needs to be a new approach.

Twelfth Night was set in an Illyria which was a dream world, an Alice in Wonderland world. The costumes were a mixture of periods, Malvolio was a Cromwellian, puritanical figure, while Toby Belch was more of a green wellington booted squire of our time. The characters were what was appropriate to them and there was no attempt at uniformity. Again this had the virtue of throwing all the rules out, the audience was prepared to accept whatever was thrown at them. The set was less successful. It was meant to be a moonscape and was a cratered dome shape. This was fine when you explained it but until then people wondered why the production was taking place on a giant pizza.

Apart from these two productions I had also done a collaborative production of *Cymbeline* which went very well but I had come nowhere near repeating the success of *Hamlet*. Then David Threlfall said he wanted to play Macbeth. I agreed to do it on the understanding that we would not schedule it until I found a way of approaching it. It seemed to me that *Macbeth* was the greatest play about evil ever written, how it involves the Macbeths and then is projected outwards onto the country they reign over. However, every production I had seen, including my own, had been a play about two great parts for actors and nobody else, and although intermittently gripping never seemed to bring this terrifying text properly alive.

I went through my usual processes and was getting nowhere when I read Primo Levi's harrowing account of life in a concentration camp, *If This Is A Life*, and its sequel, *The Truce*. *The Truce* tells about the repatriation of the Jews after the war was over. This took months as they were shunted around endlessly in trains. They were no longer in concentration camps but their condition was still gruelling. To save their society, whenever they stopped at a small town or village, they would put on a show, a satirical show to let off steam. That gave me the idea for *Macbeth*. This production of *Macbeth* would be put on by the prisoners in a concentration camp after lights out in order for them to try to

understand how the evil that had been visited on them could possibly have come about.

So yes the actors would sit around the stage because they were also spectators. Any props would be fashioned out of materials that they could scavenge. All the actors would be in prison clothes with shaved heads – male, and female. Any sound effects would be created by the actors. The only cheating would be the lighting which had to be more theatrical.

It was a harrowing and difficult rehearsal period. *Macbeth* is a famously unlucky play, which is not surprising; evil spirits are involved, witches run wild, ghosts appear. Examined properly this is bound to have an unsettling effect on everyone connected.

It worked. Without even trying, the Fourth and Fifth Acts evoked the nuclear winter that the Old Man describes and the feeling of Hitler in the bunker as Macbeth rages blindly against his inevitable fate. As in *Hamlet* the audience were not distracted by the usual paraphernalia of *Macbeth* and the language now had a context.

There was however one major flaw. Many people who knew the play said it was the best Shakespeare they had ever seen but people who didn't know the play were somewhat bewildered. Everyone looked the same, and what were they doing in a concentration camp? With hindsight I should have had some sort of introduction to make the context clear. So the production was a spectacular success and an unsatisfactory failure at the same time. For me, despite the error, it was the second time I had come near to realizing the full scope of a Shakespeare play.

I had never thought I would do *The Tempest*. I admired it but it had always seemed to me at one remove, a cerebral formal dance. Then I read a science fiction book – I can't recall its name – where the hero is dangerously ill suffering a sort of breakdown and he experiences a kind of dream where he finds himself a leper in a *Lord of the Rings*-type environment. He has various adventures, I think the book was part of a series, and when he regains consciousness he has somehow found the strength to survive in real life.

Suddenly I had the idea of how to do *The Tempest*. The play is an interior journey. The island is a symbol of introversion. Prospero comes face to face with his spirit side, Ariel, his animal side, Caliban, and his anima, Miranda. He also faces his worldly side with the Lords and his low level cowardly side with Stephano and Trinculo.

The first scene took place in Prospero's study, the study of a scientist, rational man. Then Prospero had a breakdown, the storm hit the study, the sailors invaded the space, his desk split apart hit by lightening and Caliban and Ariel came out of it. All the characters when they first appeared wore masks of Prospero who was played by David Horovitch. The play was a self-examination. It was, if you like, a Jungian adventure.

The main component of Prospero's inadequacy was his sexual attitude. At the end of the play he is reconciled with every part of himself, except Caliban. He goes back to the real world with everyone, except Caliban. All he can manage with Caliban is 'this thing of darkness I do acknowledge mine', but he leaves him on the island. I scrapped the text of the masque that is played before Ferdinand and Miranda and substituted a dance. Look-alikes of Ferdinand and Miranda celebrated their coming nuptials but the dance turned sexual and that is what drove Prospero to stop it in his furious rage.

Every nook and cranny of the play came alive and no side of the play was lost. It could still be seen as a parable of corrupt power and redemption and it remained magical. The main message was by facing oneself and letting go of one's Ariel and one's Miranda, you integrated them into your personality instead of keeping them prisoner by magic, i.e. will. The breaking of the wand was therefore a mark of gaining a new maturity.

It was a satisfying experience and I thought it would be the last Shakespeare I would do. It was his swansong and I felt I got as far as I could to understanding the soul behind the plays, the soul that couldn't integrate the Caliban side of his nature. Once again I was wrong.

Years ago I had directed *Catch My Soul,* which was a rock version of *Othello,* and I fell in love with the play. I had the idea of doing a

production in negative. Othello would be white and everyone else black. This would place the predominately white audience in sympathy with Othello's position. The only white man in a black community married to a black lady, always aware that she might find her own race more attractive than this elderly white man, always eaten away by the fact of being an outsider and perhaps being looked down upon and by some despised and hated. I even cast the production; Trevor Peacock was to play Othello and Hugh Quarshie, Iago. Then Hugh withdrew and with it the production collapsed. That seemed to me to be that.

Then Paterson Joseph came to the Exchange to play in Lorraine Hansberry's *Les Blancs* and there was the ideal Othello. Paterson has that nobility and purity that Othello needed. I knew Andy Serkis wanted to play Iago and I managed to persuade them to do it. Ironically, Paterson was the hardest to persuade, he wanted to play Iago!

I knew that this production was unlikely to fail because I had two great actors. I had never seen an *Othello* where both he and Iago were equally matched. The heart of the play was secure. My job was to do a production that allowed them full reign and was not bowed down by a director's concept.

Johanna was again designing and we agreed we needed as minimal a set as possible. Venice was played on a map of the world; Cyprus was a simple stage with lots of sun and sound effects. The military was emphasized. The bed of the last act was a soldier's camp bed. The clothes were as devoid of period as possible. Soldiers' uniforms have not changed that much down the ages and the two women, Desdemona and Emilia were designer Edwardian. Bianca and the islanders were Mediterranean and exotic. The image of an occupying army far from home was powerful.

I'm not saying this was genius but it was preferable to several concept productions I had seen where, for example, the Venetians were Fascists. Quite simply the two actors were superlative. They were up there in my personal pantheon with Robert Lindsay's Hamlet.

Then there was another one. Josette Bushell-Mingo had been wonderful as <u>all</u> the women, except the Mother, in *Peer Gynt*, and my son

told me that she wanted to play Cleopatra. Now if you asked me what my favourite Shakespeare was I would have said *Antony and Cleopatra*. I had played Antony at school. In my view it is the peak of dramatic poetry. After my 'death' I would stand in the wings just to hear the sublime speeches of Cleopatra. I had always wanted to do the play, was slightly in awe of it, and I certainly didn't know how to cast it. The idea of doing it with Josette was irresistible.

The set was very simple. On one side of the stage was the formal Roman world, and on the other side the sensual Egyptian world, thus the epic play with its cinematic sequence of scenes could unroll seamlessly. Shakespeare wrote so that there should be no pauses, unless specifically marked in the verse, during the scenes, and absolutely no pauses between the scenes. His productions were on a bare stage, we had to create the equivalent. We knew that the Romans couldn't be in togas. Knobbly-knee syndrome is just too risible and distracting. The Romans were clothed, by Johanna, in invented uniforms, cold, frightening and efficient. The Egyptians were, of course, much easier to conceive with their Middle Eastern sexuality.

The big innovation was the battles. In Shakespeare they are offstage and the audience knew and accepted the convention. I felt this wouldn't do because each battle has its dramatic point and the audience would feel cheated.

I asked Mark Bruce, a choreographer who I have worked with many times, to conceive the battles as representing the interior personalities of Cleopatra. They became movement sequences, heavily stylized. The first battle Antony loses because Cleopatra distracts him, the second he wins because she is in his mind in harmony, in the third he suffers a disastrous defeat because she has become a demonic nightmare image. The replacement of the public life of Antony the great·leader, by a passionate, totally fulfilling relationship was vividly expressed. For all their frailties by the end of the play their great love, which they knew for certain would survive death, was a thing of great beauty. 'Let Rome in Tiber melt' may have seemed indulgent and negligent at the beginning

of the play but, by the end, you felt that it should, because something far greater had replaced it.

Well there it is to date. I once again feel that I may have done my last Shakespeare. Of the Tragedies, *King Lear* remains. Because I never really knew my father, I can't connect to the central dilemma, although as a work of art it is stupendous. The great comedy I have not done is *As You Like It* because I don't think the Michael Elliott production could be bettered. I've done all the late plays except *Pericles*, and if the right actor materialized that would be a temptation. I have never done a History play and that would certainly only happen because of the right actor wanting to do one.

I hope this tour through my relationship with Shakespeare has whet your appetite. I have written this chapter this way to try to show you that you must have your unique adventure as you must with any playwright, you have to find your language. Sometimes you will succeed and sometimes you will fail but if you love him enough you will find the way to bring him alive. It is a lifelong affair and you never get tired of it. Great genius will always give, and demand, more.

GREEK TRAGEDY

I have no doubt that this is the most difficult genre to direct. If building a bridge over the four hundred years to Shakespeare is difficult, it dwarfs in comparison to the two and half thousand years that separate us from Aeschylus, Sophocles and Euripides, three of the greatest playwrights ever, whose plays still resonate on the profoundest level with us today.

The problem is in the form of the plays. The violence crucial to each play always takes place offstage and is reported by a messenger or a herdsman in six page speeches. Then there is the chorus. It is they who take the play to their deepest level but how do you do them? How do you make a chorus of Theban citizens dramatic?

As I mentioned in an earlier chapter, I did Sophocles's *Antigone* about forty years ago. It was at the Nottingham Playhouse and it had the American actress, then a well-known film star, Shirley Knight, in the lead. I read everything I could about Greek tragedy, especially how the choruses were danced and sung. I had a very good choreographer Flic Colby of *Pan's People,* and with her and the composer, Terry Docherty, I attempted to make the chorus vocally interesting by splitting up the lines between different actors or by the whole chorus chanting in unison, and by creating interesting patterns of movement. Visually and aurally, the production was rather beautiful. The acting was difficult. The cast were an amalgam of Playhouse actors and actors I knew. I used the usual method of casting.

We rehearsed with great intensity and commitment and I was convinced that the production would be a success. I was convinced until the performance started on opening night. It was perfectly respectable but utterly boring. Although everyone did their best, and there were

some very good actors in the cast, there was only one performance by Paul Dawkins as Tiresias which really worked. The chorus were simply dull and no one really listened to what they were saying. I was poleaxed. I watched it several times during the run and I couldn't see what I should have done. Therefore the thought of doing another Greek tragedy filled me with horror and I put the thought out of my mind.

However about ten years ago I became fascinated, and then obsessed, with Euripides's *The Bacchae*. Its major theme, which I took to be the imperative of embracing and blessing our Dionysiac side, our sensual, animal side, seemed to me one of the most important themes of today. There were scenes in the play like Pentheus dressing up as a woman which could have been written today. I began to think seriously about doing it but the old problem remained: especially the chorus. In this play they are the female followers of Dionysus and they represent the positive aspects of Dionysus, as opposed to the destructive side which is so powerfully experienced in the play by Agave's murder of her own son.

I knew that until I solved the chorus there was no point in going forward, and I couldn't solve them. The words they had were full of archaic references which had little meaning now, and in every version I read they remained resolutely page-bound. By this time I was discussing the play with the choreographer Mark Bruce who was also magnetized by it. We decided it was undoable and commissioned a new play inspired by *The Bacchae* and set now. It didn't work. How could you explain the Gods in modern terms? We gave up.

A couple of years later, I went to see Mark's dance company at The Place doing a programme called *Sea of Bones*. It was a great evening and one sequence in particular was a richly sensual experience. I met him after the show and said that I thought I knew how to do the chorus. If we could find the right version and the writer permitted it, we could cut the choruses down and explain their content through dance and, of course, music.

I found lying on my desk a version by Mike Poulton which had been lying there unread for at least a year. It was/is a brilliant version because,

while being faithful to the original, its use of poetic language bridges that two and a half thousand year gap in one leap. That's the first lesson. Don't attempt Greek tragedy unless you have a version that you are not constantly trying to breathe life into. Believe me, you will not find that easy.

I met Mike Poulton who agreed that we could edit the chorus. I was still nervous of the big speeches, especially the Herdsman and Messenger who report the violence of the Theban women, driven mad by Dionysus. Their speeches are six pages each and Dionysus has two speeches nearly as long at the beginning and the end of the play. I had to know I could make them work. We decided to do a week's workshop with three dancers and three actors. The three excellent actors were in a play I was doing at the time. Lesson two, which may sound obvious, was having excellent actors wasn't enough, they had to be in themselves, as human beings, the right casting. I have said before you can't cast someone who has not got for free the intrinsic qualities that their role requires. In Greek tragedy it is even more so. The actor is acting himself as he would behave in the given circumstances. The performance springs directly from the actor. He does not become another, he is himself projected in the character. That was why the Tiresias all those years ago was so good. He didn't have to act the spiritual sagacity that the character needed. It was obvious that the actor, John Kirk, who was playing the Herdsman, was the Herdsman in the way that the other two weren't (no criticism of them). I knew John could do that speech and indeed he eventually played the part. Mark experimented using illustrative movement for the dancers during the speeches but quickly found that if the actor was right, the words were the only important thing. There were now no excuses not to proceed.

Casting was going to be difficult. Apart from the need for each actor to be essentially a leading actor with the ability to explore the most extreme emotions there are: how do you act a God? Uniquely Dionysus is onstage for practically the whole play. Indeed the first actor to audition asked me, 'How do you play a God?' I said I hadn't a clue, either you had it naturally in you or you didn't. The actor did his audition and he had

it and I cast him! As I say, it's not like normal casting. You are not going to sit in rehearsal discussing character backstories. You are not, as I was startled to find, going to do for the most part, beats and objectives (there aren't any in six page speeches). You are going to try and earth the essence of the actor. The casting was actually easy. You could tell in seconds if the actor was possible.

When I had done *Antigone*, Michael Elliott had come to see it. He told me, 'What disappointed me is that you of all people didn't earth it.' That sentence haunted me all the way through the preparation and rehearsing of *The Bacchae*. I was greatly helped by doing the play in the round. Dionysus could really talk to the audience and the chorus could really confront them. You probably won't have that benefit. The audience were the undecided Thebans. The battle for their acceptance between Dionysus and Pentheus was really alive. The chorus worked as we hoped they would and the long speech actors made us really believe that they had seen the terrors they had seen. The ghost of *Antigone* was laid to rest for me.

So my advice is only do a Greek tragedy if you passionately believe in what the play is about. Do not commit to it until you are sure you have a vital way of doing the chorus and have the right people to work with. It's a bit like doing a musical. You will work with the Principals whilst the choreographer and composer are in another room with the chorus. It'll be a while before you can put the pieces together and see if they fit. Do not start without a version you know will work. Mike Poulton was very appreciative of my production but I was able to say to him in all honesty that with the same approach but without his version the production would not have worked.

I have to say finally that *The Bacchae* worked but I would still think twice before attempting another one. The choruses are so different in each play. It was immensely rewarding to do *The Bacchae* but the hardest thing I have ever done.

HOW TO HANDLE DIFFICULT ACTORS

Here are three case histories:

1. MUCH ADO ABOUT NOTHING

Because this actor is very ill at the moment I'm just going to call him 'K'. I was casting *Much Ado About Nothing* and a colleague suggested I offered Benedick to K. He was a very well-known actor who had been in the West End, on Broadway and had done seasons at the RSC; I also knew him socially. He lived near me in Richmond and we belonged to the same club. He accepted the part and we very quickly talked about the production and agreed on the casting of Beatrice. All seemed set fair.

He suggested we go to the first rehearsal together because as he said, 'Few actors realized that the director is nervous at the first rehearsal' and I might appreciate the company. That was a very nice gesture.

We arrived at the rehearsal room. The first person we met was the actor playing Don Pedro. 'Hello K,' said the actor 'we did a tele together.' K grunted. The actress playing Beatrice came over to greet him. He grunted.

When it came to the read-through, K mumbled his way through the play, giving absolutely nothing. The next day his wife phoned to say he wasn't feeling well so he had gone to bed and wouldn't be coming in. I spent the day rehearsing scenes he wasn't in and then that night I phoned him. I told him I knew that he was scared but that staying at home and avoiding rehearsing would only make him more vulnerable. He came to rehearsals the next day. Rehearsals were a nightmare. He refused to express anything, demanded his boots, his props, shouted at stage management when they reasonably pointed out that it was unusual to have your costume at the beginning of rehearsal and generally made

himself as unpleasant as possible.

Here's an example: he was doing a scene with Don Pedro. Don Pedro finished his speech and there was a silence. 'It's your turn K,' I prompted.

'I know,' he said. He paused, then turned to the actor and said, 'Is that how you're going to do it?' in tones of withering scorn.

Another example: the poor actress playing Beatrice was having a terrible time. It's a difficult part to rehearse if you're getting nothing from your leading man. 'K,' I said 'Benedict is happy in this scene, he's full of life and vitality. K looked at me.

'K's happy inside,' he said. That was that.

It was hell, made worse by the fact that every night he would ask me to have a drink with him as if to make sure that I didn't hate him. Every night I did have that drink and, needless to say, I paid for every drink every night.

Eventually we reached the last week of rehearsal. I was very tired and very desperate. We were now in Manchester and I invited him out to dinner. I was very young and he was very famous. I said to him, 'K, things aren't going well.'

'You're damned right!' he said and proceeded to slag off all the members of the cast. 'K's doing his job,' he said 'but they aren't doing anything.'

I took a deep breath and said, 'No K, they're fine. It's you who isn't doing anything.' PAUSE.

'I'll do it at the dress rehearsal,' he said.

'Please K, you must do it now. Poor Beatrice is distraught. You can't wait till the dress rehearsal.'

Lo and behold he had worked out his whole performance and very good it was too. He did do it properly in between tantrums and tirades but it was too late. The rest of the cast had no time to adjust and grow. Of course he took all the reviews.

This is a very truncated version of the full awfulness of that period. During the run I travelled up with his wife to see the show. 'He adores

you,' she said 'he wants to work with you again.' My turn to grunt. PAUSE. 'You won't work with him again, will you?'

'No.'

'He does this to all the directors he works with. Why?' At that time I had no answer.

2. WAITING FOR GODOT

I've written about this in my autobiography. The actor was Max Wall. I had done *Godot* with Trevor Peacock and Anton Rodgers but Trevor suggested we do it again with Max Wall whom he knew. Max Wall was a hero of mine. I met him, he was very eager to do it, so I agreed. About four days into rehearsal, he suddenly said, 'Right, that's it, I'm off.' I was stunned.

'Why?' I asked.

'You knew what you were getting; you booked me.' I didn't understand. 'You obviously hate what I'm doing. I'm off.' I assured him I thought he was wonderful. 'But there's nothing on your boat race.'

'What do you mean?'

'You don't think what I'm doing is funny.' I tried to assure him that I did but that whereas I smiled or laughed when he first did a gag, I simply didn't do it every time, but it didn't mean I didn't appreciate him. 'And there's another thing,' he said 'you keep on stopping.' I explained that that was so that everyone could understand what the play was about and that this was usual. 'Well how am I supposed to learn my lines then?' he asked.

I was nonplussed. 'All right,' I said 'we'll try not to stop!'

The other complication was that at lunchtime Max hit the Guinness. This meant that during the afternoon sessions he told funny, very funny, jokes, did imitations and sang to his own guitar playing. Eventually I had to rehearse the other members of the cast separately. When we came together again, I hit on a plan. I told my friend Trevor that if I needed to give Max a note about, for instance, cueing, I'd give it to Trevor instead and pretty angrily, even accusing him of ruining the scene. Amazingly it

worked very well and we stumbled towards opening night.

I also realized that he didn't understand half of what he was saying, especially in Vladimir's big speeches. At first this alarmed me, as you can imagine. However I realized that even if he didn't understand them, he said them rather wonderfully so I sat on my instincts and let him get on with it.

What he did understand were gags, though even then with the famous 'bowler hat' sequence he was reluctant to use his full repertoire. 'But it's Beckett,' he would say. 'Are you sure?'

Quite frankly he detested me.

That all changed when the show opened at the Exchange and got sensational reviews. I became a hero. The gags appeared thick and fast. By the time the show got to London it regularly overran by up to twenty minutes. I didn't mind; I was watching a genius at work.

3. MACBETH

I've written about this too in my autobiography, so I won't go into all the gory detail. Suffice it to say that Frances Barber who was playing Lady Macbeth hated me. In her own words, 'I want to cut your fucking head off.'

As with K, I had discussed the idea about the production with her and David Threlfall, who was playing Macbeth, over very pleasant dinners to make sure everyone was happy. This was the production that I have already described set in a concentration camp. Having endorsed the whole idea she took against the concept and me and tried to turn the whole company against me. It was far too late to change things, even if I wanted to, so I had to live through the entire process with the atmosphere charged with poison.

When she told me that she wanted to cut my fucking head off, she also made it clear that she had no intention of leaving the production. Since she was obviously going to be a fabulous Lady Macbeth that was a mixed blessing.

Eventually the production opened to great reviews and she, of course, received raves.

<u>So what do you do?</u>

Those are just three of many, many more stories I could tell. They are particularly extreme but variations on those themes occur with unfortunate regularity. They always come at you out of the blue because, unless you are a masochist, you do not knowingly cast someone who is going to cause mayhem. Of course there are cases where an actor has an unjustified bad reputation. I remember the great Ibsen translator, Michael Meyer saying that some actors got bad reputations because they worked with poor directors but they were actually very good to work with.

Why do they behave like that? The answer once again is 'fear.' Every actor wants to be excellent and every actor, who is worth their salt, fears to fail. Star actors have got to the top of the ladder and become afraid of risking themselves in something new and different. They think they know how and why they are where they are and they don't want to risk their reputation by straying outside known territory. I once worked with that terrific actor, Peter Vaughan on *The Lower Depths*. He had a difficult reputation but I adored working with him on the part of Luka. However on the first preview he gave a performance which had absolutely nothing to do with what we had rehearsed. When I tackled him on it he apologized profusely but said in front of the audience he panicked and gave them what they would expect of him, not what we had prepared. He was back on form the next night. With Max Wall he was on completely unfamiliar territory, with Frances it was a mixture of many things but at base it was fear.

What I unconsciously did with all of them and now rather more consciously do when faced with the equivalent problem is to keep talking to the side of them that wants to succeed, keep saying the right things that you know somewhere they will listen to. Even if they seem to resist what you are saying, it will be going in somewhere. In these three cases I have mentioned the actors all gave fine performances and, except when I have miscast an actor, I have rarely looked at a performance on stage which was wilfully wrong.

It is important for the rest of the cast to see you sticking to your guns. They too will be listening and using what you are saying. If they retain faith in you then there is more chance of the production hanging together, even if it will never either be a pleasant or rewarding experience.

Finally, and it sort of comes under this heading, there is the question of firing an actor who is not delivering. This is an awful dilemma. You have cast the actor so you may feel, as I did for years, that it's your responsibility and you have to keep faith with him or her.

I learnt my lesson in a horribly exposed way on Broadway, where I should have fired a leading actor and didn't. I felt it was my choice and my fault, and I persevered even though the management encouraged me to get rid of him. He got better but now I realize that better is not the point; it is not right it is just better. The production, which in other respects was well cast and rather good, failed and a lot of very good actors suffered as a result.

Faced with the same dilemma the next time when I was rehearsing *Peer Gynt*, I did not hesitate. I felt awful firing the actor but then a member of the cast came to me and thanked me for doing it on behalf of the company. 'It showed you really cared,' she said.

My advice then is clear. For the good of the production and all the people working on it, you have to do the unpleasant thing. One caveat: I have known directors wanting to fire people simply because the actor had a slow process and was causing the director to wobble. Be absolutely sure the situation is irredeemable but if you are sure, do it!

WORKING WITH PRODUCERS

Unless you are directing for your own company, i.e. the Artistic Director, you are not the boss; the Producer is. Although there are subtle differences, this goes for the subsidised and the commercial sectors. In the subsidised theatre, the Producer is the Artistic Director, although there is often someone called the Producer who is responsible for the organizational side of the production. The Artistic Director has final artistic responsibility for what goes on in the theatre. In the commercial theatre it is the Impresario who is the Producer. As with directors every producer is different so that it is very hard to make any rules of how to behave.

Very early in my career, at the age of twenty-one, I had an eccentric amateur as my producer in New York. Things got so bad between us that she actually sent cops into the theatre to have me thrown out. A few months' later I was sacked by a weak producer at the behest of a star actor who had a substantial amount of money in the production. Therefore, and this took me a long time to get over, I regarded the producer as the enemy. He is not. First, he has hired you because he believes you are the best man for the job. Second, it is his money so he wants you to be a success. Having said that there are crooked producers, straight producers, producers with taste, producers without taste, hands-on producers who interfere with you from the word go, hands-off producers who never give you a note, efficient producers, inefficient producers and every shade, mixture and variety of the above. So how do you deal with this problem?

It depends on your status and how desperate you are for the work. If you can, make sure you talk through as much as you can as to what you expect from each other so that at least there are ground rules. It helps if there is a good chemistry between you. If there is a natural antipathy,

the relationship can quickly degenerate into a power battle. My big rule, learnt painfully over the years, is KEEP CALM. If you regard him as the enemy, as I did for many years, the working relationship can quickly become intolerable.

Listen to what he has to say carefully. His casting ideas may be different from yours but not therefore wrong. The notes he gives you after run-throughs or previews may be very helpful. At that stage of a production you will be so close to the show that you will be blind to certain important things and he may see more clearly than you. If you follow these guidelines, and have a happy acting company, you should get through all right. If you don't have a happy acting company, then you are in a vulnerable position.

I'll tell you a story that may help if you are really up against it. This didn't happen to me. A very well-known and respected producer watched the dress rehearsal of a West End musical. He was very unhappy with the lighting which he thought was too dim. He told the very distinguished lighting designer that the show needed fundamental relighting. When he came to the next day's dress rehearsal the lighting designer made a point of asking him to give his notes after the show. The producer was delighted with the lighting and congratulated the lighting designer. Actually the lighting designer had done nothing at all. Moral: the producer may actually know very little about the creative side of theatre but will certainly want to feel that he is the boss.

It is different in the subsidised theatre where the Artistic Director is usually a director as well and therefore may be trickier to deal with when things go wrong. However, he will be hoping that things don't go wrong because he's responsible for so many shows and is directing himself so that he will be grateful for not being called upon.

However things can go badly wrong. I have been sacked twice and as Artistic Director I have had to go through the horrid process of sacking two directors. If this happens to you, and it occurs more often than you might think, my very strong advice is don't make a fuss, accept the situation with dignity and wish the company well. You do not want to compound the destructiveness of the situation. Then later when you

have recovered from the pain of it all, think it all through. It will be a big learning moment for you. Decide carefully who was to blame and if appropriate accept responsibility for your part of it. It will be a big learning moment.

Lest this should seem like a very negative chapter, I shall say in conclusion that I have had only positive experiences with producers for a very long time.

ARTISTIC DIRECTION

The health of theatre in our country depends on the quality of its artistic directors. It is a different skill from directing and for some directors it is anathema. A good director doesn't necessarily mean you can be a good artistic director and vice versa.

I fell into being an Artistic Director almost by mistake at the age of twenty-two. I had been a whizz-kid, directing in London and New York when I was twenty-one. I was terribly arrogant and thought I knew it all. Then I had a string of commercial disasters because I neither sought for, nor had, proper guidance. Then one day I was offered a new West End musical and on a strange compulsion I turned it down. I was shocked by the enormity of what I'd done. A copy of *The Stage* was lying on my desk. It contained an advertisement for a new Artistic Director of the Century Theatre, an extraordinary company who toured around the North West in its own theatre which was contained in four huge lorries and when put together turned into a full stage and auditorium. The company was also about to take up a yearly residency at the new adaptable University Theatre in Manchester, now called Contact.

I applied for the job and astonishingly got it. I hadn't a proper idea of what it meant. I learned the hard way and I've been an Artistic Director ever since. I will try to tell you what I learned bearing in mind that after forty-five years I am still learning. I assumed it would be straightforward. I'd choose the plays, find the best actors I could and put on superb productions. That is of course absolutely right, although easy to say but difficult to do and I'll come back to it. What I wasn't prepared for was that an artistic director runs the entire company. Century was a small company, the Royal Exchange employs two hundred and fifty people but the principles are the same.

The first thing is to make sure that you are the Boss. In some companies the Executive Director is the Boss or the two positions are equal. Unless you have an extraordinary sympathy with the Executive Director, don't even contemplate it. However good they are, and in Pat Weller we had the best there was at the Exchange, they will almost always come to the problems from a different angle, the angle of money.

Creativity is the life blood of a company but nothing can happen unless there is the money to carry out the vision and there is never enough so any decision about where money is to be spent in a company is actually an artistic one. If you decide to spend it on new office furniture or marketing or catering or any of the myriad things that a theatre is concerned with, there will be less left for the productions. Now all these things have to have money spent on them but what proportion of the annual budget goes on them must finally be your decision. The decisions are often difficult. There is no point in having a marketing department if you don't give them enough money to do a good job for example. The point is your artistic perspective must prevail. You will decide the priorities.

Then there is risk. A successful company has to take risks unless it is satisfied with boring conservative planning and, the Executive Director, together with the Finance Director whose job is to present the accounts to the Board, will be less inclined to take risks than you will be. So make sure you have the ultimate power.

It follows that it is crucial that you have the right Executive Director, one with whom you are in complete sympathy and who you trust. They will be running the company on a day-to-day basis and so needs to share and understand your vision because they will be overseeing all the heads of department: box office; catering; education; finance, marketing; sound; wardrobe; wigs; workshop etc. You should also be instrumental in choosing who those heads of department are when vacancies arise. You want everyone to reflect the desire to have a happy and creative team throughout the company. Effectively it is the same as casting a play and forming your creative team, except many departments are not directly

linked to the putting on of a production but you still want them to be enthused by the theatre's policy. Too often, especially in a large company, the departments become cut off from each other into little kingdoms.

To this end two crucial heads of department are the production manager and the company manager. The production manager oversees all the making departments and the company manager oversees the stage management, the rehearsal process and is generally concerned with company morale. If they are good and they get on with each other then the heart of the company is well looked after.

You will naturally come in contact with the people who are working on the production but it is important to keep good personal relations with other departments too. Look at it from two different ways.

The audience coming to see one of the productions book tickets. Are they treated well by the box office staff, are the ushers polite, did they have a good meal in the restaurant, how were the bar staff? In other words, do they arrive in the auditorium in a good state to see the play or are they irritated by their treatment?

Then there are the actors. If you want the best out of them you want them to feel cared for and important. Do the accounts department treat them well? Are they looked after in the Green Room? Is the Stage Door helpful? You see, there is no one in the building who doesn't contribute to the product of the company.

Then there is the public side of the job. A subsidised company needs to have good relations with the Arts Council and the local authority because they give you the money, without which you couldn't exist. Then there is the increasing reliance on the generosity of the public through donations and sponsorship. Sometimes you will be the most important person that can make these relationships work. You will have to become a politician and a diplomat. There will be times when you might have to fight for the survival of your company, either because money is tight or you are under attack from the press.

It's quite intimidating isn't it when you consider that you are planning seasons and directing plays and it emphasizes how important

it is to have the best possible team around you. With good people you can delegate and that makes your life tolerable. Without good people the load becomes unbearably heavy.

So why on earth might you want to become an artistic director? Well go and work in a badly run company and you will see how many obstacles you find in your way through bad production departments or sloppy stage management. Work in a building where morale is low and experience the feeling of having no back-up. If you want a finely tuned instrument which works to the highest standards in a happy creative atmosphere then you need to be an artistic director. If you want to be fully supported during the inevitably hard rehearsal process then be an artistic director.

This leads back to the initial point. You must have a vision that you believe in passionately of what you want your theatre to achieve. This will sustain you during difficult times and inspire and support the people who work with and for you.

How you choose your programme is a matter of taste but the trap is to forget that you are putting productions on for an audience but only think about what pleases you. You are likely to empty the theatre very fast. I do not mean that you should play down to your audience but I do mean you have to give them a wide spectrum of experiences. Say you are putting on nine productions a year, they can't all be tragedies. Some plays are difficult, usually the ones directors are attracted to, don't do nine of them. Bring in directors who have a different colour to you so that the audience is stimulated in different ways. A successful artistic director knows his audience, knows how much and when to push them out of their normal territory, knows when they need to laugh and when to cry. You won't get it right all the time but you'll have to get it right enough if you want to survive.

One important point is that the most dangerous moment is when you are enjoying a successful period. It's when you relax. Don't. You know at some point the cycle will turn against you and so you should

plan even harder at that moment. The wave is bound to fall, you have to be creating the next one.

That choosing of the season is the hardest bit. Finding the plays and the right directors and the right actors is a never-ending task, and just when you celebrate that you've sorted one season out you realize you've got to start thinking about the next one. It is a endless treadmill.

All that said, it is a wonderful thing to do if it's in your blood. It is a lasting sense of achievement.

I'm not going to labour this but the Royal Exchange has a different way of doing it, which in our case, and in the case of others like the famous regime at the Glasgow Citizens, works very well. The Exchange is run by a group of directors. When the Company was founded the three of us, Casper Wrede, Michael Elliott and myself had all been Artistic Directors and we knew how tough it was. In the words of the great director Tyrone Guthrie, 'Have you noticed what bad directors you have become?' Casper Wrede's idea was that since we shared a vision of what theatre should do, why didn't we run the theatre together. In this way the director who was in production wouldn't have to worry about administration duties, the others would cover for him. Equally important the repertoire would benefit from not emanating from one person's taste but would cover a wider spectrum. Moreover, probably all three directors wouldn't get exhausted at once so there would always be some with the energy to drive the company. Although there are many pitfalls and difficulties, especially with competing egos, it has been remarkably successful. I recommend it, and if you can't actually do it that way, remember the principle that, the more you can share the load with good people, the more you will survive the burden.

GOOD LUCK,

OR AS THE FRENCH SAY, *MERDE*

I end as I began. I hope this book has, and will, help you. I am a successful director so some of my advice should be good advice but use yourself as a filter. It's what you do that counts. If there was one way of directing then productions would become very boring. Releasing the creative in yourself and in other people is the be all and end all. I cannot imagine a more fulfilling and rewarding way of leading your life.

WWW.OBERONBOOKS.COM

Follow us on www.twitter.com/@oberonbooks
& www.facebook.com/oberonbook

The Driving Games Manual

Manual

The ultimate guide to all car-based computer and video games

Haynes

60 km/h

0000176

2

050

João Diniz Sanches

Foreword by Bruno Senna

The Driving Games Manual

Dedication

For João, Fernanda and David – playing video games did lead somewhere, after all.

The Driving Games Manual Contents

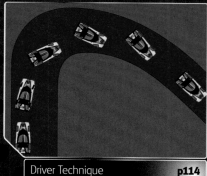
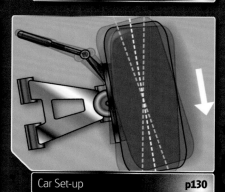

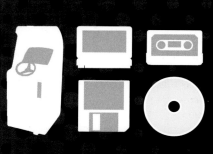

Foreword
by Bruno Senna

Over the last decade my racing career has progressed with pace; this, however, has been rivalled by the rate of development within the video game industry. In the early '90s I was wowed by Geoff Crammond's *Grand Prix*. For its time it was amazing; a game I played constantly. In fact, it was the first of many racing video games to whet my appetite for the thrill of racing virtually, as well as getting out on the track in real life.

I was recently asked, and accepted with delight, to be involved in creating a new racing game for System 3. I was in awe of the level of detail that goes into creating a realistic racing experience, tuning race settings and the AI, achieving realistic handling for the individual cars and dialling all these technical details into such advanced physics models – it is all mind boggling. The level of detail and technical advancement has moved on dramatically even within a few years. With the fast advancement of hardware, new all-singing-all-dancing consoles, I can only imagine what the future of the technology employed in making such racing games will hold.

This book takes a look through the history of racing games, outlining some of the greatest titles ever made, and journeys through the progress video games have enjoyed. It looks at the features that cement every good racing title as well as the ground-breaking features many racing games have introduced. From arcade games to simulation, it will voyage through the age of video games and look at those that have kept the racing genre alive for decades.

It has been an honour to write the foreword for this exciting new book, and in looking over what has been an incredible ride – coming to a time when racing video games can be as much of a practice tool for drivers as entertainment for racing fans – nothing excites me more than the future of this genre.

I'm just hoping my success on the track matches my in-game success!

Bruno Senna
June 2008

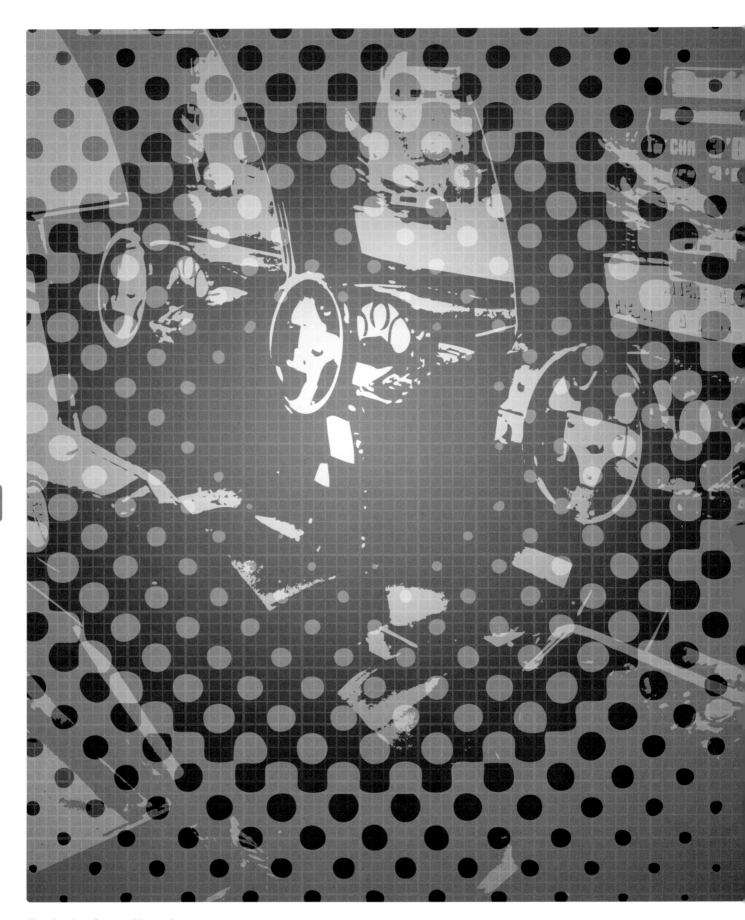

(Trakus)

(Microsoft Game Studios)

kmh

4.7
km

3
Fehler

68.2
Sekunden

Introduction

Introduction

Following their arrival on the video gaming scene in 1974, driving games have proved consistently popular. Over the past 30-odd years they have evolved from hopelessly simplistic, overhead-viewed 2D blocks of monochrome into fully three-dimensional near-photorealistic representations of the word's most famous circuits, cities and cars. It's little wonder that since the mid-'80s they have remained within players' top three favourite genres. Driving games continually lurk in the slipstream of first-person shooters and

sports titles, threatening to overtake them for dominance over a gamer's playing time.

The popularity of driving games isn't entirely surprising, of course. Cars are everywhere, they're something most people on the planet can identify with. And – for the male of the species, at least – speed laced with competition is a near-irresistible cocktail. After the Olympics and the World Cup, Formula 1 is often the most watched global sporting event on television.

But like the motorsport events and vehicles it portrays, the driving genre can be as broad in its scope as the audience it attracts. Whether it's karting, touring cars, rallying, sports cars, single-seaters, illegal street racing, drifting, drag racing, or stock car events, if it has four wheels, you're more than likely to be able to play it. And you'll be in good company. It's not unusual to hear Formula 1 drivers – particularly the new generation – saying they regularly enjoy a few virtual laps on their console of choice once in the comfort of their motorhomes. This widespread acceptance is in part a result of the continuing growth of the video gaming medium, but in this context it's arguably more

Pic 1: With video gaming moving at supercar speeds, *OutRun2 SP*'s lovely visuals will one day appear as risible as early driving games do now. *(Sega)*

Pic 2: Electro mechanical devices were popular before the rise of arcades and the microprocessor. But they didn't go out without a fight, as 1974's *Speed King* suggests. Part of the game's marketing used the dated electro mechanical make-up as a selling point, claiming the machine would be easier to fix. *(Chicago Coin)*

a result of the fact that the last few years have seen this genre evolve considerably, to a stage when even today's average driving game productions deliver a solid, playable ride.

But while the core component of 1974's *Speed Race* differs little from that of 2008's *Gran Turismo 5 Prologue*, the latter incorporates nearly four decades' worth of development. And when you look back, the fundamental aspect that has arguably altered the most is the level of realism on offer. It's why you hear the likes of Lewis Hamilton and Filipe Massa talking about how games like *Formula One Championship Edition* on PlayStation 3 can be useful for learning corner sequences of unfamiliar tracks (just as rookie UK touring car drivers admitted to resorting to the *TOCA* games of the late 1990s to help their on-track orientation).

And with realism – be it graphics-, physics- or artificial intelligence-led – comes an increased sense of player engagement and excitement. True, few games will ever top the sense of fun *OutRun* provides, but if it's the delight of battling it out on the track in a race-prepared chassis with more horsepower than

sense you crave, then you'll have a hard time bettering modern productions such as *Race Driver: GRID* or *Live for Speed*.

That's not to say, however, that past classics should be confined to the pits of history – far from it. Many of the earlier titles highlighted in this book still deserve their place on the grid precisely because they share the elements that make driving games so thrilling, rewarding and universally captivating. But, excitingly, as the genre has progressed, so has the intensity of the experiences on offer. The future of the driving game as a front-runner of the video gaming medium looks assured.

What this book covers
What we know today as arcade machines – the precursor to home console and computer games – effectively began life as electro mechanical devices in the '60s. They proved popular and therefore played their part in the evolution that saw the microchip and the TV screen

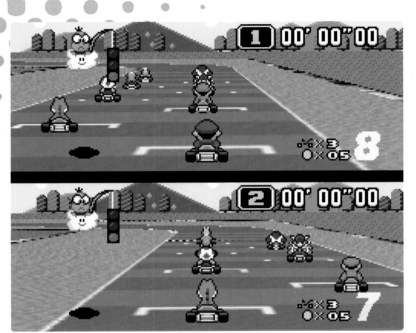

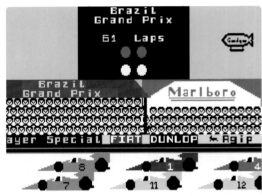

take over as the fundamental components of the video game.

Interesting as that heritage is, the focus of this book deals uniquely with the video/computer game creations that followed those early machines. In practical terms, then, it means starting with Atari's *Gran Trak 10*, released in 1974. (To put it into context, *Computer Space*, in 1971, is generally regarded as the first commercially available video game (arcade) machine. *Pong* followed it a year later.)

While estimates for racing titles since 1974 hover around the 4,000 mark when using the widest selection criteria (all formats, all subgenres), it won't

surprise you to learn that this book does not aim to cover them all – not least because a strict approach with regards to inclusion has been adopted.

The purpose of this publication is to centre on car-based virtual racing and driving experiences while providing as rich an overview of this specific sector within the wider genre as the page count will allow. That means no bikes (except when they come as a segment of a car-based experience – such as, most recently, *Project Gotham Racing 4*), no boats, no personal water craft, no futuristic hovercrafts, no robots, no trucks, tractors, chariots, planes, steamrollers, animals, insects or Chocobos. This is purely kart to production vehicle to competition car territory.

In addition, any driving or racing experience that includes weapon-based combat as a game mechanic is excluded. That means, regrettably, no *Super Mario Kart* on the SNES.

The genres covered, meanwhile, are relatively flexible as long as the underlying experience is either driving- or racing-based. So, for instance, mission-structured games are not ruled out, provided the in-game goals and progress are achieved entirely through driving. Management titles, on the other hand, have not made the cut. They're joined by interesting and inventive genre-bending examples such as 1982's *Math Gran Prix*, a top-down arithmetic-based single-seater racing 'game' for the Atari 2600.

Speaking of formats, the focus here is solely on arcade, computer and console releases (so no handheld or mobile phone titles). Further to this, aside from arcade, where games tend to have a more universal release policy, the other formats centre on games to have enjoyed publication in the West. In other words, Japan-only releases (which could threaten

Pic 1: Some excellent racing games that never made it to the West were released in Japan – *Human Grand Prix* comes to mind because although subsequently published in the US, the game's inspired original control method was replaced by a generic and less involving alternative. But many more were mediocre efforts and it would be too easy to fill this book with games that few readers would have any knowledge of. *(Author)*

Pic 2: When it comes to video game racing, just about every concept has been shoehorned into the genre. Atari's *Math Gran Prix* and its maths-based play dynamic, however, remains one of the more charming examples to date. *(Atari)*

to fill this book on their own) such as the much-underrated *F1 Circus MD* are not included.

The above may seem oppressive, but it's simply in the interests of creating specifically targeted and deliberately condensed content while achieving the kind of detail and consistency that a publication with a broader remit will be unable to match.

Yet even with the resulting 700-odd games that have made the selection, providing individual comprehensive cover is an unrealistic proposition. So instead, what is attempted here is to concentrate

on the most significant and accomplished titles to date and in doing so it is hoped that that a detailed sense of the evolution of this genre is suitably conveyed. In order to achieve this, the subsequent chapters have been divided into decades, where the prominent examples are dealt with individually, following a general overview of each era.

But this book is also a manual, and as such considerable space is dedicated to detailing real-world driving and racing techniques that can be applied in modern racing games. Their effect will ultimately be dependent on the complexity of a game's handling model, but it's worth noting that even the most arcade-like experience can benefit from resorting to a little racecraft.

Completing the history and driving technique lessons you'll find a section detailing how to maximise the virtual racing experience. The arrival of rumble technology in game controllers during the 1990s vastly increased the level of feedback enjoyed by players, most notably exploited by the original *Gran Turismo*. Indeed, the enhancement is such that playing racing/driving games without it feels like an evolutionary step

Pic 1: With its then astonishing colourful graphics, Namco's *Pole Position* in 1982 revolutionised arcades. They retain a certain aesthetic charm, but have obviously fallen a long, long way back from today's graphical achievements. *(Namco Bandai)*

Pic 2: *Formula One Championship Edition* on PlayStation 3 gives an indication of how far technology has come visually since the early days of driving games. The evolution has been as swift as the subject matter. *(Sony Computer Entertainment)*

backwards, as owners of PlayStation 3s have found out (Sony has, however, now released the DualShock 3 controller, re-instating rumble feedback).

Good as these controllers are, they pale into insignificance when next to a high quality, dedicated force feedback wheel and pedal set-up – preferably one that is integrated into a 'driving simulator' – that is, a unit specifically designed to replicate the experience of being behind the wheel of a real car, and onto which you can add anything from a subwoofer to a genuine racing seat complete with four-point harness to further create the illusion of real-world racing. If, by the time you finish reading this book, you decide that you can't possibly live the rest of your days without such a set-up, this book will have served one of its central purposes.

Technological evolution
Introduction
The fact that the driving genre is still running with the leading pack of gaming experiences after a three-decade-long race proves its durability, but more impressive perhaps is that we still see innovation in the latest titles to roll out of development. Granted, the genre has long been associated with progress, yet this has been mainly technological as game developers

relied on driving titles to showcase an arcade system's graphical prowess or, if on the home formats, their coding skills.

The power of current hardware is such, however, that visual flair is now a given. So the focus has gradually shifted onto other areas – namely the fidelity of the handling dynamics (for sim-centric titles), accuracy of race circuit replication (where applicable), the intensity, excitement and quality of the overall experience, advancements in damage modelling, the credibility of opponents' artificial intelligence (AI), the overall game structure and other additions –

Pic 1: The advancements in console technology are perhaps best illustrated by the increasing demands being placed on developers. For the first *Gran Turismo*, released in Europe in May 1998, a designer at Polyphony spent around a day to model one of the game's vehicles. *(Sony Computer Entertainment, courtesy of Edge magazine)*

Pic 2: By comparison, each car in 2008's *GT5 Prologue* for PlayStation 3 took up to six months to create. *(Sony Computer Entertainment)*

sometimes borrowed from other game categories – that aim to drive the genre forward.

The last ten years, in particular, have arguably seen the most pronounced change in these key areas, and the main elements are worth briefly detailing here.

Graphics

Just as 1982's *Pole Position* wowed the arcade-frequenting crowds when it powered in with its then-groundbreaking colourful graphics, the level of visual detail in today's leading high-definition productions can be startling.

To put it into perspective, a car model from a leading racing game dating from the end of the 20th century would be made up of around 400 polygons, the graphical building blocks of all three-dimensional objects in a game. Less than ten years later, 40,000 polygons would be used for the interior alone, with the exterior made up of another 40,000. Now supported by advanced graphics techniques, the polygon counts haven't needed to rise as dramatically because elements like texture maps and shader techniques can add more layers of detail than polygons alone manage.

In practical terms it means a contemporary in-game car model at this level can boast an accurately rendered engine bay, under-panels, inner boot, complete and fully articulated suspension assembly,

Pic 1: Modern game productions leave few stones unturned. For the leading titles, it's necessary to obtain the appropriate audio/visual information in order to include it in every facet of the game, as the crew capturing reference data for sound and graphical reproduction during *Gran Turismo 4*'s replay sequences is busy doing here. *(Sony Computer Entertainment)*

Pic 2: Sound, of course, is crucial and these days it's recorded from various sources. *(Sony Computer Entertainment)*

wheel and brake components and tyre tread. As for more immediate elements, expect meticulously recreated bodywork and an equally detailed interior featuring a gear lever, handbrake, switches and working dials.

At a glance, the cars look indistinguishable from their real-life counterparts, while the in-car cockpit views have in recent years been the focus of much attention on the part of developers, with the higher resolution graphics of the current generation of hardware enabling such eye-candy-type details as dust and dirt build-up on windscreens, most visible when hit by startlingly recreated sunlight, as well as genuine in-game improvements such as fully useable rear-view mirrors.

Clearly that's just the car, though. The environments – be they crowd-filled grandstands, dusty open country or a complex urban backdrop – are not ignored. They also play a vital role in drawing a player into the experience and, increasingly, games are ensuring they become part of the experience itself by reacting authentically to a player's vehicle.

Audio

Though rarely regarded as such, sound in a game – any game – is as integral a part of the package as graphics. In driving titles, as with video gaming in general, the breakthrough came from the use of CD as the medium onto which titles were manufactured. This allowed for a quality of digital samples previously inaccessible for the home and coincided with the genre's general drive towards realism. Previous to this, it was unusual to hear anything convincingly resembling an engine note – at least not on console and home computer titles.

Pic 1: Codemasters' long-running *TOCA* – now *Race Driver* – series has since the early days provided convincing and great AI that fools the player into believing they're up against adversaries with real personalities.
(Codemasters, courtesy of Edge magazine)

Even before the subsequent arrival of DVD as the video gaming storage of choice, surround-sound became increasingly common; but the extra data space afforded by DVD enabled 5.1-channel soundtracks, while audio budgets in game development grew to exploit these new opportunities. So developers on leading titles will be used to renting racetracks with a selection of cars in order to record engine, cabin and exhaust sound levels – for *Project Gotham Racing 3*, for example, Bizarre Creations strapped up to 30 microphones onto each vehicle – to then implement into the game. It's little coincidence that it's the engine, rather than music, that now dominates the soundtrack of many driving games.

If played back at the right level, sound obviously helps set the atmosphere of the experience, but it also provides crucial feedback in terms of what the vehicle – and each of its wheels – is up to on the track, as well as relaying other valuable information such as the position of other competitors. It is a vital component of the modern game and, thankfully, it's one area that several leading titles now reproduce in a manner that is identical to its real-life equivalent.

AI

Perhaps one of the areas that still regularly fails to convince, the artificial intelligence of computer-controlled opponents is a fundamental aspect of a driving game experience. Virtually non-existent in early titles (and still largely absent from most arcade games), it's unfortunately not unusual to see poor implementations in modern games. And if you get it wrong, all the hard work in the game's other areas could be in vain – because every time the AI fails to convince, it destroys the atmosphere by reminding you that you're playing a game.

Getting it right, however, is no easy matter. Creating AI that races against both itself and the player requires a system that understands the concept of the racing line but one that is also able to break away from that line in order to pursue overtaking opportunities. Leading titles achieve this (or at least give the illusion of it – which is just as effective) while also including parameters for each AI driver's braking and cornering ability, level of aggression and car control, as well as forcing errors in order to achieve more human-like behaviour. That does mean that in some games your opponents will give as good as they get.

Handling model

Driving games win or lose an audience based on their handling characteristics. The games from the 1970s and much of the '80s may have been content with implementing the most rudimentary form of handling dynamics, but with the arrival of 1989's *Indianapolis 500: The Simulation* on PC players glimpsed the potential for realism that lay ahead. Much of the core of authentic car behaviour modelling revolves around number crunching, which explains why PCs have led the field in this regard ever since. That said, as consoles increased in processing power, so did the authenticity of the driving models in their games.

Undoubtedly, the appearance and phenomenal success of 1998's *Gran Turismo* on PlayStation accelerated console gaming's interest in realistic handling behaviour, which in turn educated an entire generation of players to expect more from their driving titles. It's one of the reasons even contemporary arcade-like driving experiences on console offer an approximation of real-world handling. PC simulations

raced ahead, of course, but since the evolution of the sim-biased console driving title – the *Gran Turismos* and *Forza Motorsports* of the world – the gap has closed a little. The modern console sim incorporates handling data obtained directly from car manufacturers and includes hundreds of individual parameters relating to the handling model.

Far from making the experience more difficult, an accurate handling model often makes things more

Pic 1: Criterion Games' *Burnout* – here as *Burnout 3: Takedown* – series has consistently improved the visual depiction of the vehicular carnage that constitutes the games' core with each iteration, and as such has since led the field in this area. *(Electronic Arts)*

Pic 2: With improvements in hardware power comes increases in graphical detail, enabling developers to add details into driving games that were previously unattainable. *Burnout*, again showing dramatic car damage in the way only it can. *(Electronic Arts)*

accessible for the player. The problems occur when there is imprecision in the dynamics, causing a vehicle to behave in an unexpected manner. Granted, there will be a need to tweak the settings to match the control input (driving a car through a joypad isn't the same as using a force feedback wheel and pedals), the nature of the game and the expectations of its target audience, but the belief that handling complexity (at least when dealing with everyday production cars – something many are able to relate to) automatically brings with it an increase in player challenge is a misconception.

Realism

Aside from an evolution towards believable handling, increases in hardware performance have enabled developers to recreate ever more authentic interpretations of car-based experiences. This is more than a natural progression, though, the most obvious example of which would be the way Formula 1 titles started off as simplistic top-down affairs and now feature complete, fully three-dimensional recreations that include everything from centimetre-perfect rumble strips to a 22-man pit stop crew.

Rather, it's the way that more processing power has seen development studios naturally turn towards replicating real-life activities, rather than having to resort to the imaginary in order to get around programming restraints they might have faced previously. This has happened in all genres, not just driving, and the benefit is universal – both in the level of immersion and accessibility having a gameworld that players can relate to, and base their actions and reactions on what they know from real life, becomes a hugely attractive proposition.

Damage

In many driving games – certainly racing-based titles – the frailty of your vehicle actually makes for a more robust experience. The temptation by some to switch off vehicle damage will prove too great, but as with other things in life, an element of risk can spice things up considerably.

The implementation of damage in driving games has been around for a while – some of the early titles included damage, albeit in limited form – but outside of PC simulations it's been a relatively underused aspect, and from the mid-'90s it failed to develop on

console as rapidly as some of the other components to affect the genre. Developers at the time often cited contractual restrictions placed on them by real-world car manufacturers, making it impossible to display cosmetic damage on the licensed cars featured in the game. Another concern of the time related to whether the audience of primarily arcade-like experiences would accept the extra complexity and potential constraints damage can bring to a driving game.

However, the bias towards realism-based driving since the release of *Gran Turismo* has resulted in both car manufacturers and players becoming more tolerant of other real-world elements, meaning the previous issues are no longer present in the majority of today's games – which is an encouraging development, given that the visual payback to a player in being able to see the consequences of their on-track paint-swapping scrapes in *Project Gotham Racing 4*, or finishing a *Colin McRae: DiRT* stage with half of the bodywork hanging off, shouldn't be underestimated. Additionally, increases in hardware ability have also affected the complexity of real-time bodywork and chassis deformation, enabling developers to include ever more elaborate damage models in their creations – witness the evolution of the crash dynamics of the *Burnout* franchise, for instance.

But the sight of dented panels, mangled metal and smoking engines isn't the only thing to enrich the driving game experience. Damaged steering, missing gears, overheating engine, suspension failure and many more are modelled into both PC and console simulations these days, and their inclusion adds vital tension to proceedings while heightening the sense of achievement when crossing the finish line in a point-scoring position. And from the perspective of play mechanics, the strategic undertones presented by a fully functioning damage model can make for some enthralling racing (in the appropriate game, clearly).

Analogue control

For driving games, analogue control remained the domain of arcade titles and only became widely used in the home in the 1990s, through joysticks and subsequently wheels on PC, and the introduction of analogue joypads for console. Clearly it marked something of a revolution, enabling precise steering (and often throttle and brake) input where previously only a digital option existed. The enhancement was such that it prompted certain publishers to re-release titles featuring support for analogue input, as Codemasters did with *TOCA Touring Car Championship* soon after Sony launched the DualShock controller for its PlayStation console.

Digital input hasn't entirely disappeared, however, and some arcade-like titles remain perfectly playable using this method, but in general the ability to resort to analogue control has been a contributing factor in the evolution of more realism-based driving experiences.

Online play

One of the most significant evolutions since the turn of the century has been the propagation of online play amongst the console gaming crowd – the PC simracing fraternity had started considerably earlier, during the mid-'90s.

Casual online play on driving games can bring mixed results, ranging from exciting, hard-fought experiences to those that become memorable for entirely the wrong reasons – there is little that can be done to police the behaviour of some gamers more interested in ruining races than engaging in fair competition. That said, it is easy to set up a controlled environment where only those that have been invited get to play, and serious racing between fans of the *Race Driver*, *Forza Motorsport*, *Project Gotham* and even *Gran Turismo* franchises certainly exists.

On PC, the simracing community is by definition extremely dedicated and an established community has existed for years, with various online venues for

Pic 1: Modern simracing experiences such as *GTR – FIA GT Racing Game* thrive on multiplayer events. In fact, the set-up is arguably the one element that has ensured the popularity of simracing. The ability to build active communities around the games, ensuring good support for online series is obviously key. *(Atari)*

Pic 2: Online multiplayer doesn't have to be just tyre pressures and camber settings, however. *TrackMania*'s huge success is proof of that. *(Digital Jesters)*

Pic 1: It may look depressingly barren now, but in 1984 *Rally Driver* represented one of the early attempts at recreating sim-influenced mechanics within the suffocating hardware restrictions of the time. *(Hill MacGibbon)*

Pic 2: A momentous occasion in gaming and driving simulations, Geoff Crammond's Formula 3 recreation *REVS* in 1984 offered levels of handling – not to mention technical nous – ahead of everything else that was available at the time. *(Acornsoft)*

simracers to pit their skills against one another – because good as the AI in some games is, it's still got some way to go to beat a human brain.

Whether console or PC, the modern online virtual racing experience is an increasingly dependable affair that can add a tremendous new component to a driving game, sometimes transforming an otherwise competent if unexciting title into something worth playing. And when it's properly implemented as part of

a leading driving game, the results of taking that game online can be fabulous.

Arcade/simulation distinction

While the earliest driving games would be characterised as 'arcade' in nature (the fact they appeared in arcade form would give rise to the use of the term as signifying a driving experience with little grounding in realism), it didn't take long for simulation aspects to begin creeping into the home video gaming scene, arguably most notably with the likes of *Chequered Flag* (1983), *Rally Driver* (1984) and *REVS* (1984) on personal computers.

As the distinction between computer and console game widened, it wasn't surprising to find PCs, with their extra computing ability, becoming the natural home for processor-intensive simulation-based driving experiences.

The relatively simplistic handling requirements of console driving titles were in part a reflection of the limitations of the hardware, both from a technical perspective and in terms of control input restrictions. Clearly, as the performance of consoles has increased, along with better control methods (such as analogue input and decent force feedback wheel and pedal set-ups), there has been an inevitable push towards replicating real-world elements in console titles. As

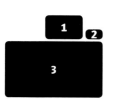

Pic 1: In a decade dominated by Papyrus creations, only Geoff Crammond's *Grand Prix* series managed to give them a run for their money. *F1GP2*, shown here, provided some formidable competition.
(*MicroProse, courtesy of Edge magazine*)

Pic 2: While since surpassed, *Grand Prix Legends* represented a simracing landmark upon its release in 1998. Its level of difficulty may also have psychologically scarred more than a few budding virtual racers. (*Sierra Entertainment, courtesy of Edge magazine*)

Pic 3: *iRacing* is the result of four years of dedication by former members of the Papyrus group to create not a game, but as authentic a simulation of motorsport as possible. It's another step closer to reality for the simracing subgenre. (*iRacing Motorsport Simulations*)

previously mentioned, the influence of the arrival of the *Gran Turismo* franchise in 1998 and its subsequent success shouldn't be discounted either (not to mention game developers' eternal quest for realism), but the overall result is that while the console sim has introduced another subgenre avenue (with *Forza Motorsport* arguably taking over from *GT* at the head of the field), even the nature of 'arcade' driving games has evolved considerably beyond their perceived notion up to the end of the last century.

Accompanying that evolution has been an ever-more-knowledgeable gaming community, meaning that today's arcade-style driving games pose a considerable challenge for developers – the delicate balance requires the inclusion of the elements of realism most gamers expect while ensuring the resulting experience remains accessible to as wide an audience as possible.

Of course, while the arcade-style experience has progressed and a handful of very competent console driving sims have rolled out of developer studios in recent times, the PC simulation hasn't had its foot on the brake. Far from it, as the field of simracing and its hugely dedicated audience proves.

Simracing

The first aspect to convey about simracing, is that these PC-based simulations are not regarded as games by the community that engages in them. In the best examples they are highly accurate recreations of car-handling dynamics that can in some cases be used as a substitute for real racing, or

Pic 1: Simracing titles pride themselves on their recreation of realism and that level of dedication from developers isn't solely restricted to the upper categories of motorsport – *Kart Champions* aims to apply that approach to kart racing. *(SE Games)*

Pic 2: *IndyCar Racing* cemented Papyrus Design Group as the leading developer of simracing titles during the 1990s, a title it would share with precious few until its final creation, the 2003 edition of *NASCAR Racing*. *(Virgin Interactive Entertainment)*

at least as a genuine training aid. That is the philosophy behind iRacing.com Motorsport Simulations, a company partly created by David Kaemmer, former co-founder of simracing specialist Papyrus, which with first title *iRacing* aims to operate as an entirely virtual interpretation of a real-world racing environment.

Papyrus is actually generally credited with the development of the first simracing experience, 1989's *Indianapolis 500: The Simulation*, before going on to create landmark titles such as *IndyCar Racing* (1993) and its sequel (1995), the *NASCAR* series (1994–2003) and *Grand Prix Legends* (1998). Clearly other illustrious sim racing contenders turned up along the way, most notably Geoff Crammond's *Formula One Grand Prix* titles (1992 and 1996).

A community built quickly around these titles, and even as early as 1995 online racing leagues were developed. Simracing wouldn't look back.

Today, development continues, with modern simracing titles being able to recreate real-world

handling dynamics to a remarkable degree – forget the role of centrifugal force; leading titles incorporate authentic tyre deformation modelling as part of their parameters, as well as provide a generously mod-based development model that enables the inclusion of a varied selection of racing categories. The community tends to be as dedicated as it is serious, with highly competitive worldwide leagues and competitions organised regularly, which can be viewed (and are commentated on) as if a real-life motorsport event. The fact that simracers refer to their activity as a sport, not a pastime, is a good indication of the level of complexity these titles integrate.

Nevertheless, while that distinction is respected, simracing titles are not inaccessible to anyone with a console driving game background and, indeed, this publication encourages console sim devotees looking to elevate their level of virtual driving to, at the very least, investigate the simracing scene. Currently, this is as real as it gets.

Relevance of classics

It is true that several of the older games detailed in this book will prove extremely difficult for players to experience first-hand if they missed them when they originally appeared. Occasionally the opportunity to purchase these arcade cabinets from specialised retailers or Internet auction sites arises, but there are obvious practical and financial barriers to this.

A more realistic option is emulation, which for years now has ensured titles that would otherwise have been lost to history can still be enjoyed by new generations. There are limitations to this approach, not least that you are often resorting to a control method assigned to your PC's keyboard, rather than the original set-up – in the case of arcade driving games, which have almost always relied on a steering wheel and pedals, this compromise can significantly affect the gaming experience.

That said, in recent years there has been an increase in the interest surrounding retro gaming, with several titles making re-released appearances on special compilations, as well as services such as Xbox Live, the PlayStation Network and Nintendo's Virtual Console. The advantage for the average consumer is that the control settings for these games will be mapped to the console's standard controller, making things more straightforward.

For those to whom only the original experience will do, there's some comfort in the fact that, generally, console and home computer titles of the past two decades are often found on auction sites along with the hardware to run them. These can obviously vary wildly in price, depending on rarity, but thankfully driving games tend to be less affected than other genres in this regard.

Ultimately, anyone wishing to relive any of the classic driving game experiences detailed in this book should, in many cases, be able to do so.

The modern driving game

As inconceivable as it may seem now, the games of the 1970s and early 1980s could be the work of a one- or two-man team (a programmer and musician), and cost little more than a bag of crisps and a handful of weeks to put together. Fast-forward to the mid-1990s and even the arcade greats of the time – such as Sega's *Daytona USA* – would average out at 20 individuals on a 12-month development cycle.

By contrast, these days teams of 100-plus (where a third are programmers and over half are artists) are the norm. Or 150-plus if you include researchers, the legal and licensing departments, brand and marketing team, and QA unit. From scratch, and depending on scope, a project will take an average of 24 months (or 18 for a sequel) and you shouldn't expect to see much change from an £8 million budget by the time you're finished.

Pic 1: A rare glimpse into the development heart of Polyphony Digital, creator of the all-conquering *Gran Turismo* series. This is where the gaming world's most beautiful car models are painstakingly pieced together. *(Sony Computer Entertainment)*

Pic 1: The highly detailed environments in *Project Gotham Racing 4* are a long, long way down the road from the 90,000 polygons that made up those of *Metropolis Street Racer*, the series' first title.
(*Microsoft Game Studios*)

Pic 2: There can't be many men in the video game industry more passionate about cars than Kazunori Yamauchi, CEO of Polyphony Digital and producer of all *Gran Turismo* titles to date, seen here in his office environment.
(*Sony Computer Entertainment*)

The vast increase in production requirements are a direct result of the vast increase in the ability of the hardware hosting the games, combined with the unrelenting drive for increased realism. We touched on the level of graphical detail of cars – each of which can take up to six months to build, as in the case of *Gran Turismo 5 Prologue*'s vehicles – as well as the advanced handling dynamics in today's leading driving games earlier, so it seems appropriate to use the efforts that go into replicating a real-world track in a game as a further example of the components that make up a modern driving title.

Generally, in-game circuits based on a real-life equivalent will mimic layout, topography and camber values accurate to one centimetre. This is obtained from survey grade GPS-based CAD data backed by architectural plans, ensuring the precise positioning of all barriers, tyre walls, grandstands and other buildings. The team then obtains visual reference data by photographing the whole circuit and every object visible by the driver on their way around the track. For *Race Driver: GRID*, for instance, this amounted to up to 50 gigabytes of material and once built the circuit environment comprised of up to 1.5 million polygons (for comparison, the environments in 2000's *Metropolis Street Racer*, noted for its visual competence at the time, were made up of 90,000), with thousands of individual objects that could be damaged by player interaction.

To pick a specific example, *GRID*'s Le Mans circuit includes every building, grandstand and campsite around the famous 13.6km track, as well as the fairground, race teams' equipment in the pit lane and paddock and 30,000 animated 3D crowd members. When it comes to the modern driving game, this is the kind of approach that characterises the rule, rather than the exception.

the
1970s

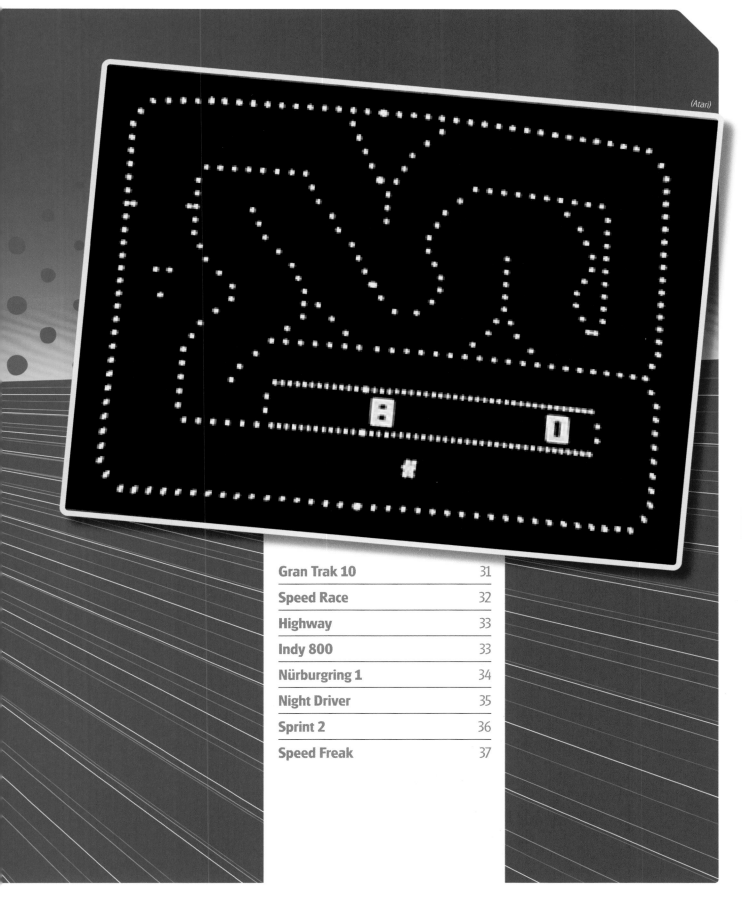

(Atari)

The 1970s

Introduction

Regardless of what you consider to be the world's first computer game, there's little disagreement over 1971's *Computer Space* by Nutting Associates (comprising the subsequent founders of Atari, Nolan Bushnell and Ted Dabney) being the first coin-operated arcade, with 1972's Magnavox Odyssey regarded as the first home game console.

Those early video gaming efforts may appear risible by today's standards but it's important to remember developers (or engineers, as they were known at the time) were only beginning to grasp the building blocks of the remarkably diverse medium we now enjoy. So the initial attempts were necessarily basic variations of space combat or the bat-and-ball antics of the hugely popular *Pong*, and the fact that it took a little while for developers to attempt something more advanced ought not to raise too many eyebrows – the leap from *Pong* to *Gran Trak 10* may not seem substantial nowadays, but in 1974 it required both a new coding and hardware approach in order for the 'new' game dynamic to be implemented, however crudely it may now seem.

Unlike the current age, despite the existence of home consoles the real developments in the 1970s were happening in the arcade sector (which also lead the battle for the medium's acceptance by a society caught off guard by the arrival of the video gaming phenomenon). It's the reason why, unlike those that follow it, this chapter doesn't contain any key entries in the driving game genre that were made specifically for the home formats – when it came to driving titles, consoles would barely get a look in during the '70s. So this seems a good time to reiterate that the aim of these chapters isn't necessarily to simply showcase the most successful, the most hyped, or even the finest titles, but rather the most influential and most notable.

The top-down view adopted by *Gran Trak 10* – an economical and simple way of representing the action – became synonymous with driving games of the '70s. This was out of necessity due to technical limitations of the era's hardware rather than as a result of stylistic concerns, a fact supported by the shift towards different approaches marked by the arrival of the more advanced microprocessor-based arcade experiences (the first-person perspective used in Atari's *Night Driver* being the most famous example, perhaps).

Better technology towards the end of the decade also enabled developers to begin considering more varied driving experiences, which up to then had mostly focused on single-seater racing. But it also got them venturing excitedly into different genres entirely, and the resulting relative abandonment of the driving game as the 1970s drew to a close is noticeable. The genre would, of course, overtake other categories again – and in impressive fashion, as detailed in the next chapter. For now, though, the key driving game releases from video gaming's first decade should be allowed their moment. After all, every driving game you play now will invariably owe some of its fine-tuned DNA to this line-up.

Gran Trak 10 (1974)

Format: Arcade
Developer: Grass Valley Think Tank/Atari
Publisher: Atari

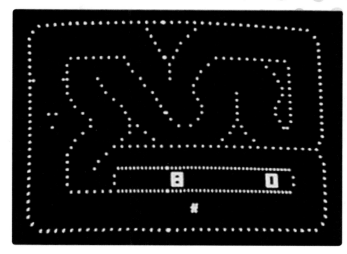

Computer Space may have been the first commercially available arcade cabinet, but the arcades of the early 1970s were full of Atari's *Pong* (1972) – the first mass-produced arcade machine – and its countless clones. So the arrival of *Gran Trak 10*, with its steering wheel, two pedals and four-position gearstick – all firsts for arcades – hardly went unnoticed.

Developed allegedly as a result of Atari's frustration at the number of *Pong*-inspired titles on the market (not to mention a decreasing interest in the bat-and-ball dynamic from both public and arcade operators), *Gran Trak 10* was commissioned from employees of engineering company Ampex who went on to form the Grass Valley Think Tank R&D lab for Atari. The design was subsequently tweaked by Al Alcorn, creator of *Pong*, prior to its release.

The racing car dynamic would prove harder to replicate by competitors than two bats and a ball, while Atari hoped the innovative nature of the game would reignite the fire of the arcade-going crowd and, in turn, its balance sheet. Alas, an accounting error saw the publisher sell the game for $995 – $100 less than it cost to manufacture – leading Atari to post losses for the fiscal year 1973–4 of $500,000 and in doing so come close to bankruptcy.

The game involves completing as many laps of the top-down viewed circuit in exchange for points as time will allow, with the player given three forward gears to assist them. The handling characteristics of the car are clearly primitive, with lightning-quick steering and a minuscule turning circle (rendering the reverse gear mostly redundant), but as the first arcade game to use ROM (read-only memory) to store graphics information, the 'realistic' single-seater car and track visuals, combined with an approximation of engine, tyre-screech and crash sounds – an impressive and considerable advancement over the beeps and blips of previous games – did a decent job of masking the rudimentary gameplay at the time.

Atari had ambitious plans for its first driving game, announcing the concept of *Gran Trak 10* 'racing clubs' for digital racers to compare their skills across the nation, with arcade operators acting as the organisers

of individual events, effectively predating the notion of online racing leagues so familiar to the simracing community (and subsequently elements of the console sim crowd) by more than 20 years.

Despite its impact, *Gran Trak 10* suffered from limitations, not least the fact that only one car featured on the track. Atari redeveloped the concept in various subsequent versions, with *Gran Trak 20* adding a second player, an on-track oil slick hazard and a 'free play' mechanic for a high score.

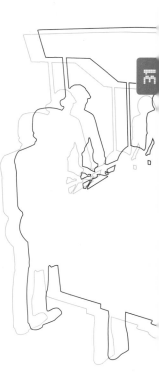

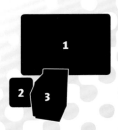

Pic 1: A complete lack of corners wouldn't hurt *Speed Race*'s popularity, which was assured through the exciting and relentless pace of its on-screen action – the vertical scrolling racer had arrived.
(Taito, courtesy of The Arcade Flyer Archive)

Pic 2: The limitations of the hardware occasionally required developers to cut corners, as Taito did by using a green plastic overlay to mask *Speed Race*'s monochrome nakedness. A technique it would later employ for *Space Invaders*, of course. *(Taito)*

Pic 3: A more compact version of *Speed Race*. Just as it remains common practice, it wasn't unusual for arcade cabinets of the 1970s to be offered in alternate versions to increase their suitability in a larger number of environments. *(Taito)*

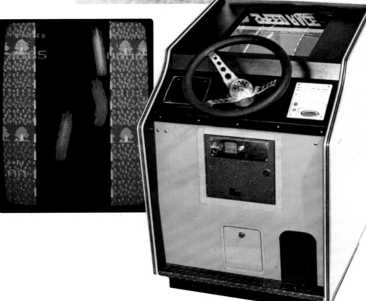

Speed Race (1974)
Format: Arcade
Developer: Taito
Publisher: Taito

While Atari was busy dominating the arcade space in the West, over in Japan Taito was establishing itself as a major player in the sector. Its first notable driving effort was *Speed Race*, a considerably more exciting offering than *Gran Trak 10*, as Western players found out when the game was exported (as *Wheels* or *Race*).

In its top-down, vertical-scrolling approach, *Speed Race* adopted an innovative driving game method that would go on to grace a number of subsequent creations. It did mean a complete lack of corners, with only the width of the road altering the endless vertical stretch of racing tarmac, but players were kept too busy in avoiding the reckless driving characteristics of opponents who zigzagged their way along the screen to notice.

The name is also appropriately descriptive, given that the faster the player is able to keep their 1960s-styled single-seater vehicle travelling, the higher the score (with play time extended at 2,000, 4,000 and 6,000 points). Naturally, the higher that score, the greater the number of rival vehicles to overtake on-screen, while 'Slip Zones' – segments offering reduced traction and requiring a more careful approach – also show up at 800, 1,800 and 2,800 points to further increase the difficulty.

It's a charmingly simplistic concept by today's standards, but upon its release *Speed Race* proved considerably more enthralling than its predecessors, a fact evident from its popularity with arcade players and the emergence of several direct sequels up until 1980.

Highway (aka Hi-Way) (1975)
Format: Arcade
Developer: Atari
Publisher: Atari

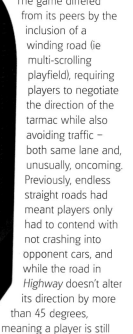

The top-down scrolling driving game concept introduced by *Speed Racer* was quickly adopted by Taito's competitors, but the first to add significantly to it was Atari with *Highway*.

The game differed from its peers by the inclusion of a winding road (ie multi-scrolling playfield), requiring players to negotiate the direction of the tarmac while also avoiding traffic – both same lane and, unusually, oncoming. Previously, endless straight roads had meant players only had to contend with not crashing into opponent cars, and while the road in *Highway* doesn't alter its direction by more than 45 degrees, meaning a player is still always heading 'up' the screen, the game's additional dynamic proved both refreshing and welcome at the time.

Also striking was the way the experience was delivered. Encased in a sit-down cockpit-style cabinet – the first arcade game to adopt this approach – it would have stood out effortlessly from a typical arcade's rows of upright cabinets (though an upright version was also released). This approach was repeated with *Night Driver*, a later game (see p35), which Atari incorporated into unsold *Highway* cabinets, before eventually becoming standard practice for almost every driving game released in arcade form (particularly as it became harder to differentiate the arcade experience from the vastly improved console driving game as the performance of home hardware accelerated ahead).

Indy 800 (1975)
Format: Arcade
Developer: Kee Games
Publisher: Kee Games

If *Highway*'s cabinet impressed gamers, the 16 square feet needed to house the eight-player (eight steering wheels, eight horns, 16 pedals) set-up of *Indy 800* must have caused a few instant cases of tachycardia. And that's before those affected saw the colour screen at the centre of the action – previously (and for a few years after) arcade games had almost entirely relied on black and white displays.

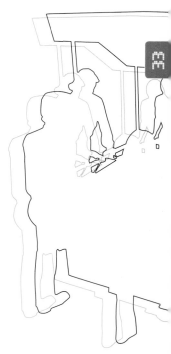

Pic 1: Even now, *Indy 800*'s remarkable cabinet would most likely command the attention at any arcade. *(Kee Games, courtesy of The Arcade Flyer Archive)*

races, but the social dynamic created by the cabinet's set-up must also be recognised as contributing to *Indy 800*'s huge success. *(Kee Games)*

Pic 2: The game's eight-player dynamic ensured frantic and closely fought

Pic 3: Alas, the *Nürburgring* games remain relatively unknown. *(Trakus)*

Today still this behemoth of a cabinet wouldn't fail to be noticed, even if its basic play mechanics – not substantially different in either feel or structure from spiritual predecessor *Gran Trak 10* – obviously belong to a time long surpassed.

Nevertheless, the appeal and reward was clearly in the multi-player dynamic, unmatched in its day, and *Indy 800*'s ability to draw big crowds (who could follow the on-track action via top-mounted mirrors while awaiting their turn) isn't surprising. Expecting something of a reaction to follow the arrival of its unprecedented cabinet at arcades, Kee Games (a wholly-owned subsidiary of Atari) gave operators the option to purchase a remote control module to start races, for those with the entrepreneurial spirit to organise special race events around their business's latest acquisition.

Nürburgring 1 (1975)
Platform: Arcade
Developer: Dr-Ing Reiner Foerst
Publisher: Trakus

While Atari's *Night Driver* is generally referred to as the first driving game to employ a first-person perspective, that

achievement actually belongs to *Nürburgring 1*. Developed as a simulation by an expert in the field, Dr Reiner Foerst, work on *N1* began in 1971 as a backdrop to creating the most advanced driving instruction simulators – Dr Foerst's interest centred on engineering and simulation theory.

The arrival of *Pong* in 1973 saw a shift in approach with regards to *N1*'s development, a prototype of which had up to that point relied on light bulbs rather than a monitor. By adapting the technology from other arcades, Dr Foerst altered the display technique and

two years later the first title in the *Nürburgring* series was ready.

Adapting a 'bonnet'-style viewpoint and using white rectangles stretching into the horizon of the black background of its small TV screen, *Nürburgring 1* was a world away from the top-down perspectives of driving games of the time. But it also led in other areas, most notably in audio. The engine sound alters according

Pic 1: *Nürburgring 1* came from the desire to create a driving simulation and the eventual game would include several innovative features. *(Trakus)*

Pic 2: For most arcade goers, *Night Driver* would represent their first

encounter with a driving perspective other than top-down. *(Atari)*

Pic 3: *Night Driver*'s promotional materials: only in the 1970s. *(Atari, courtesy of The Arcade Flyer Archive)*

Pic 4: The *Night Driver* sit-down cabinet followed Atari's own *Highway* but such a set-up was still a rare sight at the time. Its one-size-fits-all mould did mean taller players were forced to play the upright version, though. *(Atari)*

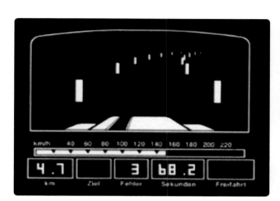

to the revs and accelerator position so that a player can discern the gear changing from the audio cues, while tyre screeching and crash effects are also simulated, along with the noise of air displacement when travelling at high speed.

The game was ahead of anything else at the time and it didn't take long for other companies to spot *Nürburgring 1* and come up with their own interpretations. Midway and Atari were two to do this quicker than most, and their ability to mass-manufacture (and therefore sell units at a cheaper rate), combined with global distribution opportunities, completely outclassed the set-up Dr Foerst and Trakus had – hence the widely held view that *Night Driver* was the first such driving game.

The *Nürburgring* series continued, however, with the second iteration turning up in 1979 (essentially a motorbike version of *Nürburgring 1*). A considerably evolved version featuring advanced graphics and audio, which also came in a version featuring a tilting cabinet, *Nürburgring 3* showed up in 1980, and was followed by, unsurprisingly, *Nürburgring 4* (1982), with significantly better visuals, now in colour.

Development of the *Nürburgring* series carried on deep into the 1980s, albeit with an increasing bias towards the training and commercial simulator sector, a field Dr Foerst and his company continue to work in. His early arcades, having rarely made it beyond Germany's borders, remain largely unknown.

Night Driver (1976)

Format: Arcade
Other versions: 2600 (1980), C64 (1982)
Developer: Atari
Publisher: Atari

Night Driver started life as *Night Racer*, developed by Micronetics after the company found itself inspired by the appearance of *Nürburgring 1*. Subsequently, both Atari and Midway made their own versions (with the latter naming its effort *Midnite Racer*, before a licensing deal with Datsun saw a swift name change to *280-ZZZap*).

It was Atari's second sit-down driving game (the first being 1975's *Highway*), and although primitive by today's standards the use of microprocessor technology (rather than ROM chips) ensures *Night Driver* runs fast and smooth with responsive steering as players attempt to get as far

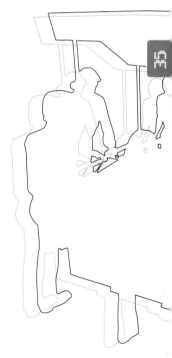

Pic 1: As a 1970s arcade operator, if for some inexplicable reason *Sprint 2*'s exciting new style or arcade racing didn't convince you to place an order for a unit, the vibrant sales flyer most likely would have done so. *(Kee Games, courtesy of The Arcade Flyer Archive)*

Pic 2: Although we take AI opponents for granted these days – until they spoil a hard-fought race, at which point their existence is cursed – when two first appeared in *Sprint 2* it was obviously a big deal. And proved a key component of the game. *(Kee Games)*

down the sinuous road as time allows, their effort rewarded with points – the game displays highest top speed and best high-score to entice competition between gamers.

Three tracks are included, which also dictates the difficulty level, and the game borrowed a concept from the electro mechanical arcades of the 1960s by using a card overlay to portray the player's car, rather than opting for a graphics-based solution (as *Nürburgring 1* did). The effect may look a little odd during some of the cornering sequences, but it didn't stop *Night Driver* from being an enjoyable experience that early video game players brought up on a diet of top-down racing lapped up enthusiastically.

Sprint 2 (1976)
Format: Arcade
Developer: Kee Games
Publisher: Kee Games

Considered by many as one of the greatest driving games of the 1970s, *Sprint 2* is in effect a remake of *Gran Trak 10*, albeit completely refreshed from the ground up due to its reliance on microprocessor technology (*Night Driver* had also made the transition, but *Sprint 2* is generally thought of as the first mass-produced game based on such technology).

The concept may have remained almost identical to *Gran Trak 10* in its top-down, lap-based challenge approach, but the result of the reworking is that it played infinitely better than its predecessor – the 'feel' of the car is much improved, along with control and overall pace – as well as including additional elements such as on-screen text and, for the first time in a racing title, AI opponents.

Sprint 2 is a one- or two-player affair (subsequent *Sprint 4* and *Sprint 8* versions upped the player count), with the computer taking care of the remaining competitors so that four cars battle it out on any one of the game's 12 speedy tracks using the four-speed gearstick. Collisions between players ends in loss of control and time.

Its simplistic nature may hide it now, but at the time *Sprint 2* offered a glimpse at the dynamism the genre would subsequently incorporate. It became one of Atari's biggest hits (and proved extremely profitable for arcade owners), ensuring that the *Sprint* franchise survived well into the 1980s, not least with the release of the excellent *Super Sprint* (covered in Chapter 3).

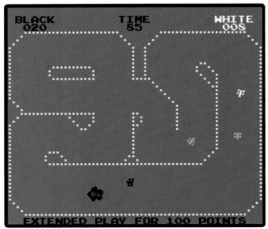

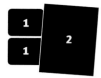

Pic 1: *Speed Freak*'s long, mostly empty road, minimalist visuals, simplistic dynamic and impressively smooth ride invoke an almost dream-like state in players – unlike the majority of today's sense-assaulting driving game productions. *(Vectorbeam)*

Pic 2: For a game that would have been so exciting at the time, the sales materials for *Speed Freak* leave too much to the imagination. *(Vectorbeam, courtesy of The Arcade Flyer Archive)*

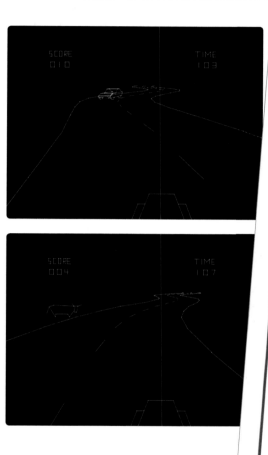

NEW **Speed Freak**

FROM **VECTORBEAM**

33441 CENTRAL AVENUE • UNION CITY, CA 94587
415/489-2000 • TWX 910-381-8075

3-D EFFECTS

Challenge the ever turning road with your greatest speed. But be careful, you're not alone on the road. A true three-dimensional car is constantly coming at you. Crashing into this car causes a spectacular three-dimensional crash in which you see true actual parts of the car exploding and spinning off into the distance. Stay on the road or you can also crash, which brings up a cracked windshield. All crashes stop game play with no loss of time, although the driver must get back up to speed by shifting through the four gears.
All this plus a four-speed gear shift, realistic scenery, hitchhikers and various other objects enhance the game. Add to that, extended play feature, selectable coinage and the ever popular Vector Monitor you have the greatest single player upright driving game ever built.
Available now through your nearest Vector Beam distributor.

Distributed by

Dimensions: 25 Wide
26½ Deep
68 High

Speed Freak (1979)
Format: Arcade
Developer: Vectorbeam
Publisher: Vectorbeam

The move to microprocessors in titles such as *Night Driver* and *Sprint 2* hinted at the road ahead for arcade (and home) titles, but by the end of the 1970s the technology still wasn't able to convincingly replicate a three-dimensional environment. This saw a few developers resort to the use of vector graphics, which managed the recreation of 3D objects and a therefore more realistic game environment at the cost of other aspects such as colour.

The most prominent example of this approach in the driving genre of the time is Vectorbeam's *Speed Freak*. It's a first-person affair in which the player uses an analogue steering wheel and four-position gearstick to drive as fast as possible along a mostly empty road, avoiding the occasional oncoming car and police road

block while trying not to get distracted by roadside objects such as cows, hitchhikers, trees or even a passing plane.

The game easily impressed upon release – a result of exciting visuals and silk-smooth nature – and is probably best remembered by players for its 'advanced' crash sequence (an animation of the player car's components spreading across the screen), but was also notable at the time for the fact that colliding with either obstacles or scenery incurs no time penalty as was typically the case (although the score, which is based on speed and distance without crashing, is clearly affected).

Despite its accomplished and exciting nature, *Speed Freak* failed to enjoy the most widespread exposure around the world's arcades.

the 1980s

TIME 36 SCORE 100 LAP 0'00"68

START

STAGE 1

(Sega)

Pic 1: Although *Pole Position* often gets credited with being the first full colour arcade game, that remark ought to be wheeled out for Sega's *Turbo*, which came out a year earlier. That aside, Namco's game offers a more exciting play experience. *(Sega)*

Pic 2: Racing in just before the end of the decade in 1989, *Winning Run* followed *Hard Drivin'* in offering a polygon-built gameworld ahead of the 3D revolution that followed. *(Namco Bandai)*

Pic 3: Technically, Sega's *Power Drift* is one of the best 1980s examples of sprite-based racers. *(Sega)*

Pic 4: Sega began the '80s intent on establishing itself as a leading driving game producer. It did. *(Sega)*

Introduction

The 1980s didn't start particularly well for driving games in the arcade sector. Whereas they had ended the '70s as one of the leading categories, as technology rapidly improved developers began focusing instead on experiences that they had previously been unable to recreate – be they real-world or fantasy-based – because previous restraints of the hardware had dictated simplistic, easily identifiable premises. This change in approach effectively forced the driving genre to take something of a back seat to space shooters, pill munching circles and platforming plumbers.

Notable appearances did nevertheless roll in, such as Sega's impressive *Turbo* and Namco's enormously popular *Pole Position*, both of which marked a new shift to the third-person 'chase cam' perspective that would typify driving games for that decade (and remain a staple component of the genre beyond), as well as igniting a rivalry between the two companies that continues to this day. But it would be the latter half of the '80s that saw the genre really get into gear in arcades, with the seminal *OutRun* clearing the way for renewed interest from both developers and the game-playing public.

On the home formats, the road up to that point had been considerably smoother. Indeed, in between *Pole Position* and *OutRun* the most exciting driving genre developments were to be found on computers such as the ZX Spectrum, Commodore 64 and BBC Micro. Titles like *Chequered Flag*, *Pitstop II* and *REVS* may not have matched the output of arcades technologically, but they could easily beat their coin-op cousins in terms of substance and player involvement. That clearly changed with Sega's *OutRun* in 1986, and the arcade sector fought back further with the introduction of multiplayer gaming (seen first in 1987's memorable *Final Lap*, the cabinets of which Namco had made linkable for up to eight players); but it didn't take long for the home formats to get back behind the wheel, and by the end of the decade the PC would power past a milestone in the form of the first

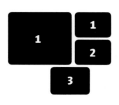

Pic 1: The iconic image of Mount Fuji scrolls smoothly past to remind you *Pole Position*'s track is indeed based on a real-world equivalent, other links to the world of motorsport could be found in the need to qualify in order to be allowed to race. *(Namco Bandai)*

Pic 2: Arcade games of the '80s took few prisoners. On the one hand they were clearly designed to deliver the best financial return for arcade operators, but their harshness also stems from play mechanics that now seem very unrefined. *(Namco Bandai)*

Pic 3: The majority of home conversions of *Pole Position* – Spectrum shown here – couldn't match the visuals and lacked steering wheel input, although several managed to transfer the essence of the game mainly intact. *(US Gold)*

true simracing title, *Indianapolis 500: The Simulation*.

As an example of how far the genre had travelled throughout the '80s, as well as an indication of what would follow, the timing of Papyrus's title – 1989 – couldn't have been more appropriate. The end of the road for 2D-based titles was fast approaching.

Pole Position (1982)

Format: Arcade
Other versions: Atari 2600, 5200, 400/800, Commodore 64, Vectrex, VIC-20, ZX Spectrum (1983); Texas Instruments TI-99/4A (1984), PC (1986), Intellivision (1987)
Developer: Namco
Publisher: Atari

History can be cruel. Although Sega's *Turbo* is arguably the first full-colour sprite scaling driving game, it is *Pole Position*, which emerged a year later, that is generally the title associated with that honour. That aside, Namco's racer isn't short on innovation in that it can claim to be the world's first driving game to be based on a real circuit – Japan's Fuji Speedway – and also the first to include a qualifying lap structure, which players have to complete in order to determine their starting

position in the subsequent (typically) three-lap race. That's assuming they're fast enough, because if you fail to qualify it's game over – a brave decision on the part of Namco but one that certainly didn't put players off.

It may be difficult to imagine it now, but *Pole Position*'s graphics mark the beginning of driving game developers' obsession with realism. It may not have been the first full-colour game on the arcade grid, but it was certainly the prettiest, one of the smoothest and easily the most authentic. When combined with a striking all-encompassing sit-down cabinet and engaging chase cam view (again, *Turbo* offered a

Pic 1: The six real circuits in *Chequered Flag* include Brands Hatch, Monaco, Österreichring, Monza, Paul Ricard and Silverstone. They join four fictitious tracks – although hardware limitations mean all look remarkably similar with regards to scenery. *(Sinclair Research)*

Pic 2: As one of the early sims, Psion's game was considerably trickier to play than arcade racers. *(Sinclair Research)*

Pic 3: The game looks basic now, with a worrying lack of track-side detail but upon release this was less shocking.

Pic 4: No official licence resulted in the inclusion of the 'McFaster Special' and the 'Ferreti Turbo'. *(Sinclair Research)*

However, the lack of competitor cars meant *Chequered Flag*'s 'races' could feel like lonely affairs. *(Sinclair Research)*

near-identical proposition on both fronts), then advanced sound effects, as well as the addictive nature of its game mechanic – which revolved around competing against computer-controlled opponents (a feature first introduced by *Sprint 2* in 1976) and avoiding hazards such as water puddles while negotiating the circuit's corners – this ensured *Pole Position* was the first driving game to seduce the general public, not just those who frequented arcades.

The game was a massive worldwide hit, was extensively converted to the major formats of the time and is rightfully considered a classic – even if its unrefined 1980s game dynamics (such as the slightest brush with a competitor or the scenery objects resulting in an instant explosion) will seem harsh by today's standards.

Chequered Flag (1983)

Format: ZX Spectrum
Developer: Psion (S Kelly)
Publisher: Sinclair Research

One of the very early first-person driving games on a home format, *Chequered Flag* is generally remembered by Spectrum owners with great fondness. Essentially a time trial simulation – there were no other cars on the track – the game requires you to drive one of three Formula 1 cars around ten tracks (six of them based on their real-life counterparts) as fast as possible while keeping an eye out for obstacles (oil, water, rocks and broken glass) that may force a trip to the pits.

Unusual for the time, care must be taken to look after certain parameters of the car. The dashboard displayed a speedometer, rev counter, gear selector, engine temperature and fuel level – keeping an eye on the latter two gauges ensured any issues such as engine damage and running out of petrol didn't prematurely end a run.

The graphics might be basic, even for the time, but the simulation aspects married to a handling model

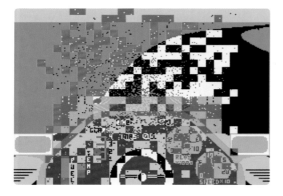

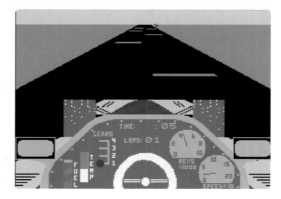

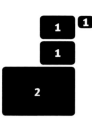

Pic 1: The envy of many a Spectrum owner, Epyx's *Pitstop II* was solely focused on the dynamic of two-player competition – even the eponymous pitstop sequence was turned into a mini-game, ensuring the level of tension was maintained. *(Epyx)*

Pic 2: The split-screen set-up – an obvious necessity at the time – undoubtedly adds to the game's excitement but also introduces a tactical layer for players unscrupulous enough to block their opponent during close-fought encounters. *(Epyx)*

that resorts to two sets of keys in order to simulate a pseudo-analogue steering system (with elements such as understeer reasonably conveyed) resulted in a memorable experience. Certainly, it would be a couple of years before anything better came along.

Pitstop II (1984)

Format: Commodore 64
Other versions: Apple II, Atari 400/800
Developer: Epyx (S. Landrum, D. Caswell, E. Murphy)
Publisher: Epyx

Proof that sequels can sometimes better their predecessor, *Pitstop II* is a defining two-player Formula 1-based arcade-style driving game based on a relatively unremarkable game first developed for the Atari 800 before being ported to the Commodore 64, where it enjoyed enough success for publisher Epyx to commission a follow-up. When the company involved wasn't able to deliver, Epyx turned to its employees to take over the project and just three months later *Pitstop II* emerged.

The concept of split-screen two-player was at the time very new and certainly *Pitstop II* would have

Pic 1: Geoff Crammond may have proved his simulation programming talents with *Aviator*, a Spitfire sim from 1983, but he had no racing experience. So for *REVS* Acornsoft partnered him with David Hunt, whose car in the 1983 Marlboro British Formula Three Championship was sponsored by the publisher. Hunt would become the game's technical advisor and can be assumed to have played a significant role in the creation of one of the most notable driving simulations of all time. *(Acornsoft)*

attracted attention for this element alone, but had it failed to back it up with such an exciting game dynamic, which, for the first time, included pit stops to replenish fuel and refresh tyres (a feature that played out in mini-game format, ensuring that the competition between the two racers would continue even off the track), it would definitely not be remembered as one of the C64's greatest achievements.

But leading graphics and sound, solid and dependable handling, a choice of six tracks, and the crucial tactical elements available to players – either through pit strategy (where conserving your tyres by avoiding collisions or running over the interminable rumble strips, and fuel through careful use of speed, can mean having to stop fewer times) or by dirty tactics on the track – ensured that on that format at least, few driving games ever overtook it.

REVS (1984)

Format: BBC Micro
Other versions: Commodore 64 (1986)
Developer: Geoff Crammond
Publisher: Acornsoft

Picking up where *Chequered Flag* left off and finding a couple of extra gears, *REVS* is a landmark in driving games notable for its then revolutionary simulation-grade handling and realism-heavy approach.

Programmed by Geoff Crammond, who'd go on to produce some of the iconic titles in the racing genre, *REVS* aimed to recreate a Formula 3 experience on what was at the time hardware offering very limited computing power. That it succeeded in delivering an unprecedented level of physics-based car feedback

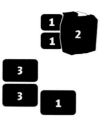
and control, while extracting exceptional, smooth graphics (which included fully three-dimensional environments complete with elevation changes) out of its modest host system is further testament to how far Crammond's approach was ahead of the field. Indeed, the next game to bother *REVS* with regards to vehicle dynamics would be *Stunt Car Racer*, another Crammond production (albeit an admittedly very different one).

The fact that it included just one track – Silverstone – didn't limit the game's appeal (an expansion pack added Donington Park, Brands Hatch, Snetterton and Oulton Park), and neither did its difficulty. Even after tweaking the wing settings – an unusual inclusion in games of the time – to an optimum level, mastering the car takes considerable effort, while some of the 19 other opponents – different characteristics for AI drivers was another innovation – present a considerable challenge. But with a game mechanic so rewarding, putting the practice in on *REVS* never felt like hard work.

Buggy Boy (aka Speed Buggy) (1985)

Format: Arcade
Other versions: Commodore 64, Amstrad CPC (1987), Amiga, Atari ST, ZX Spectrum (1988)
Developer: Tatsumi Electronics
Publisher: Taito

At a time when others were focusing on realism – both aesthetically and thematically – Tatsumi decided fun to be a more worthy pursuit. *Buggy Boy*, with its cartoon-like visuals and simple yet addictive game mechanic, is certainly that.

The game's core ingredients, which involve speeding through five courses circumnavigating obstacles such as rocks and tree trunks – or simply jumping over them via judiciously placed ramps – as well as acquiring points for collecting flags, driving

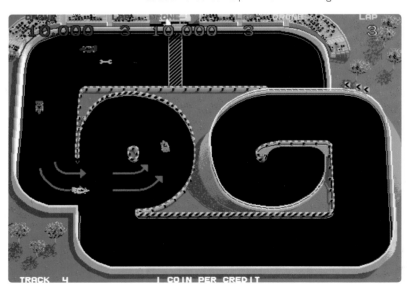

Pic 1: Anyone who missed the instantly likeable *Buggy Boy* in its impressive arcade form was given the chance to be introduced to its many charms in one of the several home conversions that followed the original release a couple of years later. *(Taito)*

Pic 2: It's the simple things in life… Atari's resurrection of the *Sprint* franchise didn't mess around with the original dynamic too much and instead added just enough sprinkle of modernity to turn it into a hugely addictive and playable affair. *(Atari)*

through gates or on two wheels, and any air time, may not sound like a recipe for long-term interest, but *Buggy Boy* is effortlessly more than just a sum of its parts, as the many who developed a mild addiction with the arcade (and its equally popular – and mostly accomplished – home conversions) found out.

Aside from its chunky, charming quality, most will probably remember the game's arcade cabinet, which borrowed the triple-screen display set-up Tatsumi had previously used for *TX-1* in 1983 (generally considered to be the first arcade unit to utilise three displays) and as such ensured its presence wouldn't go unnoticed.

Not that it can't hold your attention through the quality of its experience alone – despite the game's playful appearance, this is an expertly honed title whose character the passage of time has barely affected.

Super Sprint (1986)
Format: Arcade
Other versions: Amstrad CPC, Atari ST, Commodore 64, ZX Spectrum (1987), NES (1989)
Developer: Atari
Publisher: Atari

It's likely the majority of players who found themselves exposed to *Super Sprint*'s hugely addictive character in the mid-'80s would have been blissfully unaware of the series' inception in the previous decade, courtesy of *Sprint 2*. Yet even the game's conspicuous three-player, three-wheeled cabinet can trace its roots back to the 1970s.

Despite its illustrious heritage, *Super Sprint* was never in danger of not doing its family proud. At a time when top-down driving titles were beginning to look out of favour with a gaming crowd increasingly used to

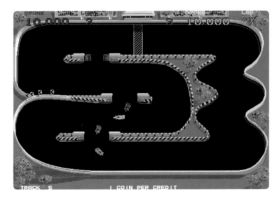

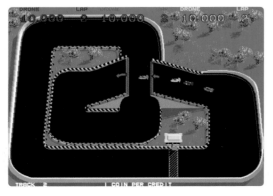

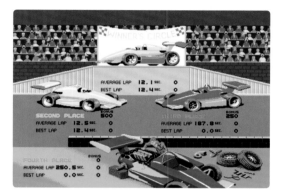

the perspectives offered by advancing technology, it says something about the *Sprint* series' tenacity and fundamental roll-caged structure that such a simple concept would have cut it in the arcades of the time.

Sure, the game's eight tracks may have now featured new elements such as jumps and the game incorporated an upgrade system (based around collecting wrench icons to exchange for better traction, speed or better acceleration), but the ancestral fun, frantic on-track action remained as the tiny single-

seater cars raced around expertly designed circuits, showcasing their fly-like direction-changing abilities. It's an undeniably straightforward proposition – which, despite having its roots in the '70s, has nevertheless inspired numerous 'tributes' over the years – and one that isn't likely to lose its charm in the near future.

OutRun (1986)

Format: Arcade
Other versions: Amstrad CPC, Commodore 64, Master System, MSX, ZX Spectrum (1987); Amiga, Atari ST, PC (1989), TurboGrafx-16 (1990), Mega Drive (1991), Saturn (1996), Dreamcast (2001), PlayStation 2 (2006)
Developer: AM2
Publisher: Sega

If a game encapsulated the materialism of the 1980s better than *OutRun* – which features a Ferrari Testarossa and blonde bimbo girlfriend passenger in a wild and carefree road trip – that game hasn't yet made itself known. Which isn't surprising, given that there isn't a title from that decade that could

1

Pic 1: Most aspects of *OutRun* appear designed with the purpose of creating a seamless and unique driving experience. That would explain the unusual decision not to allow players to insert more coins to continue their journey once the timer runs out. *(Sega)*

Pic 1: For many, the first glimpse of *OutRun*'s 350kg, hydraulic-powered, 26-inch screened 'Deluxe Type' cabinet in their local arcade was arguably as impressive as seeing the game's then astounding graphics. *(AzyxA/D Reed)*

Pic 2: The massive popularity of *OutRun* in the arcades saw the game extensively converted to the home systems but depressingly few managed to capture the essence of the coin-op original. *(Spectrum, US Gold)*

realistically claim to have been in a position to upstage Sega's groundbreaking, near-perfect creation.

An obvious technical showcase – either through its then astonishing visuals (which relied on Super-Scaler technology, Sega's marketing term for the sprite-scaling largely responsible for the game's exceptional sense of speed) or the revolutionary hydraulic-powered Deluxe arcade cabinet – *OutRun* is also a masterpiece of design and game balance.

Structured over 15 stages, each with its own memorable vibrant visual theme and laid out in a branching pattern so that any journey through the game is composed of five segments, *OutRun* was highly unusual in giving the player the choice of route at the end of each stage, which sees the road split in two (Tatsumi's *TX-1* had previously featured a similar approach). In doing so – and because routes differ in difficulty, with the right-hand forks typically leading to more treacherous journey segments – Sega effectively created a dynamic and player-controlled difficulty system. In a game where each stage is played against the clock, altering your route depending on your performance

Pic 1: One of the more impressive technical tricks up *OutRun*'s air intake was the inclusion of elevation changes. It wasn't the first sprite-based game to apply this but the effect was done in a manner that was particularly convincing. *(Sega)*

Pic 2: *OutRun* would get a series of spin-off titles, such as *Turbo OutRun* and *OutRunners* – shown here. But a direct sequel wouldn't turn up until 2003 when the aptly named *OutRun2* eventually drove into the world's arcades, to much acclaim. *(Sega)*

Pic 3: While technically very solid, *Chase HQ* didn't exactly astound visually when it rolled up in 1988. Its appeal resided instead in the quality of the play experience and a game dynamic that saw few male teenagers of the time able to resist it. *(Taito)*

suggests an unusually refined design ethos. Certainly, at the time it represented a step away from the harsh, cynical nature of many arcade games.

Not that *OutRun* wasn't designed with the intention of getting players to insert as many coins as possible – an arcade title survives on its ability to generate maximum profit for operators. But the game's hook is not in its five possible endings (each with a distinct animated sequence) or even in discovering every one of its gorgeous stages. Strong incentives as those are, it's the remarkable quality of the drive on offer that would make *OutRun* such a commercial success.

The promotional materials of the time talk excitedly about the accurate simulation of the central sports car, which is nonsense – *OutRun* is possibly the purest arcade driving experience around, boasting nothing that resembles real-world handling. In this instance that's a compliment, rather than a criticism.

Powering through the expertly designed stages, mastering their sinuous nature and avoiding (same-way) civilian traffic while having your actions supported by what is arguably the greatest soundtrack to ever grace a driving game, is one of the most thrilling and rewarding journeys in video gaming.

There is simply nothing noticeably wrong with *OutRun*. Everything from its unforgettable look and its sound to its structure and its feel is extraordinary. It is the reason it remains, arguably, the finest and most complete arcade driving game experience of all time.

Chase HQ (1988)
Format: Arcade
Other versions: Amiga, Amstrad CPC, Atari ST, Commodore 64, MSX, NES, SNES, ZX Spectrum (1989); Master System (1991), TurboGrafx-16 (1992), Saturn (1996)
Developer: Taito
Publisher: Taito

Perhaps just as iconic as *OutRun*'s Testarossa, the Porsche 928 at the centre of *Chase HQ* will forever be associated with Taito's game by an entire generation of players, such was the arcade release's impact in 1988. Based around the premise of using the 928 – an undercover police car – to pursue, catch up to and stop fleeing criminals by ramming them into submission (or, more accurately, filling their damage meter displayed on-screen), the concept proved refreshingly different upon its arrival.

Played against a two-tiered time limit system (the timer extended once the criminal car has been

Pic 1: *Chase HQ*'s mechanic is basic but that's possibly one of the reasons why it works so beautifully. *(Taito)*

Pic 2: No big deal now, but one clever touch was the inclusion of three turbos for the player to deploy. *(Taito)*

located) and through five increasingly difficult stages, *Chase HQ* is unashamedly arcade-light in terms of handling but even now it retains its highly compelling core – there's something deeply satisfying in repeatedly smashing into your AI opponent – while the action retains its relentless nature.

It may be tricky to appreciate these days, given our familiarity with its concept (which has since appeared in numerous other games), but *Chase HQ* caused a storm upon its release. Crashing its way into an oversubscribed genre mostly concerned with track-based competition, the uniqueness of the play mechanic holding Taito's game together revitalised the gaming crowd in a manner that hadn't been seen since *OutRun*.

Hard Drivin' (1988)
Format: Arcade
Other versions: Amiga, Amstrad CPC, Atari ST, Commodore 64, ZX Spectrum (1989); Mega Drive, PC (1990)
Developer: Tengen/Atari
Publisher: Atari

Simulation-based games had appeared on the home formats towards the start of the decade, yet, despite the claims of the early driving titles of the 1970s, realism had swerved around the arcades. In *Hard Drivin'*, that sector

Pic 1: It's not been proven but there are reports that not every *Hard Drivin'* player opted for the Stunt Track. *(Atari)*

Pic 2: Some of the home conversions did what they could to emulate the arcade's 3D visuals. *(Domark)*

Pic 3: The appearance of the *Hard Drivin'* arcade cabinet set-up – particularly the 'Deluxe' version – with its three-pedal and four-speed gearstick intimidated and attracted young arcade goers in equal measure. *(Atari, courtesy of The Arcade Flyer Archive)*

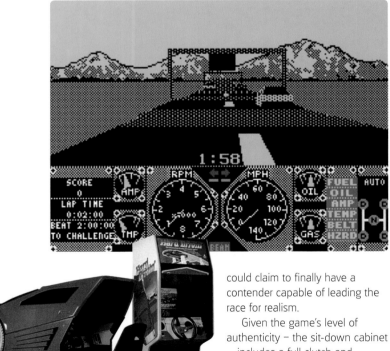

stunt track may seem odd. But the jumps, loop-the-loop and other elements actually allowed *Hard Drivin'* to showcase its advanced handling model.

Developed by Douglas Milliken, son of vehicle dynamics expert William Milliken and himself a leading figure in the field, the game's physics may fail to impress next to today's simracing stars, but in their day they made considerably more impact – Tengen and Atari's effort certainly carried off a convincing illusion of being in control of a car. Unless you were keen to regularly see its (admittedly excellent) crash replay sequences, *Hard Drivin'* required a completely different approach to other driving game arcades – speed and steering input had to be carefully judged in order to successfully negotiate its environment. The game's uniqueness and adherence to real-world vehicle behaviour earned it an enviable reputation. (Fearsome, too, if you happened to be the young learner driver who had the misfortune of stalling the car when using the manual gearbox while trying to show off your newly acquired driving skills in front of friends.)

As did the visuals, which were one of the earliest examples of polygon-based graphics. The resulting three-dimensional world with its lack of texture-mapping and mostly flat, detail-free environments may look barren to today's eyes, but, despite failing to match the splendour of the latest sprite-based creations of the time, they enabled the creation of the 3D world able to sustain *Hard Drivin'*'s revolutionary physics modelling. That they also conveyed precisely the type of weightiness suited to a simulation only added to the already remarkable experience.

Stunt Car Racer (1989)
Format: Amiga, Atari ST, Commodore 64, PC, ZX Spectrum
Other versions: Amstrad CPC (1990)
Developer: Geoff Crammond/MicroStyle
Publisher: MicroProse Software

When released, it was undoubtedly one of the most enjoyable experiences you could have on four virtual wheels at home. Created by the exceptional mind behind the excellent *REVS* and the then yet-to-be-programmed genius of *Formula One Grand Prix*, Geoff Crammond's *Stunt Car Racer* places you at the wheel (a decision that at the time bucked the trend of chase cam perspective that had persisted despite the popularity of titles such as *Chequered Flag* and, indeed,

could claim to finally have a contender capable of leading the race for realism.

Given the game's level of authenticity – the sit-down cabinet includes a full clutch and four-speed gearbox option, detailed force feedback and even an ignition key start-switch to get things going – the choice to set the action in a

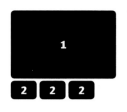

Pic 1: The Commodore 64 version of *Stunt Car Racer* isn't as easy on the eye as the editions running on the more powerful hardware, but it serves to highlight the simplicity of Geoff Crammond's concept beautifully. *(MicroProse Software)*

Pic 2: One of the great touches of the Amiga and ST versions of the game was the ability to link-up these rival systems together for two-player *Stunt Car Racer* meetings. The resulting potential in such a set-up won't have escaped many. *(MicroProse Software)*

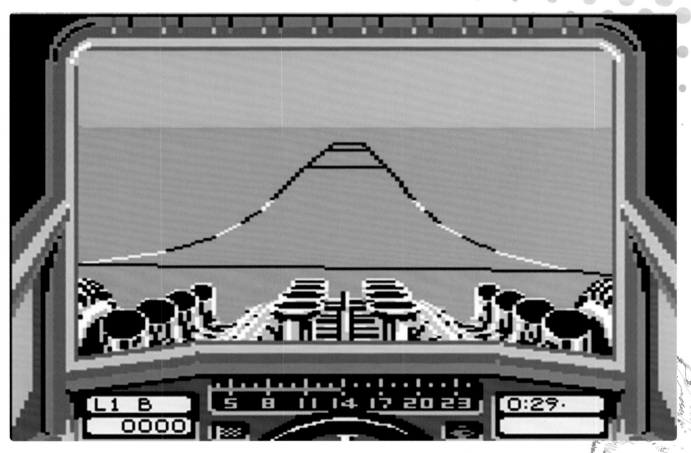

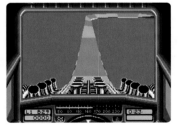
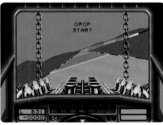

Crammond's own *REVS*) of a specially prepared vehicle and requires you to tackle tracks designed to test the limits of gravity against an opponent just as keen to become champion as you.

If the competition is tough, the tracks are tougher. A collection of barrier-less straights, banked turns and treacherous jumps just wide enough for the two competing vehicles means the smallest mistake is often punished by a trip bonnet-first back to the ground below. If that makes the experience sound

perilous, it is, but don't let it dispel the notion it isn't hugely enjoyable and worryingly addictive.

Analyse it now and *Stunt Car Racer*'s elements don't appear to add to much but the game's masterstroke was in fact its forced dashboard viewpoint, which combined with the polygon-based visuals – still a rarity at a time of 2D sprite-based racers – significantly increased the level of player immersion. The result is not unlike driving your way through a rollercoaster ride and, crucially, every bit as exciting.

Pic 1: While some brave souls persevered with key-based input, the complexity of *Indianapolis 500*'s handling model would drive players to look for better control systems and led peripheral makers to try their hand at steering wheel set-ups. *(Electronic Arts)*

Indianapolis 500:
The Simulation (1989)
Format: PC
Other versions: Amiga (1991)
Developer: Papyrus Design Group
Publisher: Electronic Arts

Upon its release, *Indianapolis 500: The Simulation* would do two things. First, it established Papyrus, on its first attempt, as a leading developer of simracing titles – a reputation the outfit wouldn't lose over its 16-game history; and second, and arguably more important, it is generally credited with establishing the simracing subgenre. Certainly, while some previous titles had displayed their simulation intentions – the aforementioned *REVS* perhaps more enthusiastically than most – nothing matching the scale and depth of *Indianapolis 500* had yet been seen.

As the title suggests, the game aims to recreate the world-famous Indy 500 event, with the player stepping into the cockpit of one of the 33 cars that took part in the 1989 and selecting between race options ranging from ten to 200 laps. Being a simulation, full practice and qualifying sessions are included, as well as a

Pic 1: Home conversions of *Super Monaco GP* couldn't hope to recreate the game's visual prowess. *(US Gold)*

Pic 2: *Super Monaco GP* still doesn't look ugly today but static shots fail to convey the intensity of the drive on

offer, which in hindsight could in part have been due to the surprisingly cluttered nature of the in-game display players faced – digesting all the information while keeping out of the barriers requires fighter pilot-like levels of perception. *(Sega)*

Pic 3: Perhaps a good example of how an arcade cabinet can contribute to a player's emotional involvement is the way the stand-up version of *Super Monaco GP* loses much of the game's essence and, by association, appeal. *(Sega, courtesy of The Arcade Flyer Archive)*

relatively comprehensive damage model (although AI drivers can also retire from races as a result of simulated component failures such as radiator and oil leaks, which do not extend to the player's car) and, crucially, extensive set-up options.

It is the last that most impressed back in 1989. Set-up options had appeared in games previously, of course, so the ability to play around with wing, gear and suspension settings, or even fuel levels and tyre compounds, won't necessarily have caught players by surprise. But camber, tyre pressure, anti-roll bars and turbo boost options, not forgetting real-time data such as tyre temperature, would have been new territory.

Of course, all the settings in the pit lane will make little difference if the handling model isn't able to implement them in-game. But, again, *Indianapolis 500* was ahead of the field, offering an unprecedented level of realism with regards to driver feedback. While not comparable to today's simracing titles (or indeed Papyrus's own subsequent releases), the game's handling physics are sufficiently elaborate that the slightest settings tweak has a noticeable effect out on the track. For the time, the above elements combined with an exceptional attention to detail delivered a drive that proved hugely demanding, uncommonly rewarding and, undoubtedly, revolutionary.

Super Monaco GP (1989)

Format: Arcade
Other versions: Mega Drive, Master System (1990); Amiga, Amstrad CPC, Atari ST, Commodore 64, ZX Spectrum (1991)
Developer: Sega
Publisher: Sega

While *Hard Drivin'* introduced arcade players to the world of polygon-based visuals, *Super Monaco GP* would put forward what was arguably the best case for sprite-based graphics of the 1980s. Viewed from a first-person in-car perspective, this F1 driving game couldn't claim to convey much relating to realism in terms of handling (or certain other aspects – the

Monaco circuit layout in the game is at best an approximation of the real thing), but with regards to displaying one of the richest graphical environments yet seen it would hear few counter arguments.

The visuals, along with an excellent sense of speed (an evolution of the sprite-scaling prowess Sega had showcased in *OutRun* and subsequently *Power Drift*) ensured *Super Monaco GP* delivered one of the most intense arcade driving experiences seen at the time. The atmosphere was considerably heightened by the enclosed cockpit style cabinet, which in its grandest version housed an impressive four-channel sound system, force feedback steering wheel with paddle shift gears (then only recently introduced to F1 cars) and convincing vibration effects.

The game's structure played its part, too. Taking inspiration from *Pole Position*, *Super Monaco GP* requires players to first qualify before the main three-lap event, where it introduces its own dynamic of imposing a checkpoint-based position limit on the player, adding to an already remarkably tense experience. Games of the early '90s would progress the sprite-based driving game further still, before the inevitable universal switch to polygons, but Sega's *Super Monaco GP* – appropriately the sequel to likeable 1980 top-down affair, *Monaco GP* – deserves to be remembered as an example of how far the genre had progressed technologically during this decade.

the
1990s

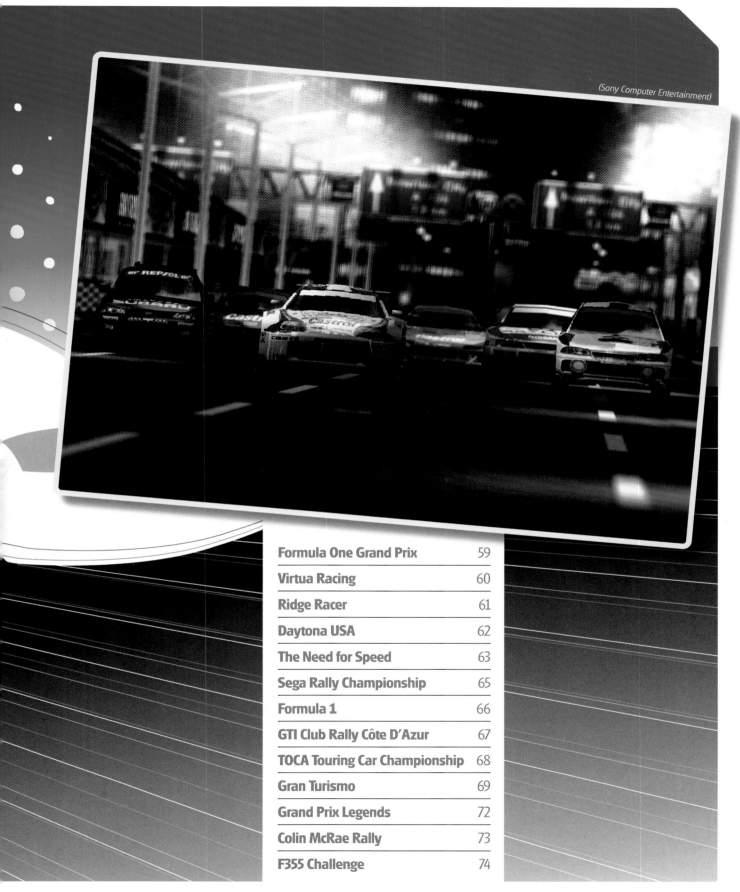

(Sony Computer Entertainment)

Pic 1: Rolling out of development in the mid-'90s, *Ace Driver* and *Ridge Racer* are perfect examples of how quickly companies like Namco got to grips with the rapidly evolving technology of the decade. *(Namco Bandai, courtesy of Edge magazine)*

Pic 2: *Daytona USA 2*, from 1998: a considerable graphical gulf still existed between arcade and console titles before the start of the 21st century. *(Sega, courtesy of Edge magazine)*

Pic 3: *Destruction Derby 2* illustrates

developers quickly getting used to 3D for console games. *(Sony Computer Entertainment, courtesy of Edge magazine)*

Pic 4: Console interpretations of arcade giants suffered technically. *(Virtua Racing Deluxe, Sega, courtesy of Edge magazine)*

Introduction

Has there ever been a more exciting decade for driving games than the 1990s? Possibly not. *OutRun* may have ruled the '80s and, indeed, still delivers the most well-rounded arcade driving experience, but even it would run out of limelight when the focus shifted onto the genre-altering revolution that would epitomise this decade: 3D graphics.

Polygon-based games were not new – Atari's *Hard Drivin'* and Namco's *Winning Run* were arguably the two most prominent examples already showcasing the technology towards the end of the '80s, but it would be 1992's *Virtua Racing* that really got the arcade crowd paying attention. Sega's landmark title put into motion a technological race that saw game developers overtake each other's efforts with the kind of intensity

that hasn't been seen since. Just seven years separate *Virtua Racing* and *F355 Challenge*, a time span that will appear unfeasibly short when you consider the technical gulf that exists between the two titles.

But then, by the end of the 1990s you would need something spectacular to make any kind of sizeable impact, because silently riding the arcade 3D slipstream were home consoles. The 1995 release of PlayStation, with its near-identical version of *Ridge Racer* – a game that only 18 months previously had wowed arcade players with its then unmatched visuals and intense play experience – caused a sensation. For the first time, home driving game experiences ported across from the arcade original were no longer anaemic representations of the source material.

Not only that, as developer teams got into their three-dimensional stride, console and home computer driving games began to lead, not follow. Early indications had come with the likes of *The Need for Speed* on 3DO, followed by *Screamer 2* on PC and *TOCA Touring Car Championship* on PlayStation (and PC). Suddenly, the home game sales charts, which in

Pic 1: The 1990s played host to some memorable driving titles, such as the impressively accomplished *V-Rally*, which predated *Colin McRae Rally* as the off-road experience of choice for the PlayStation crowd.

(Atari, courtesy of Edge magazine)

Pic 2: Even before *Formula One Grand Prix*, Geoff Crammond had already established himself as something of a sim-biased star with *REVS* and *Stunt Car Racer*. But this creation would propel him onto a considerably wider international stage. *(MicroProse Software)*

Pic 3: Crammond returned in 1996 with *Grand Prix 2*, another Formula 1 affair – based on the 1994 season – which again pushed the simracing segment onto a new level, both technically and in terms of handling. *(MicroProse Software, courtesy of Edge magazine)*

the 1980s and early '90s had rarely featured driving games, saw a transformation in the retail performance of the genre.

But it was the knock-on effect of the arrival of the pioneering *Gran Turismo* in 1998, again on PlayStation, that would most seriously bend the arcade driving game's axle. The increase in realism and intricacy Polyphony's game brought with it was a leap too far for the arcade sector to match. Thematically it was also beyond its remit of entertaining for three minutes, true, yet as the console and PC community became increasingly accustomed to the authenticity and substance offered by the games they could buy, arcade titles struggled and ultimately failed to keep up with their home counterparts.

The next development race for the driving genre would be disputed in the living room.

Formula One Grand Prix (aka World Circuit) (1992)

Format: PC, Amiga, ST
Developer: MicroProse Software
Publisher: MicroProse Software

When *Grand Prix* rolled out of MicroProse's garage, the simracing world had never seen anything like it. Programmed by Geoff Crammond (of *REVS* and *Stunt Car Racer* fame), it offered a level of simulation laps ahead of standard driving titles and arguably bettered its most immediate predecessor – *Indianapolis 500: The Simulation* – with revolutionary elements, a level of detail and what was effortlessly the most realistic handling dynamics at the time thrown into the hugely impressive mix.

Based on the 1991 Formula 1 season and featuring all 16 tracks and the cars of that year, the game featured cutting-edge polygon-based visuals, detailed

scenery (modelled, to a degree, on the real-world locations), working rear-view mirrors, extensive (for the time) tuning options and intricate aspects such as tyre wear, damage and a customisable replay option.

But it was the inclusion of driving aids, designed to be selected dependent on the player's ability, that ensured much of *Grand Prix*'s success. Sure, the simulation aspects were thoroughly convincing (with

Pic 1: *Virtua Racing*'s simplistic polygonal visuals retain an undeniable charm but upon the title's release gamers had never seen anything as exquisite. Anyone lucky enough to have tried out an eight-player link-up race is unlikely to ever forget it. *(Sega)*

Pic 2: If you're going to wow the arcade going crowd with your technical marvel, you better do it with a cabinet design up to the task. *Virtua Racing*'s Deluxe version didn't disappoint and is one of the first titles to use a widescreen display. *(Sega)*

only the behaviour of the AI occasionally spoiling the illusion) and the detail of the 3D visuals unprecedented, but by enabling the use of delicately implemented steering, brake and throttle assists, for instance, Crammond made it possible to play a high-level simulation via the keyboard, something owners of *Indianapolis 500* would have looked upon enviously.

Unsurprisingly, *Grand Prix* developed a following and competitions were held online (though not in the way we know them today) soon after its release. These days the limitations of its handling dynamics would see it languishing at the rear of the modern simracing grid – or even fail to qualify altogether – but such comparisons are inappropriate for a true classic of the driving game genre. It's perhaps indicative of how much esteem some still hold for Geoff Crammond's masterpiece that a small but dedicated *Grand Prix* community remains active even now.

Virtua Racing (1992)
Format: Arcade
Other versions: Mega Drive (1994), Saturn (1995)
Developer: AM2
Publisher: Sega

There's little danger of overemphasising the impact the appearance of *Virtua Racing* had in arcades across the globe. It wasn't the first arcade racing game to feature a dedicated polygon engine (*Winning Run* had passed that checkpoint first) but it screeched into the scene with the usual Sega fanfare, capturing the hearts, minds and eyes of players everywhere with its then exceptional showcase of technology.

Essentially a single-seater (featuring unofficial Formula 1 cars), the game is a high-speed thrill ride through a gloriously vibrant, angular landscape. But the initial excitement was certainly due to its revolutionary four-view option (achievable due to the game being entirely three-dimensional, of course), enabling the player to select the perspective they most favoured.

By today's standards the game maintains a certain visual charm despite its primitive polygons, and may feel ridiculously arcade-like in its handling dynamics (although it was preferred by a substantial segment of the hardcore gaming crowd over its spiritual successor, *Daytona USA*). Yet even in its day it could hardly have been described as realistic, as four-time

Pic 1: Namco would quickly tweak the *Ridge Racer* formula. Only released in Japan, *Ridge Racer 2* adds multiplayer – up to four 'twin' cabinets link-up – a rearview mirror function, a night-time setting, and more efficient vehicles. *(Namco Bandai, courtesy of Edge magazine)*

Pic 2: *Ridge Racer Revolution*, an *RR* effort developed with a console rather than arcade focus. It's notable for being one of the early PlayStation titles to support the vastly underused link-up option. *(Namco Bandai, courtesy of Edge magazine)*

Pic 3: *Ridge Racer* will be remembered as an exceptionally thrilling arcade. *(Namco Bandai, courtesy of Edge magazine)*

Pic 4: The game that sold PlayStation – Namco's near-perfect *RR* conversion. *(Namco Bandai, courtesy of Edge magazine)*

F1 World Champion Alain Prost found out to some embarrassment when he crashed his virtual single-seater under the watchful eye of the press during an event to commemorate the opening of a new Sega arcade centre in the UK.

That said, *Virtua Racing* was actually relatively well researched. In charge of a team of around 20 who worked flat out for a year to put the game together, project leader Yu Suzuki did his homework by studying 1992 Ferrari and McLaren-Honda engines, spoke to drivers and engineers and hired a Honda NSX for a period of time. The finished handling model in the game actually includes 120 advanced parameters such as air density, slipstream and aerodynamics.

Once the novelty of the technology wore off, however, as a gaming experience *Virtua Racing* found itself quickly overtaken by successors and only its two-player competitive mode ensured any genuine long-term appeal.

Ridge Racer (1993)

Format: Arcade
Other versions: PlayStation (1995)
Developer: Namco
Publisher: Namco

Hospitals around the world must have faced an influx of broken jaws once Namco released *Ridge Racer* into arcades in 1993. Its graphics were easily the most astonishing yet seen (outclassing even

those of the gorgeous *Daytona USA*, effectively Sega's response to *Ridge Racer*), and when combined with the absurd speed of the player's car hurtling through the game's expertly designed track (featuring tunnels, a suspension bridge, a jet plane, helicopter, beach-fronted road, mountainous passes, roadworks – all elements that would rapidly become racing game clichés), it created an irresistible assault on the senses. Throw in an arcade cabinet featuring a fully working clutch and six-speed gearbox set-up (or a real-life Mazda MX-5 and a curved six-metre wide screen in the Full Scale version) and *Ridge*

Pic 1: While certainly a rewarding single-player game, *Daytona USA* becomes exceptional the moment you begin adding more human racers into the mix. It's the very reason you still often find the game in arcades around the world. *(Author)*

Pic 2: Typical of Sega's arcade games of the time – certainly those from the AM2 division – *Daytona's* scenery was packed full of detail that would initially be lost on players too engrossed in the action on-screen to notice. *(Sega, courtesy of Edge magazine)*

Pic 3: A work-in-progress and therefore graphically subdued *Daytona USA* gets snapped at a Japanese arcade trade show, revealing the building blocks that would go on to underpin one of the great arcade multiplayer experiences of all time. *(Edge magazine)*

Racer had little trouble in seducing anyone who saw it into playing it.

It took a team of 40 programmers, designers and musicians a year to develop the game. Unfeasibly small and short by today's requirements of leading console racing titles, it nevertheless represented a massive leap over the production resources of arcade games up to that point.

The result was not only technically astounding, but for its time *Ridge Racer* offered the most convincing feeling of powersliding yet seen in an arcade game (the Japanese fascination with drifting was by then long established, although it would be several years before it made the transition to the West). It is absurdly exaggerated, true, but the effect is helped immeasurably by the 'first-person' perspective adopted by Namco.

Inarguably exhilarating, the experience was nevertheless not perfect. A single track (effectively), seemingly non-existent AI for the 12 computer-controlled opponents (who possess an incredible ability to often get in your way), poor crash effects and no visual damage effectively robbed *Ridge Racer* of some of the substance offered by the titles produced by arch-rival Sega and as such the game harnessed relatively short-term appeal.

That said, its ability for instant gratification was near-perfect while no one would dispute that its appearance proved instrumental in driving the genre forward; and for that, if nothing else, it deserves its standing in gaming history.

Daytona USA (1994)

Format: Arcade
Other versions: Saturn (1995), PC (1996)
Developer: AM2
Publisher: Sega

It would be no exaggeration to say *Daytona USA* should be considered a giant of arcade gaming. A follow-up to *Virtua Racing* and viewed by most as Sega's reply to Namco's *Ridge Racer*, *Daytona USA* was always going to deliver in technical terms. It took a year to create (in addition to the time required to develop the hardware it ran on) and was the company's first texture-mapped 3D effort. That it arguably failed to match Namco's effort on a purely graphical performance level was easily balanced out by a more varied and rewarding visual journey, helped by significantly greater attention to detail and the option of three tracks to *Ridge Racer's* one.

Pic 1: *Daytona USA*'s tracks look deceptively simple but they've been very carefully designed. Even gentle curves can only be correctly negotiated at full speed after much practice, which gave the game unusual depth. *(Sega)*

Pic 2: *The Need for Speed* was one of the highlights of the 1990s but remains relatively unknown due to its host format – 3DO – having failed to establish itself as a viable platform before the PlayStation turned up and gobbled up the market. *(Electronic Arts)*

Daytona's real advantages, though, lie elsewhere. The game offers a better, more extended learning curve than its closest rival (the drifting of *Daytona*'s NASCAR-based 750bhp machines takes a while to get to grips with), and while the AI of your computer-controlled opposition (up to 39 per race) may not have won awards it remained amongst the better examples on arcade at the time, with a semblance of deliberate blocking on their part – or at least its illusion – evident.

Nothing beats human competition, of course, and *Daytona USA*'s single greatest achievement was its eight-player cabinet link-up ability (the game, then under the working title of *Daytona GP*, was initially unveiled as a 13-cabinet link-up affair at Japanese trade shows but eight cabinets is the maximum commercial set-up). This turned an already exciting and rewarding virtual racer into what is arguably the ultimate multiplayer arcade racing experience. It's the reason the game is still found in numerous arcades around the world (usually in four-player link-up form, although additional variations such as the Champion Cam feature displaying the face of the leading driver on a screen in six-player set-ups introduced in 1995 are not uncommon), where it remains impressively popular – something that can hardly be said of nearly all of its contemporaries.

The Need for Speed (1994)
Format: 3DO
Other versions: PC (1995); PlayStation, Saturn (1996)
Developer: Pioneer Productions/EA Canada
Publisher: Electronic Arts

An evolution of the promising but ultimately dreary *Test Drive* games that appeared before it (and the first iteration of EA's now vastly different *Need for Speed* series), *The Need for Speed* couldn't have been further down the road from its inspiration. Largely under-appreciated in its time, it actually delivered an astonishing and utterly engrossing

Pic 1: *The Need for Speed* offers three viewpoints but predictably it's the in-car option that is by far the most convincing, both visually and in terms of 'feedback' experienced from the game's accomplished handling model.
(Electronic Arts, courtesy of Edge magazine)

Pic 2: While hardly *Burnout Paradise*-like in their complexity, for the time *TNFS*'s crash dynamics proved brutal enough for players to wince at the carnage on-screen – or at least those sufficiently engrossed in proceedings.
(Electronic Arts, courtesy of Edge magazine)

sections – feels more like being on a journey, but here the concept was plainly amplified by a realistic setting and relatively authentic feeling of speed.

The illusion was helped, of course, by the fact that this was technically one of the finest looking, finest sounding and smoothest games of its generation. The gorgeous visuals resulted from digitised surface bitmaps produced from real photographs, wrapped over a polygon skeleton. And a unique 3D rendering system enabled the team to draw the road out to infinity, resulting in a convincing vanishing point.

Underpinning one of the best driving environments seen at the time was an impressive and hugely rewarding handling model. The car data was provided courtesy of US magazine *Road & Track* and the physics model system used statistical information recorded by the publication to simulate the characteristics of the cars. The result was a handling dynamic considerably 'weightier' than the majority of other driving games, further increasing the level of authenticity.

The real-world connection was even further enhanced by the use of licensed vehicles – the Ferrari Testarossa 512TR, Lamborghini Diablo VT, Porsche 911 Carrera, Dodge Viper, Chevrolet Corvette ZR-1, Honda NSX, Mazda RX-7 and Toyota Supra – which in itself was an unusual proposition in games of the era, as well as the attention to detail in conveying the characteristics of the car selection through extensive FMV sequences.

Also unusual for the time was the inclusion of elaborate crash dynamics, and while this element failed to include visual damage such as crumpled bodywork (only the addition of smoke issuing from the engine bay), the way the often spectacular accidents book-ended segments of intense virtual driving only added to the already hugely engaging (and then unique) *The Need for Speed* road trip.

driving experience that transcended the then concept of driving games.

The Need for Speed may have presented itself as a race, with the player competing against an AI vehicle while avoiding relatively convincing civilian traffic and outrunning police patrols, but this is effectively a driving experience that enabled car aficionados to savour the thrills of driving a fine selection of automotive exotica within an utterly absorbing setting. Like the previous decade's magnificent *OutRun*, travelling through the game's three environments – urban, coastal and alpine, each composed of three

Pic 1: Glorious arcade-like handling, relentless action and one of the most rewarding powerslide dynamics ever implemented ensure *Sega Rally Championship* will retain its status as one of the finest examples the driving genre has seen. *(Sega)*

Pic 2: For the ultimate *Sega Rally* experience, only four linked-up Deluxe arcade cabinets – complete with 50-inch screen to best enjoy the Model 2 CPU board's 300,000 texture-mapped polygons per second – will ever do. *(Sega)*

Sega Rally Championship (1995)
Format: Arcade
Other versions: Saturn
Developer: AM3
Publisher: Sega

Certainly, two cars and three stages (or three and four respectively if you count the bonus vehicle and track) sounds like too miserly and generic a list of ingredients to make one of the greatest driving games of all time. Yet that's exactly what Sega's AM3 division achieved when it took just ten months (including a research trip to the 1994 Indonesian rally where sound was also recorded) to develop the hugely influential *Sega Rally Championship* arcade title.

These days, the game's 300,000 texture-mapped polygon/second figure – along with elements such as animated crowds and transparent windows – may fail to impress, but upon its release they ensured *Sega Rally* was one of the most visually astounding arcade titles available, helped, no doubt, by the inclusion of two iconic rally cars: the Lancia Delta Integrale '92 WRC and Toyota Celica GT-Four WRC.

Technology aside, the game would be remembered for its beautiful, cleverly designed tracks as well as its then remarkable handling model. Through the collaboration of Toyota and Lancia engineers who happily provided car dynamics and performance data (reportedly no licence fees were discussed between Sega and the two car manufacturers), the feeling of changing vehicle behaviour depending on the surface being driven on – stages focused on desert, forest and alpine settings – was for the time exceptionally conveyed. The powersliding may have

Pic 1: Rather angular these days, but *Formula 1* looked astonishing when it powered onto PlayStation in 1996. The attention to detail and use of real-world elements such as official timing graphics helped. *(Sony Computer Entertainment, courtesy of Edge magazine)*

Pic 2: AI opponents in *Formula 1* aren't too concerned by your position on-track. Although less revolutionary, the game's sequel – *Formula 1 97* – offered players a considerably improved experience. *(Sony Computer Entertainment, courtesy of Edge magazine)*

been the most difficult aspect for the team to recreate, but ultimately it's the game's greatest achievement and the principal reason for its massive popularity.

The passage of time hasn't significantly altered this and today (as one of Sega's most successful coin-ops, *Sega Rally Championship* can still be found in numerous arcades around the world in either two- or four-player link-up form) the game remains hugely enjoyable. By modern standards the AI is possibly more apparently obstructive than before, granted, but then even in its day the game's computer-controlled cars amounted to little more than moving chicanes; effectively, they were markers to give players an

indication of how well they were doing at the end of each stage (*Sega Rally* employs a structure that requires the player to overtake their way up the competitor field, with each new stage starting in the position the previous one is finished in).

But any criticism is driven away once sat in front of the arcade cabinet's dual-motor force feedback steering wheel while experiencing the use of 'Active Shock Generator', which ensures the seat reacts according to the on-screen action. Fast and furious, like all of Sega's best arcade racers *Sega Rally Championship* is a hugely energetic driving experience from which only those without a pulse are likely to emerge unimpressed.

Formula 1 (1996)

Format: PlayStation
Other versions: PC (1997)
Developer: Bizarre Creations
Publisher: Psygnosis

The first title in what became Sony's long-running *Formula 1* series is quite a few horsepower short of being the best, but it is arguably the most significant. Based on the 1995 season, it was memorable for introducing the idea that simulations – then only at

Pic 1: Ahead of its time, what *GTI Club* may have lacked in handling dynamics it made up for with charming visuals, great course design and intense, checkpoint-based play – as well as the game's crucial free-roaming aspect.
(Konami, courtesy of Edge magazine)

home on the more powerful PC platform – could work on console. Whereas F1 games on that format had previously been resolutely two-dimensional in their approach, the capabilities of the PlayStation opened up a 3D realm for driving games (as it did for other genres).

As the first polygon-based F1 title to appear on console, *Formula 1* certainly impressed, both technically and in its attention to realism. Each of the 26 cars was individually modelled from real data and made up of 450 triangles when displayed in high detail (switching to 100 in low), the 17 circuits were recreated from official surveyors' maps, with the visual reference for advertising hoardings coming from more than 100 hours of video footage, while all 35 drivers (including substitutes) made it onto the CD.

The attention to detail – a trait developer Bizarre Creations would go on to display impressively in its *Metropolis Street Racer/Project Gotham Racing* series – continued with the camera angles during race replays adopting the placement of their TV counterparts. The sound, meanwhile, had been recorded on a DAT strapped to a driver's body during a test session and then sampled into the game, while over an hour of Murray Walker commentary (for the UK edition) was also recorded and included.

For the time, and on console, the handling model proved accomplished and reasonably rewarding, while the ability to fool around with pit and fuel strategies (in addition to general set-up) was an uncommon inclusion. The experience wasn't trouble free, however, with graphical glitches resulting from the developer's relative unfamiliarity with the host hardware, while disappointing AI which stuck stubbornly to the racing

line, regardless of your position on the track, significantly affected the game's potential.

Anyone experiencing it today will regard it as little more than an historical curio, but as the first 3D F1 driving title on console, coupled with its ambition, *Formula 1*'s achievement is worth remembering.

GTI Club Rally Côte D'Azur (1996)
Format: Arcade
Developer: Konami
Publisher: Konami

The concept of free-roaming gaming may be a road well travelled these days, but back in 1996 it hadn't been applied to an arcade driving title prior to Konami introducing *GTI Club Rally Côte D'Azur* (*Turbo Esprit* did effectively manage it ten years earlier but on the home computer formats).

The revolutionary (Atari's *Hard Drivin'* doesn't count) approach of go-where-you-like freedom – coupled to the smart decision to base the game's car selection around European hot hatches and setting these within

an environment that requires players to tear through a seemingly intricate Southern French town looking for the fastest route (which inevitably involves discovering short-cuts and making good use of the arcade cabinet's included handbrake to negotiate the tighter turns), while also avoiding civilian traffic – created a hugely enjoyable driving game experience.

Excellent graphical detail and great crash sequences (two aspects Konami would embellish on when taking the concept further with *Thrill Drive* in 1998) added to an already intense atmosphere but it was one that proved somewhat short-lived, possibly due to an overall lack of substance and a functional, rather than engaging handling system.

Konami would subsequently boost the game's lifespan with added multiplayer elements such as a bomb-based game of 'Tag', but despite its relatively short-lived time in the limelight, *GTI Club*'s standing as the blueprint for the subgenre to which the likes of *Burnout* belong remains assured.

TOCA Touring Car Championship
(1997)
Format: PC, PlayStation
Developer: Codemasters
Publisher: Codemasters

A hugely significant release, *TOCA Touring Car Championship* signalled the start of Codemasters' exceptional foray into 3D driving games (which to date shows no signs of slowing down), but it also

demonstrated – before *Gran Turismo* was able to – that the console community was more than capable of appreciating a sim-focused approach to driving titles.

The timing of the release – at the height of the British Touring Car Championship's popularity – certainly explains the game's huge success (it remained in the UK charts from its release in the winter of 1997 and through nearly all of 1998). Or at least part of it, because the excellent, demanding physics matched to accurately modelled circuits and one of the most convincing in-car

Pic 1: Astute timing on the part of Codemasters saw the publisher capitalise on the height of popularity surrounding the TOCA Touring Car Championship. As interest dwindled, the series simply changed name. *(Codemasters, courtesy of Edge magazine)*

Pic 2: The moment everything changed. The arrival of Sony's *Gran Turismo* redefined the console driving game landscape and is responsible for the subsequent realism-based focus the genre underwent. *(Sony Computer Entertainment, courtesy of Edge magazine)*

Pic 3: *Gran Turismo*'s 4WD version of the Mitsubishi FTO is actually a creation of the development team achieved through tweaking parameters in a bid to make the ideal sports car. *(Sony Computer Entertainment, courtesy of Edge magazine)*

views seen up to that time ensured the drama and excitement of the sport was thoroughly conveyed.

It may have been graphically inferior to racing stars of the era (on PlayStation), but it certainly compensated for this with the speed and quality of racing on offer. Added to the game's real-time damage model, it ensured some of the most exciting virtual racing to be had on console at the end of the 1990s, with hugely competitive opponents making it impossible to predict the outcome of the race until past the finish line. It remained, until its superior sequel a year later, one of the most relentless, action packed driving experiences.

Gran Turismo (1998)
Format: PlayStation
Developer: Polyphony
Publisher Sony Computer Entertainment

It's easy to forget the impact *Gran Turismo* had when it arrived in May 1998 (or December 1997 in Japan) –

Pic 1: The later cars in *Gran Turismo* tip towards the race-prepared machines traditionally found in driving titles, but it's the initial focus on everyday production cars that partly explains the game's success. *(Sony Computer Entertainment, courtesy of Edge magazine)*

we're so used to the series, not to mention its effect, that it's difficult to remember what the driving game scene was like pre-*GT*. One way to put it into perspective, perhaps, is to mention that the franchise (comprising eight titles to date) has sold over 50 million copies worldwide, 11 million of them being the first game. Another is to remember that Nissan UK attributed the sudden widespread awareness of its Skyline GT-R to the car's prominent association with the game (in another game-to-real-world crossover instance, Polyphony has since produced the dashboard display graphics in the 2008 GT-R), just as Aston Martin acknowledged increased brand awareness for its vehicles in the US following the game's incredible popularity on that side of the Atlantic.

But arguably the strongest reminder is the realisation that *Gran Turismo* has influenced nearly every driving game that has emerged since.

It wasn't so much the fact that the game turned up

Pic 1: Although the realistic physics modelling found in *GT* proved revolutionary for console titles upon release, it's not entirely without constraints – it's not possible to flip cars, for instance. *(Sony Computer Entertainment, courtesy of Edge magazine)*

with 170-odd cars (the team originally aimed for 'just' 87) – a figure that ridiculed any other driving game's offering up to that point – or that the Japanese edition featured a 54-page reference guide to convey the necessary information relating to driving technique and set-up, in addition to an already substantial game manual. The appeal of *Gran Turismo* centred on the fact that it delivered the most realistic, detailed and rewarding console driving experience of its time.

Clearly, the handling played its part in this. The dynamics were, for the day, exceptional, with facets such as the weight transfer, body roll, lift-off oversteer and power understeer remarkably conveyed. The physics engine was effectively the result of four years' work (it was a development of the one used in Polyphony's first PlayStation game, *Motor Toon GP*, released in Japan in 1994) and modelled each wheel independently, resulting in a revolutionary realistic feel for a console game.

But the visuals were also key. *Gran Turismo* featured the best graphics for a console driving game up to that point, the result of the developer's almost tangible passion for the motor vehicle (combined with the obvious technical advantage an in-house Sony team possessed over rival developers when trying to extract the maximum performance from the PlayStation hardware). Indeed, replays and car behaviour were so convincing that it became standard practice amongst players to watch the entire playback after each race.

Ironically, the races themselves proved the game's weakest point. Even by 1990 standards, the AI is appalling – and continues to be the series' Achilles' Heel – showing a complete disinterest in the player's position on the track while happily carrying on, drone-like, towards the finish line. It's also possible to enter race events with a wildly overpowered car and be leading from the first corner to the chequered flag with relatively little effort.

Then again, the *Gran Turismo* series has never really been about racing, but rather about taking a car and its driver to their limits, while wrapping the experience up within a highly engaging structure more commonly found in role-playing games (RPGs). While the *TOCA* games focus on the experience of battling it out with competitors equally hungry for victory, *GT* has typically concerned itself almost exclusively with the purity of a 'car-versus-track' approach.

It's one of the fundamental principles of its approachability. The real genius of *GT*, however, is that it focuses on production cars. While previous titles at the time aimed mainly at recreating the antics of race and rally stars (and subsequent *Gran Turismo* titles have admittedly leant towards that approach – or at least ignored some of the more pedestrian inclusions of the franchise's first game), Polyphony's effort enables players to get behind the wheel of their family car; and being able to recognise and identify with that machinery (rather than a sponsorship stickered-up, supercharged racing equivalent – although those obviously also feature later in the game) is one of the reasons why Sony Computer Entertainment's *GT* appealed to an audience that eventually ended up containing so many non-gamers.

Sure, you can subsequently upgrade your family saloon to absurd power and handling levels via the game's exceptionally detailed tuning system, but the importance of starting out in standard 'car dealership' spec shouldn't be underestimated – it effectively acts as a natural difficulty curve, integrating the player into the game's demands in an unusually gentle and encompassing manner. The resulting RPG-styled structure (where cars, rather than characters, get their characteristics upgraded as the game progresses) may not have been initially planned – it came about from the team's problem-solving meetings and discussions – but its ability to capture the largest audience and keep it playing for the longest possible time is undeniable. The driving game genre would be changed forever.

Pic 1: No downforce, hard rubber tyres, trees as crash barriers… The life of a 1960s F1 driver was tough, something *Grand Prix Legends* had little trouble in conveying when it appeared in 1998. The title remains a genuine challenge.
(Sierra, courtesy of Edge magazine)

Pic 2: Things have dated a little visually, but in its day *Grand Prix Legends*' recreation of the Formula 1 cars of 1967 looked as beautiful as the glorious real-life vehicles the simracer focused its attention on.
(Sierra, courtesy of Edge magazine)

Grand Prix Legends (1998)
Format: PC
Developer: Papyrus Design Group
Publisher: Sierra

Following on from the very successful (primarily in North America) and hugely accomplished *NASCAR Racing 2* came *Grand Prix Legends*, yet another superlative simracing entry by specialist Papyrus (which had effectively got the subgenre rolling with *Indianapolis 500* back in 1989).

Based on the 1967 F1 season and including some of the most beautiful racing cars ever built, such as the Eagle-Weslake T1G and Lotus-Ford 49, the game undoubtedly offered the most advanced driving simulation at launch. The physics engine had taken over a year to perfect but incorporated gyroscopic torque forces, as well as the application of true physics.

Because of the focus of its subject matter – pre-downforce-assisted Formula 1 cars with great power and very little weight, running on narrow hard rubber

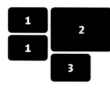

Pic 1: Slide into *Grand Prix Legends'* cockpit with anything but the most respect for it and you're guaranteed to be facing the wrong way on the track before long. Success comes from hours and hours of practice.
(Sierra, courtesy of Edge magazine)

Pic 2: Inspired by the great rally games that had gone before but adding a little more realism into the mix, *Colin McRae Rally* kicked off the gaming industry's – and players' – renewed interest in rallying. *(Codemasters, courtesy of Edge magazine)*

Pic 3: The in-car view utilised in console titles may be commonplace these days but it was still considered relatively risky when *CMR* was released. Codemasters was brave, thankfully, because here it's a triumph.
(Codemasters, courtesy of Edge magazine)

tyres – it also meant this simracing entry would gain a reputation for being one of the most difficult.

Mastering it isn't impossible, however – Papyrus founder David Kaemmer demonstrated his considerable ability behind the wheel of one of his near-finished game's gorgeous machines at one 1998 video game trade show at least – but it does require dedication, not least in terms of acquiring the delicacy required to pilot the tricky vehicles while getting used to their different braking ability in order to survive 11 of the world's deadliest tracks (such as the high-speed Monza, the treacherous Monaco and the infamous Nürburgring Nordschleife).

In addition to getting to grips with the handling, it's crucial to get the set-up right, and for its time *Grand Prix Legends* offered impressively comprehensive options, while the realism extends to a damage model that, though detailed in 1998, is understandably less noteworthy now.

But the one thing the game hasn't lost over the years is its difficulty. The tracks remain incredibly demanding, the cars are no less of a handful, while the AI drivers still provide a stern challenge in the higher settings. The physics modelling may have been long overtaken, but *Grand Prix Legends* retains much of its charm.

Colin McRae Rally (1998)
Format: PC, PlayStation
Developer: Codemasters
Publisher: Codemasters

Fresh from conquering the track tarmac with *TOCA Touring Car Championship*, Codemasters turned to the dirt, gravel, mud and snow of the World Rally Championship. Rather than opt for the licence (which would later be acquired by Sony), the publisher cleverly signed the late Colin McRae, then easily one of the more exciting drivers on the WRC circuit.

McRae would offer feedback throughout the series with regards to certain aspects – notably handling – and while later games would inevitably become increasingly concerned with accurately replicating

The 1990s

quality to the physics modelling, but in every other respect *Colin McRae Rally* aimed to provide an authentic recreation of the WRC, with international stages, super-stages (a novelty at the time), laser-scanned car models, sampled engine and road noise, standard set-up options, an impressive damage model and a cleverly thought-out yet reality-inspired repair system which saw time exchanged for making your vehicle rally-worthy.

Then there was the brilliant – and brave – decision to stick to the WRC single-car run format, a move that drove against the grain of established giants of the time such as the aforementioned *Sega Rally* and then recently released (and deservedly successful) *V-Rally*. Yet rather than follow console rally convention of stages run alongside competitors, Codemasters' game adopted a real-time checkpoint-based system whereby the times of competitors and your position in relation to them get regularly displayed during a stage. The resulting tension and excitement of seeing your progress at each time check is immense. Which sums up the *Colin McRae Rally* experience rather aptly.

F355 Challenge (1999)
Format: Arcade
Other versions: Dreamcast (2000), PlayStation 2 (2002)
Developer: AM2
Publisher: Sega

When it arrived across the world at the end of the 20th century, Sega's *F355 Challenge* made something of an impact. Clearly, the massive 600kg cabinet, with its three-pedal set-up, six-speed replica Ferrari gearshift and three 29in monitors (to provide a 170-degree view and a realistic sensation of speed), displaying cutting-edge visuals, would have had something to do with it.

But once the initial shock of seeing this behemoth in the local arcade wore off, the attention turned to the game itself. And it's in this respect that a long-term association with *F355 Challenge* would form for many players. In conjunction with the input of Ferrari and a selection of racing drivers, long-time Scuderia fan Yu Suzuki – the Sega producer behind *OutRun* – and his team had produced not only an impressively ambitious game but a simulation two and half years in the making. And a rather serious one – aside from Ferrari's technical support and professional drivers' feedback,

vehicle behaviour (2007's *Colin McRae: DiRT* being the pinnacle of Codemasters' efforts), the first *Colin McRae Rally* can't begin to describe itself as simulation-heavy.

That said, its arcade-style handling model is realism-based – in addition to the input of a WRC champion, the team spent time at a rally school with 200bhp Sierra Cosworths to ensure the right elements were included in the game. But the inspiration was very much *Screamer Rally* and *Sega Rally*, two distinct and considerable achievements in this sector.

Colin McRae Rally beat them both, however. For feel, accessibility and reward in terms of handling, Codemasters' creation proved the most playable rally title up to that point.

But it wasn't just wonderfully engaging and intuitive car behaviour. There may not have been simracing

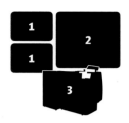

Pic 1: The exceptional quality of *F355 Challenge*'s graphics upon release ensure the game still looks good now. *(Sega, courtesy of Edge magazine)*

Pic 2: The three-screen, 170-degree view of the action presented by the arcade cabinet, combined with its enclosed nature, raises the level of player involvement considerably. *(Sega)*

Pic 3: You can't miss *F355 Challenge*'s imposing set-up and the experience is still mostly unique in arcades. *(Sega)*

team members spent track time with an F355, and those without driving licences were told to acquire them.

In an arcade environment where many players assume the brake pedal in cabinets is there for decorative purposes, that kind of approach is bound to stand out.

Equally, in a setting where each play has to be paid for, it's also not necessarily the wisest. Undeterred (perhaps remembering that Atari had hardly crashed commercially with *Hard Drivin'* back in 1988), Sega combated any intimidation players might feel by including a series of driver assists – stability control, traction control, ABS and 'Intelligent Braking System' – that could be implemented in real-time, even when the hardest difficulty setting was selected, thereby preventing the brave from being unmasked as foolish.

With no aids, the experience of driving a Challenge-prepared F355 in one of six world-renowned circuits is certainly demanding, and although not up to the standards of today's leading simracing examples it remains a convincing affair, helped in no small part by the atmosphere created by its remarkable cabinet. It was also one of the last arcade games able to make a significant impact in a sector that by this time had become dominated by console-led titles.

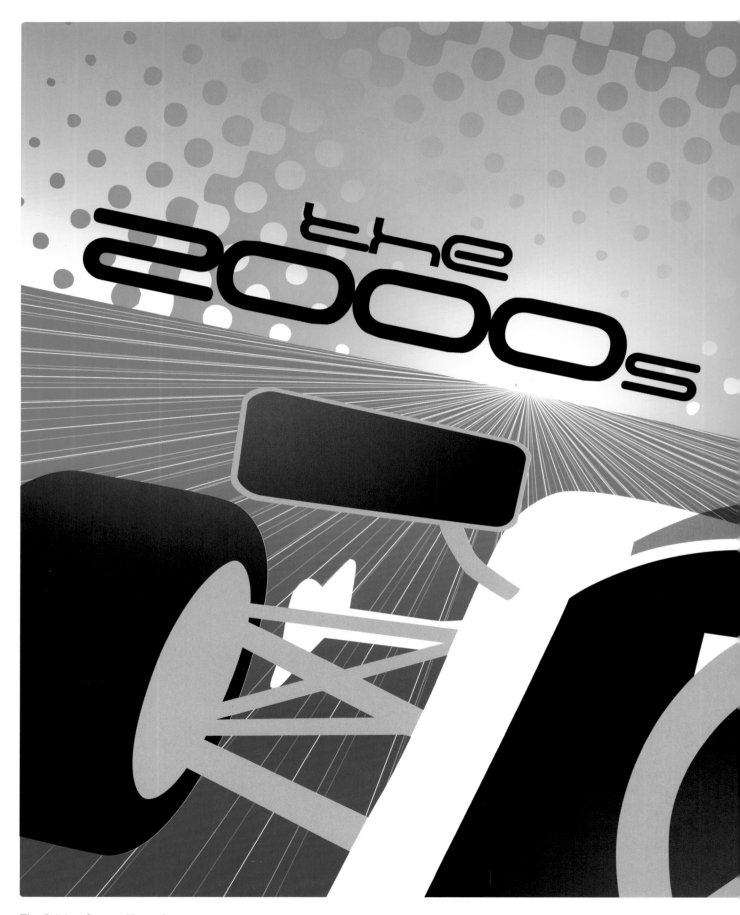

The 2000s

Pic 1: The console driving game has accelerated with each generation of consoles – witness *Gran Turismo 3 A-Spec*. *(Sony Computer Entertainment)*

Pic 2: The arcade sector may have slowed down since home consoles increased in power and popularity, but titles such as Sega's *Initial D* series have still enjoyed much success. *(Sega)*

Pic 3: A new decade brings with it the opportunity to revisit past classics while using the latest technology to bring them up to date, as the 2007 edition of *Sega Rally* proves. *(Sega)*

Pic 4: The number of driving games is such nowadays that worthy titles such as *WRC: Rally Evolved* get overlooked. *(Sony Computer Entertainment)*

Introduction

If the 1990s oversaw the transition into 3D, the opening years of the 21st century truly are the decade of the driving game. Sure, classics like *OutRun* and *Sega Rally* will always be playable, but this was when the genre really began to drive forward. The arrival – and remarkable commercial success – of *Gran Turismo* at the end of the '90s unleashed a more widespread interest in digital driving than it had previously experienced, both within the industry and amongst consumers.

In fairness, the movement had started a little earlier. The home console charts of the '80s and early '90s had hardly featured racing games (*Super Mario Kart* being the exception), but that started to change as consoles gained in power and arcades began to fall behind in the performance race and the spiralling costs of arcade technology put the brakes on the kind of development seen in the 1990s. (Nowadays it's not uncommon for some of the bigger console franchises to be converted into arcade games, but the process

previously flowed very much in the other direction).

But it was the hardware moving up a gear that facilitated the arrival of realism-obsessed efforts such as *GT* and its legion of followers. The increase in performance of new consoles in the early 2000s soon saw developers implement previously underplayed elements such as real-time deformation, more convincing AI opponent behaviour and, of course, increasingly complex handling dynamics. This resulted in the drive towards console sims, titles that

Pic 1: *Le Mans 24 Hours* on Dreamcast – not to be confused with other versions – kicked off the decade in the form of a standout driving title. *(Atari)*

Pic 2: Development of the simracing scene has also sped up since the start of the '00s, with major releases such as *rFactor* gaining a considerable following. *(Image Space Incorporated)*

Pic 3: *TOCA World Touring Cars*, another excellent start to the 21st century for the driving genre. *(Codemasters)*

Pic 4: The popularity of the *Need for Speed* series just keeps growing. *(Need for Speed Most Wanted, Electronic Arts)*

Pic 5: The arcade sector is down but not out – new titles continue to make an appearance. *(Sega Race TV, Sega)*

approximate the simracing elements found on PCs (in the interests of equality, PC owners have also been benefiting from an increase in the appearance of arcade-style racers such as *Burnout Paradise* and *FlatOut: Ultimate Carnage* on their platform).

Another aspect from simracing to evolve considerably on console in this decade is the implementation of online components, not only from a multiplayer perspective – which obviously introduced an entire new level of competition for console players – but also in the way that downloads now extend the longevity of a game. Developers increasingly release additional cars, tracks and game modes that can significantly alter the dynamic of their creation. On PC this has already been taken to the next level, with some of the leading simracing examples effectively in continuous, staged development.

Perhaps the most significant development, however, has been the overall increase in quality. Indeed, the modern gaming audience is so wise, the market so unforgiving and competition amongst game developers and publishers so tough (with development processes so honed) that it's rare for a driving game to

roll off the production line and prove to be a disaster. At worst it'll be a reasonably competent, if uninspired, effort that finds itself lapped by the competition – which says more about the level of the leading driving game experiences.

And with better quality has come a thematic evolution. Ironically, it was the arrival of *Gran Turismo* and the subsequent industry bias towards console racers and the quest for realism that slowed things down for the first half of the decade. *Burnout* was one of the early rebels and played its part in opening the toll gate to thinking about the genre in a more advanced manner, but others soon followed, resulting in even reality-influenced efforts such as *Race Driver: GRID* being keen to turn up on the start line offering something new in what had threatened to become a worryingly stifled environment.

So where do driving games go from here? Well, the focus will almost certainly be on enhancing the experience rather than improving the games' technical aspects. But technology will play its part too, and online is bound to be the frontier for those developments. For instance, there is at least one company offering developers the ability to integrate the position of cars from a real-world racing event into a game, so that players compete head-to-head against the real drivers in real-time. Whichever path driving games take, the certainty is that the road ahead will be at least as exciting as the route travelled thus far.

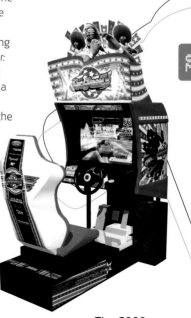

The 2000s

Pic 1: Arriving a year before *Gran Turismo 3 A-Spec*, Bizarre Creations' *Metropolis Street Racer* enjoyed its time in the limelight as the most realistic-looking console driving title. Thankfully it had much substance to back up its then very pretty face. *(Sega)*

Pic 2: One of the game's interesting features includes the way races are affected by the timezone difference of the location of the race. So a UK *MSR* player driving around one of the Tokyo tracks in the afternoon UK-time would always find a night-time setting. *(Sega)*

Metropolis Street Racer (2000)
Format: Dreamcast
Developer: Bizarre Creations
Publisher: Sega

The phenomenal popularity of 1998's *Gran Turismo* (and its sequel a year later) got publishers and developers racing to get their own reality-biased efforts on the grid. But very few of the driving games that rolled out were of a high enough standard to get noticed by a public so engrossed in Polyphony's series.

Metropolis Street Racer was one exception. Built by the team that had previously impressed with the first two *Formula 1* games for PlayStation, *MSR* was the first indication of the power harnessed within the then new generation of hardware – Sega's Dreamcast

and Sony's PlayStation 2 (Nintendo's GameCube would follow). It was easily the most technically advanced driving title up to that point, boasting exceptionally detailed car models and astounding real-world environments – London, San Francisco and Tokyo – which were based on some 32,000 photographs taken by the development team for visual reference purposes.

Of course, the appeal of *MSR* was more than just technological. The game introduced the concept of 'Kudos', a system that rewards street racers for stylish or skilful manoeuvres such as powersliding and slipstreaming in addition to the standard drive-as-fast-as-you-can requirements, and which continues in the *Project Gotham Racing* games (which are evolutions of *MSR*). The entire game mechanic revolves around unlocking further events and cars with Kudos points through a series of challenges.

By today's standards *MSR*'s progression system is perhaps a little too restricted, relying on a considerable investment from the player before access to the more rewarding cars is granted – an aspect that's since been refined in the subsequent *PGR* games.

Pic 1: In a genre obsessed with realism and in danger of ignoring the fun element that originally attracted many to play driving titles, the arrival of the almost anarchic nature of *Burnout* in 2001 couldn't have come at a more crucial time. *(Acclaim)*

Pic 2: Each iteration in the series has seen a considerable technological leap combined with a thematic tweak. *Burnout 2: Point of Impact's* obsession with speed – while taking care to keep carnage levels up – is unlikely to have found many critics. *(Acclaim)*

Pic 3: *Burnout 3: Takedown* shifts the focus onto 'car combat' but does so without losing sight of the race-based core of the original game and as a result is arguably the pinnacle of the series pre-*Burnout Paradise*. *(Electronic Arts)*

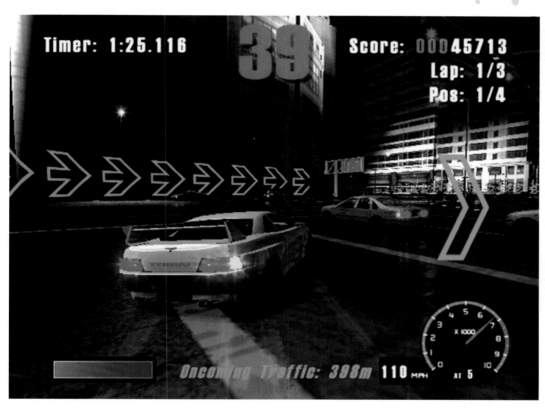

Also showing its age is the handling dynamic, which, while still certainly accomplished, lacks the subtlety of modern equivalents. Yet it remains notable for representing Bizarre Creations' first effort at delivering a system that sits comfortably between arcade and simulation characteristics – an approach that would have played a considerable part in the game's excellent critical reception, and which formed the basis from which the developer would further evolve the franchise.

Burnout (2001)
Format: PlayStation 2
Other versions: GameCube, Xbox (2002)
Developer: Criterion Games
Publisher: Acclaim

It's easy to look at *Burnout* today and underplay its importance in driving game evolution. To put its arrival in perspective, it's worth remembering the industry had been obsessed with realism since *Gran Turismo* turned up on the scene at the end of the 1990s. For a title to

deliberately drive against the genre's flow of traffic would require something brave, something special.

Sure, today *Burnout* looks hopelessly low-key. The presentation is minimal, almost non-existent, giving the game an unrefined, tech demo-like feel. The structure is risibly basic too, and the game's audio/visual merits won't impress anyone. Compared to the later productions in the series published by Electronic Arts (a master of production values, as well as possessing a finely tuned understanding of creating player-focused affairs), the first *Burnout* appears decidedly primitive.

But, crucially, the core components of the *Burnout* experience are undeniably present. Mixing elements of *Thrill Drive* and *Runabout* yet very much establishing its own personality, at the time of its release the frenetic and brazen nature of Criterion's game – which encourages players to drive in a wonderfully irresponsible manner while racing three other competitors on civilian traffic-filled roads at absurd speeds – coupled with universally accessible pick-up-and-play handling characteristics encapsulated as unashamedly an arcade experience as *OutRun*.

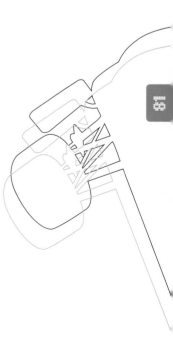

Later *Burnout* games would go on to vastly progress the fundamental aspects – not always successfully – but even on the first attempt the series' signature risk/reward element is firmly grounded. Beating an opponent to the finish line having survived countless near-misses with oncoming buses, taxis and commuters is undeniably thrilling. And when mistakes occur – and they inevitably do – the payoff is a flagrantly glorified crash sequence that, although tame by today's standards (set by each iteration of the *Burnout* games, admittedly), didn't fail in delighting driving game aficionados of the time.

Aside from the breath of fresh octane it so obviously provided, it didn't take long for those who first encountered *Burnout* to recognise the beginnings of something exceptional.

OutRun2 (2003)

Format: Arcade
Other versions: Xbox (2004)
Developer: AM2
Publisher: Sega

How do you follow what is arguably the greatest arcade driving game of all time? It's a question that Sega took 17 years to answer. And when it did, the reply was undeniably convincing. Bypassing the considerable tweaks and alterations seen in the series' *Turbo OutRun* and *Outrunners* arcade spin-offs, *OutRun2* doesn't mess with the structure of the 1986 original. Doing so would be sacrilege, after all.

So the 15-stage branching set-up is wisely retained and again the environments are irrepressibly vibrant, featuring as wide a thematic range as its predecessor. *OutRun2*'s visuals may not have caused as much of an impact upon release, but that's more to do with the gaming public's increasing familiarity with high-end graphics as a result of the power of the home consoles than a criticism of the arcade title's technological ability. Even now, *OutRun2* doesn't look out of place amongst its more modern peers, and its officially licensed Ferrari line-up rarely fails to turn heads.

If the graphics underwent an understandable evolution, so did the handling. That it's accessible is a given, but by taking the aspect of the original game that was perhaps least well

Pic 1: The appeal of sliding a Ferrari sideways through visually gratifying scenery has to be universal. *(Sega)*

Pic 2: *OutRun2*'s core dynamic barely differs from that of its predecessor – sometimes less is more. *(Sega)*

conveyed – the powersliding – and focusing the game mechanic around it, AM2's successful approach proved two-pronged. On the one hand, the ability to take every corner sideways in ridiculously long drifts at triple-figure speeds while at the wheel of one of the Scuderia's finest is as enjoyable as it sounds; on the other, nothing would ensure *OutRun2* is the perfect embodiment of the *OutRun* lineage more.

Sure, it's a one-trick prancing pony which lacks the depth of console driving titles, and one that neither matches the success nor betters the experience of the original. But that doesn't stop it being an impressively composed, often delightful and worthy successor.

TrackMania (2003)
Format: PC
Developer: Nadeo
Publisher: Digital Jesters

Notable for both its almost aggressive anti-realism stance and the fact that it appeared on the PC, home of simracing, *TrackMania* proved something of a revelation when it rolled into view in 2003.

Initial impressions were positive. The core mechanic, based on the concept of driving a car through stunt-based circuits featuring loop-the-loops, absurdly banked turns and ambitious jumps, promised a diverting drive. But it's the ability to create your own tracks (to share with fellow *TrackMania* players) that ensured the game achieved the impact it deserved; and it has since enjoyed a number of sequels and updates, each bettering the original's ccomplishments.

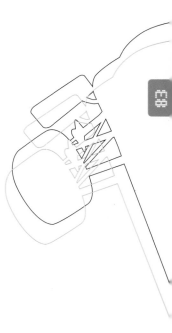

The follow-ups may improve the experience, but the original is hardly without merit. Although the high-speed on-track action is instantly accessible to as universal an audience as you're likely to find a driving game able to cater for, the handling model is deceptively delicate – intricate enough to convey the necessary semblance of realism, while maintaining the essential simplicity the nature of the game demands. It's a very rewarding balance and powering through the daredevil circuits (not to mention those conjured up by the humbling ability of some members of the *TrackMania* community) is undeniably thrilling.

That explains the uncommonly robust 'one more go' attraction of the *TrackMania* experience – at least partly. The real, underlying reason turns out to be almost as simplistic as the mechanic of the game itself: it's extraordinary fun.

Live for Speed (2003)
Format: PC
Developer: Live for Speed
Publisher: Live for Speed

In these days of gaming super-productions, there's something wonderfully comforting in seeing a tiny three-man development team still able to create what is currently one of the leading simracing experiences. Released in three stages – a wisely orchestrated approach given the limitations of the condensed team size – with each iteration aiming to add to the number of vehicles and tracks, as well as improve core elements such as the physics modelling and the audio/visual components, *Live for Speed* is generally considered by members of the simracing community as the title offering the best mix of handling dynamics and force feedback implementation.

Critics may point to a limited number of vehicles (few of them licensed), relative shortage of circuits (not to mention their fictitious nature – you won't find an opportunity to lap the Nürburgring Nordschleife here) – and the team's reluctance to release car or track editors, thus locking the mod community out of creating their own content as is common with many other simracing titles (indeed, some of them thrive on such a model). But anyone who spends even the briefest time with *Live for Speed* is likely to walk away with nothing but praise for the game's exceptional handling model, which is undoubtedly one of the most convincing examples the genre has seen. That shouldn't deter potential entrants, however. Naturally, as a simracing title *Live for Speed*'s demands on a player are significant – it's considered advanced enough to serve as a training tool for real-world racing drivers – but the diverse characteristics offered by the selection of vehicles available ensures newcomers will find something suited to their abilities.

Once sufficiently familiar they ought to replace the (certainly decent) AI opponents with real-life

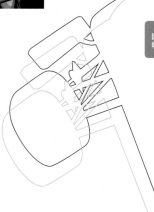

Pic 1: Fun in the sun. *RalliSport Challenge 2* may have passed most players by but that obviously doesn't detract from celebrating its easygoing and carefree approach to rallying, not to mention some great online console battles, here. *(Microsoft Game Studios)*

equivalents – no modern simracing example is complete without the ability to race fellow enthusiasts online, and *Live for Speed* is no exception. As one of the most supported such titles, finding online racing leagues to take part in is straightforward and the reward for such commitment is that the resulting experience is seldom less than outstanding.

RalliSport Challenge 2 (2004)
Format: Xbox
Developer: Digital Illusions
Publisher: Microsoft Game Studios

In the absence of a decent arcade-flavoured rally game – little of note had emerged since the fabulous *Colin McRae Rally 2.0* in 2000 – the track was left relatively empty for Digital Illusions' second *RalliSport Challenge* to speed down unchallenged.

Which is perhaps an unfair way to represent this very competent effort because despite the lack of serious competition *RSC 2* still had to propel itself into gamers' affections in convincing fashion. And even if you disregard the dizzying sense of speed, the

1

Pic 1: Technically, *RalliSport Challenge 2*'s environments were, for the time, very impressive. *(Microsoft Game Studios)*

2

Pic 2: Little could have prepared console gamers for the dedication needed for *Richard Burns Rally*. *(SCi)*

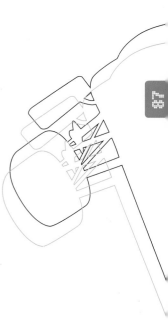

remarkable environments – easily some of the best technically and largest in any genre at the time of its release – the undemanding yet thoroughly flattering handling model, the initially daunting single-player content, the various and engaging types of events offered (from rally to rallycross to hillclimb to ice racing), and the distinctive selection of vehicles, it would be impossible to ignore the fabulous multiplayer option.

In either online or even in splitscreen situations, the injection of human competition transforms *RalliSport Challenge 2* from an impressively accomplished and worthy driving game into a highlight of the last 25 years – a significant alteration. With the right level of opponents races are thrillingly close affairs, while speeding through the vast locales never gets tiring. It's as fun and rewarding as the single-player experience – arguably even more so due to human rivals.

The lack of licence undoubtedly limited *RalliSport Challenge 2* from achieving its full potential but the community that showed up online suggests a considerable number were astute enough not to miss out on this driving gem.

Richard Burns Rally (2004)
Format: PC, PlayStation 2, Xbox
Developer: Warthog
Publisher: SCi

Although rare, rally sims were not a new departure for the PC when *Richard Burns Rally* turned up – *Mobil 1 Rally Championship* from Magnetic Fields had previously impressed hugely in 1999. However, they hadn't previously ventured onto console (the *Colin*

Pic 1: A brave and unusual step, *Richard Burns Rally* applies simracing style dynamics to a rally game destined for consoles as well as PC. For those prepared for the challenge on offer, Warthog's accomplishment is definitely worth checking out. *(SCi)*

McRae games may have got progressively more intricate handling-wise, but they've yet to reach a level that can be termed simulation grade), mainly because the hardware hadn't previously been powerful enough to host such intricate physics modelling.

To say that the console demographic wasn't ready for the realism – from set-up to handling – offered by *RBR* is something of an understatement. The degree of

authenticity of the driving model is such that anything other than the most precise, most delicate approach results in an excursion into the scenery. Usually backwards.

Which, far from a criticism, is meant as an indication of the game's demanding nature. On PlayStation 2, just as with the PC version, recourse to a force feedback steering wheel and pedal set-up alleviates matters (just as it significantly enhances the experience); but on Xbox, where there was no official wheel to support, Warthog's uncompromising approach will have shocked a few used to the broad comfort zone offered by arcade-influenced rally experiences.

But anyone who persevered would have discovered a title requiring an unusual level of dedication, exactness and concentration – qualities that now seem a fitting tribute to the rally driver whose name the game carries.

Test Drive Unlimited (2006)

Format: Xbox 360
Other versions: PC, PlayStation 2 (2007)
Developer: Eden Games
Publisher: Atari

While the vast majority of the *Test Drive* games have been disappointing – the early sim-heavy attempts,

although inspiring, often demanded more from the host hardware than it was able to deliver, while later entries in the series all but lost the ethos of the original concept – the early iterations did effectively lead to the creation of *The Need for Speed* on the 3DO, a landmark title of the 1990s.

Test Drive Unlimited doesn't necessarily turn back the clock, but it is notable for its attempt to create a persistent online world for petrolheads to explore – 1,000 miles of the Hawaiian island of Oahu, in fact,

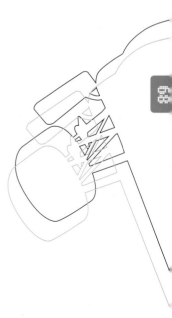

Pic 1: In attempting to recreate the lifestyle of owning the rides of the rich and famous – not just a persistent online multiplayer arena for gamers to challenge each other – *Test Drive Unlimited* ensures its car dealerships sell the right kind of product. *(Atari)*

modelled from satellite imaging. The game, labelled MOOR (Massively Open Online Racing), offers a believable environment that engulfs players in a lavish lifestyle of fast cars and matching mansions, while encouraging competition within a set-up that is otherwise refreshingly without structural constraints – progression within the game exists, naturally, but the impetus for development rests entirely with the player, meaning the game can be enjoyed at an individual's preferred pace. A wise design choice, given that many will appreciate the time to digest the believable and

attractive alternate existence *Test Drive Unlimited* is intent on delivering.

If the gameworld is convincing, the handling from one vehicle to the next is perhaps not always as accomplished, although any discrepancy in car behaviour is arguably counterbalanced by the impressive sense of community the game achieves. As an important and memorable first step in revitalising a franchise that had long stalled, *Test Drive Unlimited* earns an inclusion as one of the key driving game titles or recent times.

GTR 2 – FIA GT Racing Game (2006)
Format: PC
Developer: SimBin Development Team
Publisher: 10tacle Studios

Swedish simracing expert SimBin had already given an indication of its intentions by the time *GTR 2*, an official simulation of the FIA GT championship, turned up on the grid, so the fact the game is an uncompromising recreation of a closely fought category of motorsport shouldn't have surprised anyone.

But that the resulting production could prove as captivating and so difficult to prevent it from interfering with everyday responsibilities turned out to be a less predictable scenario.

Pic 1: Building a leading simracing experience doesn't mean alienating all but the ultra dedicated, as SimBin's expertly crafted *GTR 2 – FIA GT Racing Game* demonstrates so convincingly. Though you'll still want to play it with a steering wheel... *(10tacle Studios)*

GTR 2 succeeds because it entirely focuses on creating as realistic a simulation as it can, while cleverly tweaking the aspects of its occasionally harsh predecessor – 2005's *GTR* – and refining them so as to make this second attempt more enjoyable and, by association, more engaging.

A master stroke is the inclusion of a mode offering tuition in driving techniques, strengthening the belief in those who already possess a smattering of ability,

while successfully building the confidence of the complete novice, who may not have previously built the courage to venture into the simracing world.

Those already versed in that universe will further benefit from *GTR 2*'s active community and the custom content its members create – as is typical of most leading simracing titles – but SimBin's greatest achievement with this effort is the game's ability to captivate the serious and casual alike.

MotorStorm (2007)

Format: PlayStation 3
Developer: Evolution Studios
Publisher: Sony Computer Entertainment

MotorStorm would initially secure the attention of the gaming crowd through the quality of its visuals. Yet, while undeniably impressive upon release, the attraction of the game lies under the graphical hood.

Developed by Evolution Studios, the team behind the mostly accomplished *WRC* titles, *MotorStorm* mixes seven types of vehicle and throws them into races taking place across a dusty canyon expanse. There are no yellow flags, marshals, penalties or much in the way of rules, other than getting past the finish line first in order to win. So events become frantic, no-holds-barred vehicular arguments where opponents get shunted into the nearest obstacle or over the edge of a vertigo-inducing drop.

Adding to the experience is the layout of the tracks. While the general direction is clearly evident – usually

Pic 1: If it's in your way, run it down or run it over – anything goes provided you win. *(Sony Computer Entertainment)*

Pic 2: An oil change for the *Colin McRae* franchise in the form of the very accomplished *DiRT*. *(Codemasters)*

dictated by the topography of the terrain – the areas are wide enough to allow players the freedom to choose their own trajectory. And with each lap the terrain profile alters as a result of the vehicles' paths, introducing an additional level of consideration (this system of real-time deformation was subsequently also used by the 2007 iteration of *Sega Rally*, in perhaps more evident fashion).

It's a solidly entertaining and notable addition, and the beginning of a franchise with great potential.

Colin McRae: DiRT (aka DiRT: Colin McRae Off-Road) (2007)

Format: PC, PlayStation 3, Xbox 360
Developer: Codemasters
Publisher: Codemasters

Since racing towards a peak with Colin McRae 2.0, Codemasters had lost some of the control that underpinned the excellence of the franchise. The subsequent yearly updates improved on certain elements, admittedly, but they also diluted the experience to the point of risking the reputation of the first two, great, releases.

So the *CMR* team put on the brakes and took a couple of years to refocus on the franchise. And in *Colin McRae: DiRT*, the decision was duly justified.

DiRT succeeds in reinvigorating the series but on a more general note it also sets a standard for console rally games to aim for, both technically – its audio/visual elements are excellent – and with regards to a hugely accomplished handling mechanic. It's detailed enough to accurately convey what the chassis is up to at all times – and certainly those with steering wheel and pedal set-ups will gain from an additional level of feedback compared to joypad users – but it also works on a far more basic level, making it accessible to those not prepared to get that deeply involved in vehicle dynamics. Not an easy balance to achieve.

Pic 1: As *Race Driver: GRID* would also adopt, the decision to include a variety of vehicles in *Colin McRae: DiRT* that refuse to stick to the usual menu of categories found in rallying titles ensures the game establishes its own distinct identity. *(Codemasters)*

Pic 2: Want the finest sim-based console experience currently available? You'll want *Forza Motorsport 2*. Although no one expected it to happen, the franchise managed to overtake Sony's mighty *Gran Turismo*. *(Microsoft Game Studios)*

Also attractive is the openness of the tiered progression structure, which enables a welcome level of freedom when deciding on which of the varied off-road activities you should engage in next. And as for those activities, they've been cleverly and carefully selected to provide a set of experiences sufficiently different to the frankly overserved selection that is offered by the majority of rally titles, while still retaining a connection to the *Colin McRae* titles so as to guarantee *DiRT* doesn't waver too far off the track beaten by the series – which it does, if nothing else, through the exhilarating racing on offer. That it manages this while emerging as a distinctive experience in its own right is a credit to the developer.

Forza Motorsport 2 (2007)
Format: Xbox 360
Developer: Turn 10 Studios
Publisher: Microsoft Game Studios

In years to come, the *Forza Motorsport* franchise will be remembered for being the first to convincingly overtake *Gran Turismo* for the lead of the console sim subgenre. With expertly judged handling, excellent structure, believable AI, real-time damage and online play, the first game easily outpowered *Gran Turismo 4* in all areas bar graphics upon its release 2005.

By focusing on evolving those core elements, Turn 10 Studios has ensured the sequel again pulls away from Polyphony's equivalent effort in every respect (again, with the exception of visuals – a race the *GT* series is unlikely ever to lose).

Along with *Richard Burns Rally*, *Forza Motorsport 2* is the closest consoles have to an example of simracing. True, aesthetically and mechanically the damage model is inferior to *Race Driver: GRID*'s and the race experience is certainly not as intense, no doubt partly due to the lack of a cockpit view – increasingly a

Pic 1: *Forza Motorsport 2*'s damage system isn't the most advanced visually, but it does the job. The AI can also be a little heavy handed at times, but think of it as evidence of character. And compared to some online racers, they're angels. *(Microsoft Game Studios)*

standard inclusion for driving games hoping to thoroughly engross players in the events on-screen, and a considerable stumbling block when omitted. Elsewhere, the overall audio/visual production values – while decent – also fail to match those of some of the game's more lavish competitors.

In response, *Forza Motorsport 2* delivers a more rewarding and comprehensive realism-based driving model than any other circuit-based console contender, one that is capable of communicating every nuance of the road to an exceptional degree – particularly when using the official Xbox 360 force feedback wheel. And to the delight of those who relish getting their joypad-holding hands dirty, it backs this with some of the most advanced set-up options found outside of a simracing title. However, with that subgenre it shares an element of the soulless nature that can on occasion creep into single-player proceedings, in this case because the limited number of tracks have a tendency to possess little in the way of features. That said, an excellent online mode eradicates such worries and even for the lone player, decent – if not always convincing – AI, together with a well thought-out and rewarding structure ensures that the level of discipline and commitment required here is never as high as that of a PC-based simracing affair.

But make no mistake: dedication is necessary to get the best out of *Forza Motorsport 2*, and those that put in the effort can do so safe in the knowledge that they will be rewarded with the best driving experience available on console.

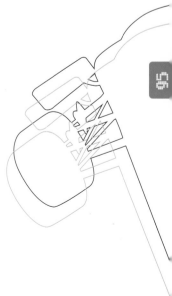

Pic 1: *Project Gotham Racing 4* continues Bizarre Creations' long reputation for technically accomplished creations, while also showcasing the latest evolution of the series' now trademark, accessible handling model. *(Microsoft Game Studios)*

Project Gotham Racing 4 (2007)
Format: Xbox 360
Developer: Bizarre Creations
Publisher: Microsoft Game Studios

The *Gotham* games are notable because of the way they integrate the complexities of real-world racecraft in a way that ensures they remain accessible to all players. It's a considerable skill and a segment of the genre – somewhere between console sim and

Pic 1: The car selection, as ever, is a veritable Who's Who of the exotic automotive world. If it's impossibly desirable, it's more than likely to be found in *Project Gotham Racing 4*. And it means you get to eventually drive it, of course. *(Microsoft Game Studios)*

Pic 2: Dynamic weather is a feature that, inexplicably, has been mostly overlooked by developers. Even a basic implementation – and games like *F1 Circus* were doing this in the early '90s – can thoroughly enhance a race situation. *(Microsoft Game Studios)*

The fundamental principle of racing around some of the world's famous urban settings hasn't altered, of course, but the addition of dynamic weather – a feature depressingly underused by driving game developers – and a carefully balanced Career mode, together with other elements such as an increase in environmental factors that further enhance the player's involvement in the *PGR* experience effortlessly justify their inclusion by the obvious benefits they deliver.

The level of content is also impressive, with numerous options to keep players occupied, while the multiplayer – already an accomplished feature of previous *PGR*s – has been further tweaked to provide an extensive arena of play that is likely to retain considerable activity for some time yet.

Ultimately *PGR4* feels complete. Perhaps the best way to explain just how much of an accomplishment this game is would be to say *Project Gotham Racing 5* can take all the time it needs before turning up.

out-and-out arcade racer – Bizarre Creations has found itself occupying almost exclusively since first releasing *Metropolis Street Racer*, the series' spiritual predecessor, on Sega's short-lived Dreamcast.

Project Gotham Racing 4 is arguably the pinnacle of its efforts, the point the franchise has been building towards. Visually it's gorgeous, displaying the attention to detail, level of polish and confident presentation its developer has become renowned for, but every other area has been refined, too.

Pic 1: As it's become expected of the franshise, *Gran Turismo 5 Prologue*'s graphics are exceptional – arguably the finest recreations of car and scenery currently delivered by a driving game on any system.

(Sony Computer Entertainment)

Gran Turismo 5 Prologue (2008)
Format: PlayStation 3
Developer: Polyphony Digital Inc
Publisher: Sony Computer Entertainment

Similar to other 'Prologue' *Gran Turismo* releases in that it's not a full-scale game, *GT5 Prologue* aims to keep those eagerly awaiting the release of *GT5* relatively happy until developer Polyphony Digital is ready to let

its main creation out of the workshop. Not known to rush its work, Polyphony's titles often suffer delays due to the developer's insistence on delivering the finest console sim experience it can. It's what has guaranteed the franchise's ability to lead its category since turning the ignition key in 1998.

As an indication of what gamers can expect, then, this latest offering is mostly encouraging. The graphics – traditionally a *GT* forte – are unrivalled, delivering the most detailed and impressive representation of vehicles seen on console, PC or arcade (each car is said to be composed of over 200,000 polygons and takes up to six months to model, compared with 4,000 polygons and one month for 2005's *GT4*), along with environments to match. The in-car view, a first for the series, is exceptionally accurate and utterly convincing – as an example, consider the driving avatar's Sparco gloves, which often look real.

The genre-beating visuals are backed by an unsurprisingly accomplished handling model, boasting an excellent feeling of weight transfer and very precise steering input – the slightest motion of the controller is transferred directly to the game. True, the understeer characteristics of some of the 70-odd cars featured can

Pic 1: While there is nothing to beat it visually, in terms of handling *GT5 Prologue* is able to keep up with the leading pack, but the franchise is no longer the current undisputed number one sim-influenced title on console.

(Sony Computer Entertainment)

be too pronounced on occasion, and the brakes can feel excessively efficient (which remains preferable to the alternative scenario), but this is nitpicking given that the *Gran Turismo* games have consistently delivered the most authentic handling dynamics on console. Or at least used to, as *Forza Motorsport 2* now holds that honour. But with the driver aids switched off, *GT5 Prologue* comes a close second.

Two areas that were long overtaken by the competition, however, are damage and AI. The *Gran Turismo* series' damage model has mostly been non-existent. The revolutionary quality of the first game, and even the second title with its rally stages and staggering 650 vehicles, managed to skirt around the issue; but as rival games began to include advanced damage dynamics, demonstrating the resulting improvement in the experience from the visual and game mechanic payback players receive, Polyphony's games have increasingly looked several places down the driving game evolutionary grid.

The AI, meanwhile, has at least made a little more progress. Typically drone-like entities stubbornly sticking to the racing line regardless of your on-track position, in *GT5 Prologue* they display a little

personality in the form of aggression and off-line venturing (as well as occasional mistakes). However, their behaviour is erratic and you end up driving around the track never too sure what your seven to

Pic 1: Easily one of the most graphically impressive driving games yet, *Burnout Paradise* is also one of the most intense. The open world dynamic suits the series well, and the promise of additional content should help long-term interest. *(Electronic Arts)*

eleven opponents will do next. When compared to the behavioural consistency of the competition in *Forza Motorsport 2* or, better still, *Race Driver: GRID*, the AI in *Prologue* remains unconvincing.

Inevitably, then, *GT5 Prologue* reverts to what the series has consistently excelled at: pitting the player and car against the track. It does it fractionally better than its nearest predecessor – a significant achievement given how honed the series has become – and the vastly improved visuals certainly help carry the *GT* franchise onwards, although subsequent iterations will need to move up a gear in key areas if the *Gran Turismo* brand plans on building the momentum to catch up with rivals.

Burnout Paradise (2008)

Format: PlayStation 3, Xbox 360
Developer: Criterion Games
Publisher: Electronic Arts

A second *Burnout* title justifies its inclusion here because *Paradise* represents a considerable evolutionary step over past games in the series. Gone is the structured and paced nature of in-game events, replaced instead by an open gameworld spanning an impressively vast surface area – from the twisty passageways of the hills to the wide tarmac stretches hugging the seafront, *Burnout Paradise*'s universe becomes an intricate playground gamers are free and actively encouraged to explore wrecklessly.

And there's plenty to find. Every traffic light holds a game event, every street offers opportunities for air-based acrobatics and seemingly every other

building is hiding a secret short-cut. There's layer upon layer of content in *Paradise* and although much of it is similar the promise of more drastic additions to follow – via downloads – should ensure the game's lifespan is as considerable as the experience is thrilling.

Yet all the content in the galaxy is of little use if the ultimate experience holds little interest. That, thankfully, isn't the case here. *Paradise* sticks to the *Burnout* franchise's pure arcade-inspired handling like superglue, not ever messing with the eloquent simplicity of those dynamics.

Where there's been progress is in the game's crash mechanics, with the move to a new generation of hardware enabling the development team to achieve a level of automotive destruction previously unseen. Crashing in *Burnout* has always been an integral part of the experience but here it's so beautifully depicted that it becomes an almost desirable occurrence.

Unless it's been caused by an opponent. Whether AI or real – *Paradise*'s online options are exemplary – the need for revenge here is no weaker than in past *Burnout* games. Perhaps stronger, even. And you wouldn't want it any other way.

Race Driver: GRID (2008)
Format: PC, PlayStation 3, Xbox 360
Developer: Codemasters
Publisher: Codemasters

Having come from an uncommonly distinguished lineage stretching back to the formidable *TOCA Touring Car Championship* on PlayStation (and PC), *Race Driver: GRID* would have disappointed if it had turned out anything but excellent. But as one of the premier driving game development studios in the world, Codemasters isn't in the habit of letting one of its key

Pic 1: If you're not playing *Race Driver: GRID* in-car, you're not playing it at all. Unnecessarily harsh, perhaps, but like most of the games featured in this book the experience is heightened when adopting the view that most closely resembles real life. *(Codemasters)*

Pic 2: Provided you stick to the a difficulty level that will test your virtual driving ability, *GRID*'s races are always hard-fought, drama-filled affairs. Get to know it well and you'll find precious few games able to deliver a worthy and satisfying alternative. *(Codemasters)*

franchises roll out of the garage with only half a tank of fuel. It also tends to be very focused in its approach to racing titles, and *GRID* may be its most determined example yet.

Daringly, realism isn't the underlying principle here. Sure, the visuals hint at impressive authenticity, with exquisitely recreated vehicles and both urban and racetrack environments, but the essence of the game is reflected in the gorgeously vibrant gameworld. *GRID* isn't about real-world simulation but rather the distillation of the thrill of motorsport, and it's something it does better than any game before it. So, gone are the series' past (occasionally comprehensive) set-up options and the demanding handling model – at least

with the default driving aids left on. That will undoubtedly disappoint some of the franchise's more hardcore followers, but even the briefest amount of track time on *GRID* is likely to convince most that the focus of this game experience lies elsewhere. From the first event, the game recreates the intensity of racing remarkably, matching exceptional atmosphere with superb AI, a genre-leading damage model, and a city-based track design that showcases moments of brilliance.

Yet it's only after several more miles that the touches of genius reveal themselves. The variety of categories, despite mostly revolving around GT, open-wheel and drift variants, deliberately eschews the overly familiar and instead delivers a diverse, different and refreshing series of events, helped immeasurably by a delicate yet expertly crafted progression structure. The micro management of sponsorship, together with elements of team ownership, add subtle but critical layers of game mechanic that further deepen a player's involvement in a game that is already more engrossing than any of its contemporaries.

Then there is Flashback, a dynamic borrowed from another genre that enables mistakes to be corrected by rewinding events to a pre-disaster point, offering the gamer another chance at taking a corner or attempting an overtaking manoeuvre without needing to restart the event. It may come across as a minor

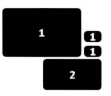

Pic 1: *iRacing*'s structure attempts to mirror real-world racing, so that simracers have to build their experience before being allowed to get behind the wheel of more powerful and faster machinery.

(iRacing.com Motorsport Simulations)

Pic 2: Though the developer plans to expand the selection going forward, the current circuit listing is mostly comprised of US-based tracks, with only a sprinkling of international racetracks available.

(iRacing.com Motorsport Simulations)

inclusion, but like every other element in *GRID* it plays a crucial role within an already hugely accomplished and currently unrivalled package. If *Forza Motorsport 2* offers the most convincing driving feel on console, *Race Driver: GRID* undoubtedly delivers the finest, most stimulating racing experience yet.

iRacing (2008)
Format: PC
Developer: iRacing.com Motorsport Simulations
Publisher: iRacing.com Motorsport Simulations

Perhaps the first thing to note about *iRacing* is that it's not a game. Rather, its developer is keen to point out, it's a training tool for racing drivers – both professional and amateur – wishing to get some track time without the expense and hassle of doing it for real.

As such, the team set out to create the most accurate handling simulation yet, while applying a similarly dedicated approach to the recreation of the tracks available for training – by laser scanning circuits the dimensions are translated precisely into the simulation and the result is a sense of depth and distance that is rare in its ability to convey the most subtle of nuances, even by the already exacting standards of the simracing subgenre.

The seriousness of *iRacing*'s approach continues in its structure, which aims to replicate the progression racing drivers experience in the real world. The subscription model enables drivers to gain experience in the lower formulae before being given the keys to faster, more demanding vehicles. And for those not playing by the rules, a penalty system awaits.

Overall it's a bold and slightly different move, but not one that places *iRacing* beyond the remit of the simracing community, of course. Indeed, it should be seen as a possible evolutionary step for the sector.

The Driving Games Manual

(Microsoft Game Studios)

Track Technique

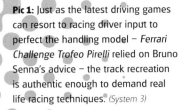

Pic 1: Just as the latest driving games can resort to racing driver input to perfect the handling model – *Ferrari Challenge Trofeo Pirelli* relied on Bruno Senna's advice – the track recreation is authentic enough to demand real life racing techniques. *(System 3)*

Pic 2: The increase in accuracy of in-game circuit replication demands a better understanding of racing technique. And few circuits represent a more difficult challenge for the digital driver than the Nürburgring Nordschleife. *(Microsoft Game Studios)*

Introduction

Racing games that required little to no braking ran out of fuel a long time ago. Even the handling dynamics of today's arcade-like titles are underpinned by complex physical models deliberately toned down to approximate, rather than accurately mimic, real-world car behaviour, and as such any player wishing to improve their lap times will inevitably benefit from some insight into real racing techniques.

The extent to which these are then applied clearly depends on the level of simulation offered in the game – *Burnout* fans can easily get by with a cursory knowledge of racing lines and rudimentary (or just rude) overtaking techniques, while, at the other end of the scale, simracing devotees will probably get through this chapter and go on to digest publications dealing uniquely with, say, tyre dynamics.

Clearly, you can fill entire books with several of the areas dealt with in this chapter, but this still aims to be a relatively comprehensive guide to the key elements that will hopefully help average digital racers to

1 2
3
   4

Pic 1: Even the most arcade-like of modern releases – such as *TrackMania United* – can benefit from the application of basic racing line techniques. *(Focus Home Interactive)*

Pic 2: Current games, and particularly

simracing titles such as *iRacing*, recreate every nuance of real-world circuits. *(iRacing Motorsport Simulations)*

Pic 3: Limited by hardware, early sims such as 1988's *Nigel Mansell's Grand Prix* could still be engrossing without

focusing on racing lines. *(Martech)*

Pic 4: Notice the difference between the constant radius line – dotted – and the racing line which takes a later but sharper turn-in, followed by a later apex point, enabling a quicker exit.

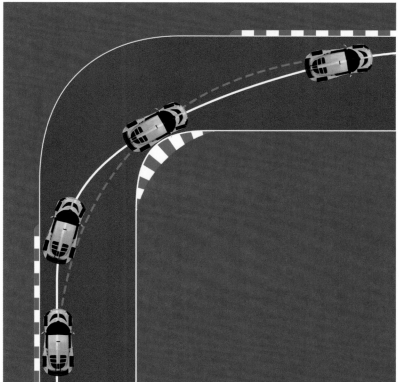

considerably improve their virtual driving and, by consequence, their lap times.

Note that the majority of this chapter relates to track- and road-based racing. That said, fans of rally games will also be able to apply some of the approaches detailed below.

The basic racing line

There's little point learning what to do around the various components of a track if you don't know where your car should be positioned on the circuit – in other words, what and where the racing line is. The basics of the racing line are actually pretty straightforward: it's the trajectory around a track that will give you the quickest route. That doesn't necessarily mean the shortest, of course.

Essentially, the racing line attempts to 'straighten' out every corner of a track, because the straighter the corner, the faster you can drive through it. So we talk of corners in terms of radius. A fast, open bend has a wide radius, while a hairpin presents a narrow radius and dictates a much slower speed from drivers. It stands to reason that the 'wider' we can make that

hairpin, by adopting a trajectory that makes this possible, the faster you'll be able to drive through it.

With that understanding in place, we next need to consider the components that make up a corner.

Pic 1: By the end of this chapter you'll be taking variable radius corners such as this in your stride. Here the apex is taken early as it allows for the maximum exit speed possible, making full use of the track available as the corner unwinds in front or you.

Pic 2: Making full use of the track to maximise your speed – the second car in this *GTR2* shot deliberately runs over the kerb on exit. *(10tacle Studios)*

Pic 3: Once you've found the apex, make sure you don't miss it – notice

this perfect example from *Forza Motorsport 2*. *(Microsoft Game Studios)*

Pic 4: Leading simracing titles may be used as driver training, but modern console sims can also relay a circuit's characteristics. *(Microsoft Game Studios)*

Turn-in

As the name suggests, this is the point after the initial braking zone at which you should begin turning into the corner. Different corners require different rates of input but, generally, the position at which you start turning combined with the amount of steering influence the next two elements of a bend: the apex and the exit.

Apex (or clipping point)

The apex is the point that separates the turn-in and exit phases. Roughly speaking, it is the middle point of a corner and the area that sees you closest to the inside edge of the track before the racing line guides you to the outside of the circuit as you begin to get back on the throttle.

Exit

The exit point is where you should be aiming to have your car after negotiating the corner. In order to maximise the radius of a turn, the exit point is likely to require you to use all of the track available and sometimes a little more. It's not unusual to run right over the kerbs at the exit of a turn in the pursuit of the fastest line through it.

The real racing line

With the concept of the fastest line through a corner being the line with the constant widest radius established, we're now able to determine the racing line. It may sound like the same thing, but there is in

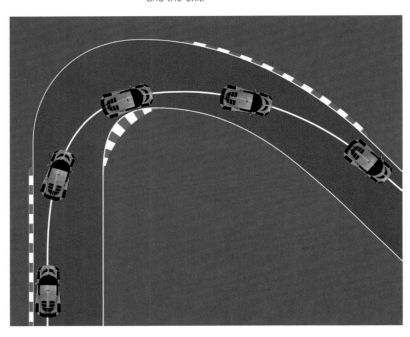

Pic 1: Extreme examples of a beginner's approach to negotiating a corner. Taking too much speed, combined with too relaxed a turn-in will see them heading for the Armco. Turn-in correctly but too late, though, and they'll never see the apex.

Pic 2: If the racing line dictates it, don't be shy when it comes to hugging kerbs – that means getting intimate, not keeping your distance. Great lap times are all about utilising all of the available track surface – and occasionally a little more. *(RACE Pro, Atari)*

Pic 3: Go in too 'hot' into a corner and not only will you miss the turn-in point, the apex and run the risk of going off-track, your opponents will fly past on the inside while you compose yourself. And you will carry that error until the next corner. *(RACE Pro, Atari)*

fact a difference. Essentially, a circuit represents a collection of turns linked by straights; so while the theoretical fastest line through a single corner is the one described in the section above, in the context of a corner being just one component of a circuit and the need to spend as little time as possible on the straights – the track's longest and fastest segments – a little adaptation is required.

Think of it as minimising the amount of time you spend in corners so that you can get back to rushing through the straights. You do this by maximising the amount of time you're on the throttle before having to get on the brakes to slow yourself down for a bend. And doing so inevitably means you're going to delay your turn-in point as much as possible, which in turn extends your apex point further along from where it would be in a constant radius situation. But the beauty of doing this is that it also straightens your exit line, meaning you can get on the power earlier and carry more speed out of the turn into the next straight, to then repeat the sequence at the next bend.

It won't come naturally to most but once it clicks into place you'll find yourself approaching all corners with a view to minimising your overall lap time.

Common errors

The potential exists for getting the line through a corner wrong in a variety of ways, but on the assumption that you've understood and are trying to implement the components that make up the racing line, you're likely to find errors stem from apexing either too early or too late.

Getting to the apex too early usually means you've turned in too soon or too abruptly. The consequence of this is that you'll run out of track on your way out of the corner, unless you're prepared to make some significant corrections (inevitably resulting in a great loss of exit speed).

If you're hitting the apex too late then you've taken too much speed into the corner. You've missed your braking point, which delays your turn-in and forces a sharper steering input. In this scenario you actually end up with a straighter exit out of the corner, but simply won't have the speed to exploit it.

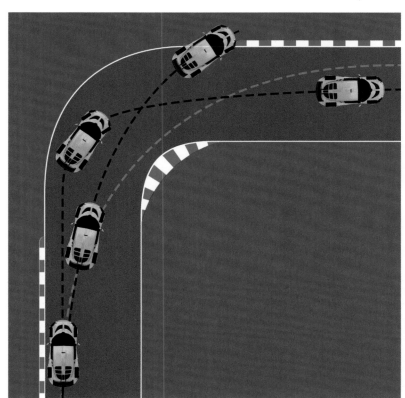

Pic 1: Master constant radius corners first, as they tend to feature heavily in circuits. *(RACE 07, SimBin Studios)*

Pic 2: The thechniques discussed in this chapter apply almost exclusively to road-based racing, meaning that on other surfaces corners can be taken in more dramatic fashion, as *Colin McRae: DiRT* illustrates. *(Codemasters)*

Pic 3: Hairpins and tight constant radius corners are best handled with a later and sharper turn-in. The speed you lose on the way in is more than compensated by the quicker exit this approach guarantees.

Pic 4: Categories of racing such as oval have their own approach, but the principles remain similar. *(GTR, Atari)*

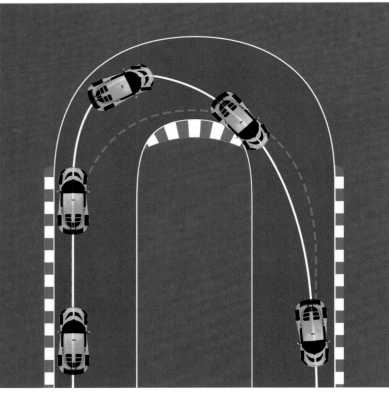

Single apex

A relatively straightforward corner where the main difference relates to the angle of the turn. If preceded and succeeded by a straight, the racing line should remain unaffected. You're aiming for a late turn-in, followed by clipping the inside kerb (again later than feels natural at first), and then straightening up as you get back on the throttle, aiming towards your exit point on the outside edge of the track.

Hairpin

The approach is similar in structure to the single apex corner but the tighter radius involved requires an even later, sharper turn-in, before apexing very late. This enables a straighter exit, meaning you can be on the power earlier than with a faster, single apex turn.

Types of corner

Of course, not every corner of every track will fall neatly into the descriptions below, but knowing the basics will enable you to adapt the correct approach in order to deal with the individual characteristics of any bend you have to negotiate.

Double apex

On a standard example of this type of corner the 'real' apex becomes an imaginary point on the track between the two turns making up the double apex bend. That tends to happen naturally if you think of them constituting a single apex turn and draw a

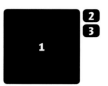

Pic 1: With double apex bends, the idea is to treat the two as one bend while aiming for an imaginary apex between the two. So you're effectively treating a double apex corner as a constant radius bend. Note that the length of the corner has been reduced in this illustration for the purposes of fitting it alongside the other images.

Pic 2: You don't always get textbook-like corners in the 'real' world, as shown by this example of a double apex turn in SimBin's *RACE Pro. (Atari)*

Pic 3: While lacking the real-world kudos of authentic race tracks, unashamedly arcade-like efforts such as *Burnout 3: Takedown* have the benefit of including corner sequences limited only by the imagination of the game's developers. *(Electronic Arts)*

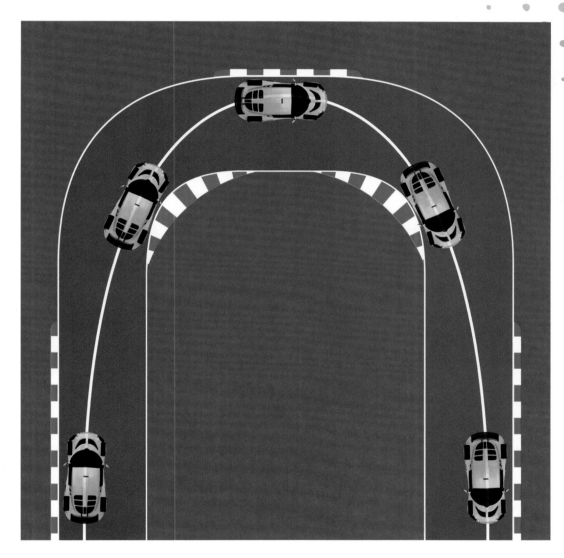

mental curve extending from the first apex to the second. Take care not to take too much speed on your way in or you risk messing up the second part – the approach for a single apex turn applies here, with you aiming for the 'virtual' apex.

Variable radius

This is a bend that either opens up or closes in as you go through it. In the latter case, resist the temptation to steer towards the centre of the track as it starts to bend and instead stick to the outside for a late and sharp turn-in. This gives you the ability to get back on the throttle early as you clip the apex and exit the corner using a wide, speed-friendly radius. For corners that start tight before opening up, take a slightly earlier and gentler turn-in, aiming to apex a touch early, and then exploit the track as it unwinds in front of you by feeding in the power, knowing that you won't run out of road.

Chicane

Chicanes that you can't straightline get a bad reputation but can be hugely rewarding when navigated correctly. The first thing to do is think of them as two separate corners that have lost the straight segment you'd normally find connecting them.

Pic 1: Once you work out the required approach and apply it systematically, chicanes aren't as bad as many think. True, they take skill to negotiate with the smallest amount of time lost, but they're often not as technically demanding as they look.

Pic 2: If the kerbs and your suspension allow it, many modern circuit chicanes can be straightlined, as aptly demonstrated by one of *Gran Turismo 4*'s gorgeously detailed sportscars – it's obviously the fastest way through.
(Sony Computer Entertainment)

Second, you need to accept that you're likely to have to compromise one of the corners in order to achieve the quickest line through both.

If the two corners are identical in radius, it's normally a case of establishing which of the preceding and succeeding straight will benefit your lap time the most. Often this simply involves picking the one that is longest, though the complexity of a circuit will ultimately determine this. Nevertheless, if the preceding straight offers the advantage, then it stands to reason that you should maximise your time on the throttle while there, and so go into the first corner deeper than usual, come out wider and therefore sacrifice your line through the second part of the chicane. If the straight of most benefit – the one on which you'll achieve the higher speed for longer – is the one succeeding the chicane, then compromise your first corner line in order to position your car so as to maximise your exit speed out of the second.

In cases where the radius of the two chicane components differs, you should normally focus on adapting your racing line so that you can take the most speed through the corner offering the widest radius. For example, if the first corner is displaying the tightest angle you should alter your turn-in to apex much later in order to keep your exit line towards the inside of the turn (which becomes the outside of the next turn, of course). This will then give you the best approach to tackle the second corner in such a way as to ensure the fastest exit speed possible.

Learning the track

In real-life racing, one of the best ways to learn the track is to walk it. In games that's not an option, but being able to practice a track before entering the race event often is, and if you're serious about your digital racecraft then it's an opportunity you shouldn't miss. Again, this is an area where you can apply real-world techniques, by progressively increasing your speed as you gain confidence, lap after lap, while learning the intricacies of the circuit – camber, differences in surface, run-off areas, the nature of kerbs, and more. Blasting out of the pits and outbraking yourself at every corner for ten laps until you eventually get the hang of it works, sure, but a considered approach tends to deliver better results considerably faster.

Pic 1: The quest for authentic recreations of real-world race tracks ensures characteristics such as camber are included, as demonstrated by *Gran Turismo 4*'s Nürburgring interpretation.

(Sony Computer Entertainment)

Pic 2: Although arcade-like racing games tend to place objects near the track to increase the feeling of speed, the accuracy of modern simulations such as *GTR* means simracing fans still get reference points on which to base their on-track behaviour. *(Atari)*

Pic 3: In a variable radius corner that progressively tightens, stick to the outside for longer than feels natural, then follow this with a sharp turn-in towards the apex, before utilising all of the tarmac at your disposal during the exit phase of the corner.

Finding the limit

While practice at a new track is invaluable for learning its orientation, once you're familiar with a circuit you'll want to start pushing so that you fall off the track. It's the only way you can learn how late you can brake without missing your turn-in, how much speed you can take into a bend before you're wide of the apex, and how soon you can get back on the power without running out of road – if you don't go past the limit, you'll never find out where that limit is. (Note, this isn't the same as the excess criticised in the previous section – even here a considered approach is necessary to learn a track efficiently.)

This is exactly what experienced drivers will do at a new track, although the immediate advantage games have over real-life situations is that you won't be faced with huge repair bills or a visit to the medical centre as a result of off-track excursions.

For those that are serious, remember that in addition to finding the limits of the racing line it's also worth practising the limits of overtaking zones – the latest off-line braking point that still allows you control of the line to the apex when putting a move on a rival.

Reference points

Away from the exhilaration of the acceleration, braking, and engine noise, the process underlying any racing driver's lap of a circuit is actually a monotonous affair. Drivers work to the same braking, turn-in, apex and exit points, lap after lap – that is how they achieve consistency to within hundredths of seconds. (That said, alterations are made to take into account changing aspects such as tyre wear, fuel load and handling issues.) That is the purpose of finding the limit, so that you can then hit the same points time after time and post near-identical lap times.

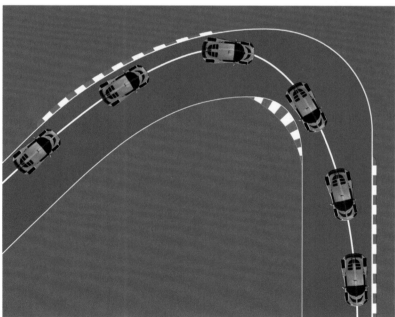

In a game the concept works in the same way, and picking those reference points becomes key to both quick and consistent lapping. But the advantage, particularly for braking points, is that game developers tend to include objects closer to the track than they would appear in real-life as a way of increasing the feeling of speed, and these items can often be used as very obvious references by which to guide your on-track actions.

Track Technique

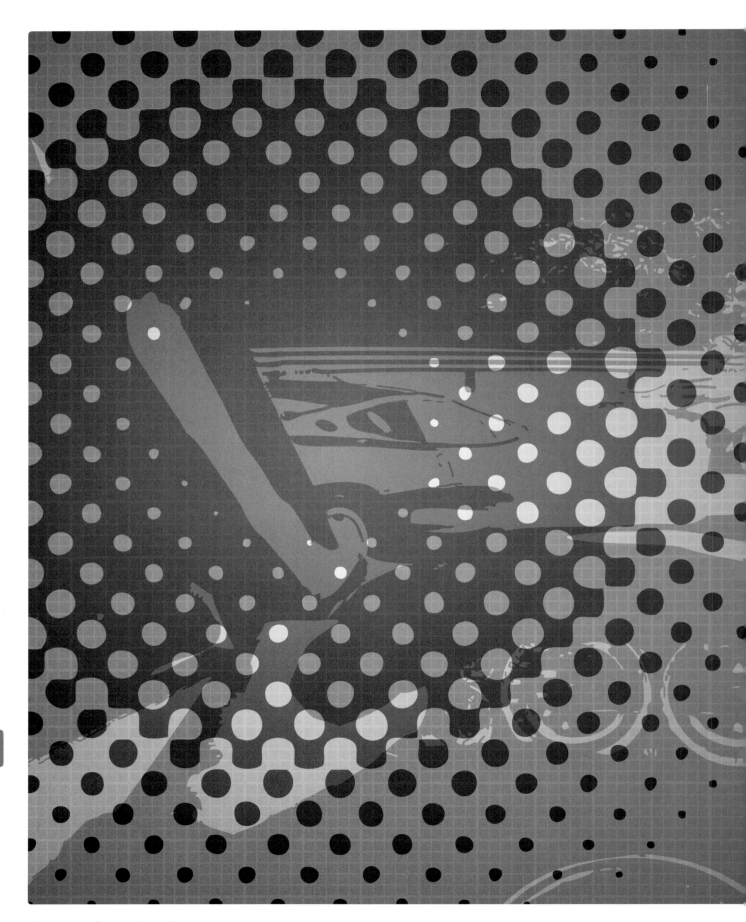

(Sony Computer Entertainment)

Driver Technique

Pic 1: With increasingly sim-heavy titles appearing on console, the need for a fundamental understanding of driver technique is obvious. *(Atari)*

Pic 2: Understeer manifests itself by the way a car 'refuses' to follow the direction of the front wheels when steering input is applied. Instead, the car ploughs straight on, or at least on a trajectory that doesn't correspond to the steering angle applied. It's not a condition as treacherous as oversteer, but it will spoil any timed run.

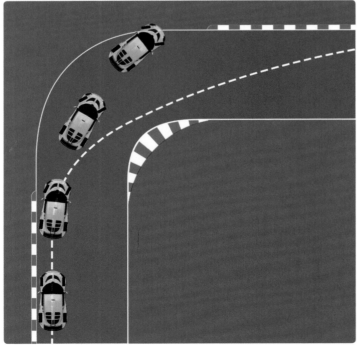

Introduction

Having an understanding of where you're supposed to be on the track as you're going round (see Chapter 6) means you can then shift your focus onto ensuring that your driving skills are up to the task. This means being fast but consistent – either one on its own won't win you many races.

Consistency is the result of not only a controlled driving style but also an understanding of the handling dynamics that govern the vehicle you're controlling. Chapter 8 covers the elements most directly linked with car set-up, and some of those (particularly tyre dynamics) come into play here too, but at its most basic a car's behaviour on the track can be categorised by a tendency to understeer or oversteer.

Understeer

When the front tyres have a lower level of grip than the rears, turning the steering wheel will see the car push straight on and refuse to follow the direction the front wheels are pointing towards. This is most costly

Pic 1: Oversteer occurs when the front tyres have more grip than the rear. There is therefore a tendency for the back end to try to overtake the front and if not corrected – countersteered – it's a characteristic that will see a the vehicle spin out.

Pic 2: The choice of vehicles at your disposal – sometimes within the same game – is vast. The basics remain the same, however. *(MotorStorm Pacific Rift, Sony Computer Entertainment)*

Pic 3: Whatever your preferred digital racing, the techniques in this chapter will apply in some form and should help you on your way to better, more consistent driving and – in turn – faster lap times. The secret is simply practice, practice and more practice. *(rFactor, Image Space Incorporated)*

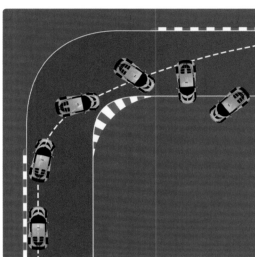

in slow corners, where the inability to negotiate the turn will lose you time. On fast open bends the effect is minimised and a small amount of understeer can actually prove useful as a way of predicting the car's trajectory and planning your line accordingly.

Oversteer

The opposite of understeer, oversteer occurs as a result of the front wheels having more grip than the rears. This doesn't affect the steering wheel's request to change direction but the back end of your car will obviously have a tendency to step out and will force a tighter turn radius than expected; or, worse, it can easily result in a spin if not caught in time. In certain corners – such as hairpins – an oversteering quality to the handling will help turn the car around quicker, but it can prove a handful in most situations.

Car technique

The great Juan Manuel Fangio once recounted that he only became truly fast when he realised that he needed to drive using his 'fingertips' – in other words, holding the steering wheel in a controlled, relaxed manner rather than trying to strangle the life out of it. Much may have changed since Fangio's racing days, but the need to be as smooth as possible at the wheel of a car in order to be fast around a circuit remains as applicable now as it has always been. And it shouldn't surprise you to learn that it's equally as relevant to video game racing, whether you use a joypad or steering wheel set-up.

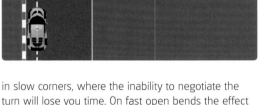

Steering

Steering in a car, whether virtual or real, needs to be done in a progressive, controlled fashion. That's because see-sawing at a wheel or waggling the analogue stick inevitably destabilises the vehicle with regards to the weight transfer that takes place and the effect that this has on the suspension. This in turn will affect your racing line, therefore severely slowing your lap time.

In a simracing title the consequences of such an approach become immediately and painfully evident, but even on console sims like *Gran Turismo* and *Forza Motorsport* the effect is obvious.

Throw into the mix the fact that every time you change direction you're scrubbing off speed and it's soon apparent why you really want to do as little steering as you can get away with. And that means being precise, needing as few corrections as possible

Pic 1: Vision is critical to race-winning lap times. You need to be looking ahead at where you want to be going, rather than directly in front of you. It takes a while to feel natural but when it does you will find you drive both quicker and smoother. *(RACE Pro, Atari)*

Pic 2: Being abrupt with either the brake/throttle or steering will, in most realism-influenced driving titles, result in a loss of control. Racing cars react eagerly to your every input so drive them decisively yet carefully.
(TOCA Race Driver 3, Codemasters)

Pic 3: Increases in hardware performance mean in-game circuits are detailed replicas of their real-life counterparts. Throw in realistic handling into the mix and you can then apply genuine racing techniques.
(Ferrari Challenge Trofeo Pirelli, System 3)

and looking as far ahead as possible (discussed later in this chapter).

Remember, too, to relax your grip on the joypad as this will help increase your precision. Owners of force feedback wheels gain an additional benefit in this regard, as relaxing the grip on the wheel will help better interpret what the chassis is up to (assuming the handling and force feedback model of the game are up to scratch, of course).

Throttle/brake input

Like steering, 'pedal' use needs to be done delicately and gradually. That's because just as when the car is changing direction, altering its momentum results in a significant weight transfer which has to be managed with care so as not to adversely affect handling.

True, the majority of racing games – certainly on console – allow for drastic braking or accelerating without great penalty to the player, either through fancy electronic driving aids or a toned down handling model. But for simracers and those who like their console driving experiences to offer a challenge, the need to learn to roll off the throttle and onto the brake and back again in a determined yet fluid, progressive motion will vastly improve their driving.

Fluid and progressive doesn't mean slow, incidentally. The very nature of racing dictates that you're only on the brakes for the absolute minimum of time, so you need to develop the sensitivity required to perform those functions quickly, but smoothly.

Inevitably, this becomes far easier to achieve using an analogue pedal set-up rather than the buttons or stick on a joypad, but the principle remains the same whichever method you happen to favour.

Vision

Human beings have a tendency to go where they look. It's what's meant by movement following vision. Ever wondered why so many real-world racing drivers appear to follow another racer off track? It's often because they were focusing on the car in front and their body instinctively adapted to get them where they were looking.

Of course, the idea is to look at the track and further enough ahead so that you effectively allow your subconscious to take over – it's not unlike driving on instinct. This is a genuine racing technique but far less nerve-wracking to practise in a game.

Essentially you want to be looking at where you want to go before you get there, and allow your body to make that happen without having to consciously resort to the here and now. So, for instance, as you approach your braking point, you already want to be

Pic 1: Trail-braking involves a shortened but intense period of braking – in red – followed by a progressive easing of the brake pedal – in amber – while turning towards the apex. You're still scrubbing off speed, and continue to do so on your way to the apex, at which point you're back on the throttle – in green.

Pic 2: Getting your braking right is a crucial skill – you won't get decent lap times without it. *(Forza Motorsport 2, Microsoft Game Studios)*

Pic 3: All of the techniques discussed here focus on a dry track. When conditions get wet, however, much of the theory is the same but obviously much greater care must be taken – smoothness is key, particularly with regards to braking. *(GTR2, 10tacle Studios)*

looking at the turn-in. Once there, your vision is focused on the apex, and moments later on the exit, before subsequently concentrating on the next braking spot. It's a continuous process that will feel wholly unnatural at first but if practised enough it's something you'll suddenly find yourself doing without realising it is happening.

The most immediate advantage is a considerably faster lap time, but you'll be smoother, too, as you react instinctively to throttle and brake application, as well as steering adjustments. It's how the real-world racing stars achieve their impressive consistency around a track and it works in exactly the same way in a game situation.

Advanced techniques

While the above basics will certainly get most players to significantly improve their digital racing ability, those seriously looking to eke out the very last hundredth of a second from their favourite driving game can read on and absorb a few more real-world techniques with which to dazzle the competition.

Trail-braking

Technically, trail-braking is an advanced control method, but its effectiveness in reducing lap times is such that those even relatively serious about digital racing may want to get to grips with it sooner rather than later.

Trail-braking is a way of maximising your entry speed into a corner, while minimising the amount of time lost through braking on the preceding straight. As such, your braking point finds itself further along the straight than a conventional braking point. This requires braking very hard for a short concentrated period on the straight (known as threshold braking), using all of your tyres' traction ability (easily done if your virtual ride is fitted with ABS, of course).

Then once you begin the turn-in you'll want to ease off the brake pedal. You do this progressively rather than coming off the brake fully, meaning that you're continually reducing the level of braking as you close in on the apex. This effectively means that you find yourself balancing the steering against the braking, taking care not to exceed your tyres' level of traction.

Normally just before the apex, once the car has rotated into the correct position, your steering input should be diminishing, you'll be nearly completely off the brake pedal and you can start feeding the power.

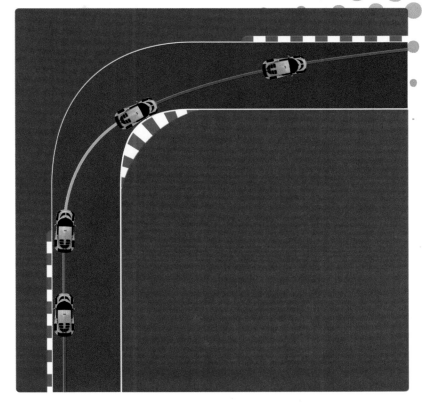

In a real-world situation this would briefly overlap the brake input as you roll off one pedal and onto the other but it's not always the easiest thing to do on a joypad (although possible with a steering wheel and pedal set-up). Once you clip the apex, you should be off the brake and on the throttle.

A further advanced technique, which is useful for some corners but is dependent on the type of car

Pic 1: Handbrake turns are relatively straightforward. Remember to apply the handbrake – never the foot brake – almost immediately after turning and don't start accelerating until you can see your exit, otherwise you'll just carry the slide into the scenery.

being used, is to deliberately break traction with the rear tyres during the turn-in stage so as to allow the back end to step out. This gets the vehicle to rotate towards the apex more quickly than waiting for the front wheels to do their job and should in turn enable you to get on the throttle earlier. It's a neat trick but easily overdone, so take care not to spin out.

Left-foot braking

Not as useless to lovers of joypads as it sounds, because although the technique does refer to the use of the left foot to operate the brake – thereby saving time by keeping the right foot handling the throttle at all times (which obviously does apply to owners of wheel and pedal set-ups) – it also extends to occasions when both throttle and brake have to be deployed simultaneously.

Applying the brake while remaining on the throttle can be used to correct a car's trajectory during mid- to high-speed corners where lifting off would induce a spin. Staying on the power but using the brake can create oversteering characteristics that will 'tuck' the car back into the corner. Meanwhile, more considerate application can be applied in similar corners to combat understeering.

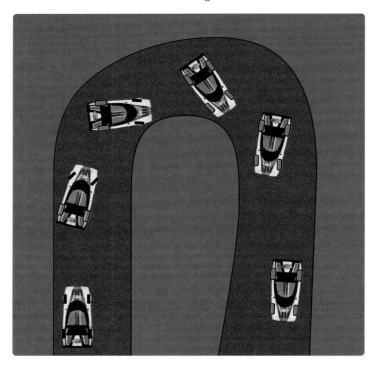

Heel-and-toe

This is another real-world technique that will apply to the simracing end of the spectrum, and specifically set-ups that include a clutch pedal (although a few console games do support the clutch function, and at least one wheel on the market includes it on its pedal layout). Heel-and-toe not only increases the smoothness of performance driving when downshifting, but also enables a driver to incorporate very late gear changes as part of their braking zone (rather than having to build in the time and distance for downshifting). This means you can maximise the amount of time you're on the throttle coming up to the corner.

The technique involves operating both the brake and throttle with the right foot so as to blip the throttle while braking and downshifting. The idea is to get the engine revs to match the gear being selected. By operating the brake with the ball of the foot, a driver can rotate the heel to depress the throttle and time this to coincide with the clutch action of the left foot. It sounds clumsy but it's actually surprising how quickly it becomes intuitive once you start using it.

Rally driving

While rally games are less frequent than their road- or track-based equivalents, their development hasn't lagged behind, with the handling models employed in this subgenre proving just as complex and accomplished. Some of the principles mentioned so far in this chapter work for rallying, certainly, but the style of driving incorporates techniques that are unique to it in terms of negotiating corners on loose surfaces in the fastest manner possible, and therefore warrant its own individual section.

Handbrake turn

In rallying, handbrake turns are used to get the car to negotiate a very tight turn as quickly as possible. joyriders and boy racers are no doubt au fait with the technique, but for those who've led a more law-abiding and quiet lifestyle, rest assured that the process is a relatively simple one to perform and claim proficiency in.

To instigate a handbrake turn in a front-wheel-drive car, begin turning (if you're using a steering-wheel set-up just half a turn will do) after braking for the corner, so you'll already be in a low gear. The steering input will normally start a little earlier than a standard turn-in. As the car rotates, the weight shifts to the outside

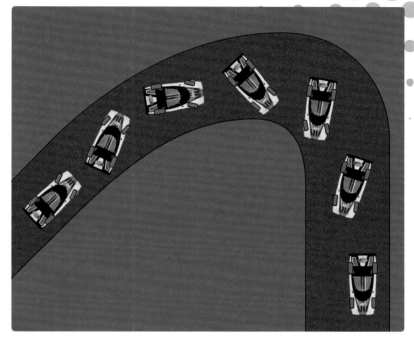

Pic 1: In medium and fast corners where handbrake turns are inappropriate, consider lift-off oversteer to swing the back around.

Pic 2: The Scandinavian flick requires great timing and takes much practice to perfect but is hugely satisfying when performed correctly.

Pic 3: Even thoroughly arcade rally experiences such as the modern *Sega Rally* will respond to most of the techniques described here. *(Sega)*

wheels and you should now sharply apply the handbrake (the standard brake shouldn't be touched at this point) to deliberately get the rear tyres to lose traction and skid. The moment you see the corner exit release the handbrake and get back on the throttle, controlling the vehicle in a sideways slide by balancing the power and the steering (which would have required an initial amount of opposite lock to prevent spinning out).

In a rear- or four-wheel-drive car, one extra consideration is the fact that applying the handbrake will stall the engine unless the clutch is pressed (most games do this for you, however).

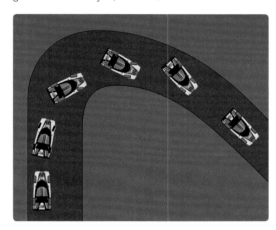

Lift-off oversteer

A rally car thrives on oversteer – it's what enables it to navigate corners in a four-wheel drift that ensures you end up losing little speed. You can accentuate a car's oversteer characteristics through the handbrake turn technique detailed above, but for fast or medium-fast corners where little braking is needed you can resort to lift-off oversteer. As its name suggests, this involves lifting off the throttle (going from full throttle to no throttle) just before turning into the corner. This shifts the weight of the car from its back wheels (while under acceleration) to the front (due to engine braking); and as you turn, the back end – now light – will easily break traction and start to slide.

Immediately, you should countersteer (opposite lock) – ensuring the wheels are pointing in the direction you want to go – and get back on the throttle. This transfers the weight back onto the rear axle and increases traction, straightening the car out of the slide.

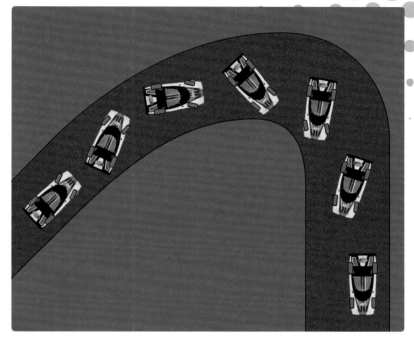

Scandinavian flick

Also known as the pendulum turn, this is a technique that involves, on the approach to a wide exit corner, briefly turning the car in the opposite direction while under braking (although maintaining the throttle) in order to start a slide facing away from the bend. The steering is then flicked in the direction of the turn, along with the release of the brake, which gets the car to change direction and propel itself into the corner in a powerslide (as a result of the momentum already built). The slide is then held by balancing throttle and steering input.

Pic 1: Perfect for medium to fast chicanes, power oversteering requires the timely and delicate application of both throttle and steering.

Pic 2: Developers' interpretations of the drift dynamics tend to vary wildly.

More so than the standard handling model, in fact. And within the same game the two can be distant cousins – *Juiced 2*'s drifting mechanic may not be the most realistic, but it is memorable. The same can't be said of its other racing events, however. *(THQ)*

Left-foot braking

In rallying this refers to a technique similar to handbrake turning that's used in front-wheel-drive cars to induce oversteering characteristics and help rotate a car into a turn. The brake is heavily applied on the approach into a corner while the throttle is maintained, which, along with steering, is then used to navigate the car through the bend. By keeping the engine under power the car should propel itself forward once the brake is released. Left-foot braking is also used in the initial phase of the Scandinavian flick.

Drifting

Drifting – the form of motorsport involving extreme powersliding through corners – gained popularity in Japan in the 1980s. It took a little while for this style of competition to invade the West, but organised events are now relatively commonplace as the sport grows in status outside of its homeland. Video games caught on relatively early, and increasingly drifting turns up alongside other categories in what can be considered very mainstream racing games – the *Need for Speed* series has had drift events for a few iterations, *GRID* and the latest *Gran Turismo* include the discipline, and drifting mods of popular simracing titles also exist.

Given its nature, however, drifting comes with specific techniques that need to be mastered (at least when it comes to simracing and high-end console racing experiences).

Handbrake drift

As you begin turning, apply the handbrake to break rear traction (if the game demands it, you'll need to depress the clutch too or the engine will stall – drift cars are rear-wheel-drive). Once the back end starts to slide, countersteer and apply the throttle to maintain the drift.

Power oversteer

As drift cars are powerful beasts, it's possible to break rear tyre traction by simply stamping on the throttle. Power oversteer refers to a drift induced by this method and is usually applied when dealing with a series of linked bends, as a way of setting up a drift for each subsequent corner without the need to brake. It takes delicacy to then balance the throttle (and steering) once in a power oversteer.

Clutch kick

This involves rapidly coming on and off the clutch to jolt a car's powertrain and affect the balance, causing the rear tyres to slip. It's of limited use in games given that it requires a clutch function (which to date hasn't been a common inclusion in console titles, although this is likely to change going forward).

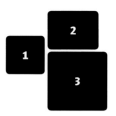

Pic 1: Similar to rallying's Scandinavian flick but without resorting to braking, the feint drift involves turning away from the intended apex and then snapping the car back on course, so that the momentum built in weight transfer helps establish a drift.

Pic 2: It's difficult to find a modern racing game without drift disciplines. *(Race Driver: GRID, Codemasters)*

Pic 3: The braking drift involves hard braking into the corner, immediately followed by throttle and steering.

Shift lock

A technique you'll be glad to practise in video game form because the real-world equivalent can cost you a car engine when misapplied. It involves violently downshifting into a very slow corner instead of braking and without blipping the throttle to match the revs, so that the shock to the engine momentarily locks the rear wheels. As the car begins to drift, you're then back on the throttle to maintain the slide and power out of the bend.

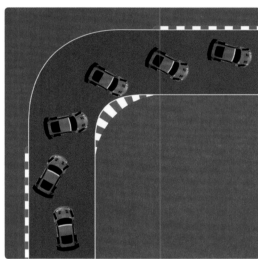

Feint drift

An advanced drifting technique similar to the Scandinavian flick used in rallying (see earlier), where the car is first turned away from the corner and then quickly back towards it so that the inertia carries the back end around and into a drift more easily, while also providing better drive out of the corner as a result of the momentum built up.

Braking drift

Relying on weight transfer, this involves braking into a corner to shift the weight onto the front end and instantly getting on the throttle while turning so that the rear wheels, now unloaded, break traction. With a little help from the steering (and throttle), the car will then begin drifting.

Kansei (Lift off)

A technique sharing its essence with lift-off oversteer (see earlier). Drift is initiated by coming off the power in

the middle of a high-speed bend so that the resulting weight transfer to the front sees the back end step out of line. Then it's a question of controlling it with steering and throttle.

Pic 1: Trying to pass another car but taking too much speed into a corner or simply leaving the braking too late will see you go in too deep and lose your speed while you get back onto the racing line. Meanwhile, the other car will have regained the position.

Pic 2: Hard but fair. Having overtaken a competitor in a bend, it's legitimate for the car in front to 'squeeze' the passed car off the racing line, forcing them to either run wide or lift off. AI drivers don't always relent, however. *(TOCA Race Driver 3, Codemasters)*

Pic 3: Try not to think too much about what is happening behind you. Racing driver schools teach cadets never to look behind them – obviously be aware of threatening rivals but it's far better to focus your concentration on the tarmac ahead. *(GTR2, 10tacle Studios)*

a little theory and a lot of experience – there are no shortcuts.

While racing games from yesteryear made the process of overtaking look easy, recent advancements in AI and the increasing popularity of online gaming have offered many virtual racers a glimpse at what real-world racing drivers have long known: overtaking competitors is hard work.

Thankfully it's also hugely satisfying – even when beating artificial (but worthy) adversaries – which makes all the practice fun. The most common ways of getting past the opposition are either to out-drag (slipstream – see ahead) them on a straight (usually as a result of taking more speed out of the previous bend) or to outbrake them into a corner. Other opportunities undoubtedly present themselves (as a result of opponents' handling issues, mistakes, accidents and so on) and it obviously pays to remain alert and capitalise on these when they occur.

Planning

Aside from the unexpected opportunities mentioned above, nearly every overtaking manoeuvre is pre-planned. You get the chance to think about it as you gain time on a competitor, lap after lap – it's just something you'll inevitably think about as you close in on them. So the trick is to ensure that you're in the right place at the right time. There's no point steaming up to the exhaust of a competitor when there's no way to get past and so lose your momentum, when you can apply that speed advantage to the moment when an overtaking opportunity presents itself.

Pressure

It sounds silly to talk about putting pressure on the driver in front in situations that don't involve real

Overtaking

With enough practice, more or less anyone can end up with impressive lap times. The difference between a good driver and a good racing driver comes down to racecraft. And like anything else, it's

Pic 1: Always attempt a passing move while remaining as close to the racing line. Otherwise your trajectory through the corner will be too tight – and slow.

Pic 2: The start and the opening lap are the best opportunities for making up the most amount of places because the field is packed and it's often chaotic. They're also the most accident-prone segments of a race. *(rFactor, Image Space Incorporated)*

Pic 3: Remember that elements such as slipstreaming aren't necessarily confined to single-seater driving games. *(BAJA: Edge of Control, THQ)*

Pic 4: Try to plan out where best to make a move on a rival. *(Project Gotham Racing 3, Microsoft Game Studios)*

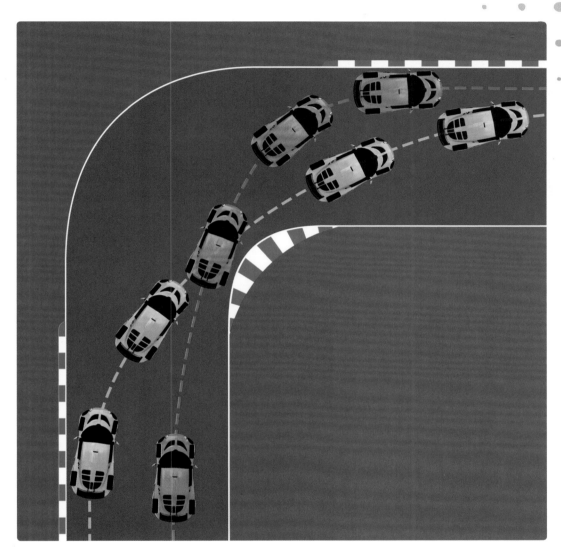

players (as you have in simracing competition or even online console racing), but the AI of certain games is such these days that some virtual racers will lose their nerve and crash out if you keep hassling them on the track. Okay, they're obviously programmed to do so, but the effect is nevertheless convincing.

Slipstreaming

An invaluable technique, particularly in same-series categories of motorsport, slipstreaming refers to the effect that sees a following car experience considerably less drag (air resistance) than the vehicle in front of it. This effectively means the chasing car is

Driver Technique

Pic 1: Outbraking an opponent into a corner requires precision timing – but provided you stop in time to still make the apex, you can get away with leaving the braking a touch later than you really ought to. *(Project Gotham Racing 3, Microsoft Game Studios)*

Pic 2: While knowing and applying the theory detailed in ths chapter is ideal, some overtaking moves are simply the result of exploited opportunities so keep your eyes open for any gaps that suddenly develop. *(Gran Turismo 5 Prologue, Sony Computer Entertainment)*

Pic 3: The key to making an outbraking manoeuvre work is in ensuring you place your car far enough alongside your opponent before turning into the bend. You don't need to be ahead, necessarily, to control the apex and therefore benefit from the fastest exit.

using less power to achieve the same speed, so that when the time is right it's able to pull out from the slipstream and use the 'extra' power to out-drag the competitor and take their position.

Outbraking

The way to successfully outbrake a competitor is to ensure you're positioned alongside them during the braking zone of a turn. This ensures that you have the inside line, and therefore control of the corner. It forces them to the outside of the turn where they pose little threat and it also ensures they don't turn in on you (it depends on how intelligent – or fair, in

the case of human drivers – the AI racers are, of course).

When moving to outbrake another car, try to remain as close to the racing line as possible, so as to not disadvantage your own line into the corner too much. If you move too far across, you'll compromise your corner entry speed (because your entry radius is too tight and you won't be able to get round without shaving off considerable speed) and your opponent is likely to be able to beat you on the exit.

Also, don't leave your own braking too late and end up running too deep into the corner. The essence of the move requires you to brake later than the

Pic 1: Defending your position from a competitor trying to pass you requires a more central line. This forces the other car either to the outside or inside. If the former, you maintain control of the apex and should therefore have the faster exit line.

Pic 2: Don't panic if your competitor passes you on the inside while defending – you still have the wider radius and so quicker line out of the corner. Consider even sneakily moving back to the outside of the turn before turning in for an even faster exit.

Pic 3: Being overambitious in your overtaking can often end in tears – if you're racing online, you won't be popular. *(TOCA Race Driver, Codemasters)*

Pic 4: If there's a gap, don't miss the chance to get your car in it. *(RACE, Eidos)*

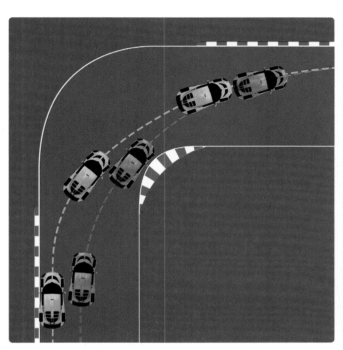

competitor (who'll presumably be on the limit of the braking point for that corner) so that you move alongside them, but as long as that is judged correctly you can then actually brake for longer because you're able to control the line to the apex and, to a certain extent, the pace out of the corner.

Defensive line

While overtaking rival cars is greatly rewarding, nothing quite bursts the bubble more quickly than being overtaken yourself. In games you can obviously punt another car off without serious repercussions, but assuming for a moment that you aim to do everything

above board (or that the game will penalise that kind of behaviour), let's focus on how best to try and keep a competitor behind you.

The correct way is to drive a defensive line. This differs from the racing line in that you position your car on the track so as to make it near impossible for someone to get past you. Generally speaking it involves

taking a more centralised trajectory on the approach to corners, forcing rivals to either commit to the inside (a useless venture because of the lack of speed they'll have at the apex) or the outside (which still gives you control of the corner, as long as you're careful on the exit). Take care not to move too close to the inside edge of the track as you get to the corner or an opponent will simply stick to the outside and slingshot past you on the way out because of the excessively tight (and necessarily slow) line you've taken into the turn.

The problem with driving defensively, however, is that your lap times suffer because of the tighter lines you're taking into corners, requiring you to scrub more speed in order to still make the apex. The obvious solution is to focus on the road ahead, rather than what's happening behind you, and put in some cracking laps. If you're fast enough, competitors won't be able to catch you and you won't have to think defensively.

Accidents

The nature of motorsport makes accidents an eventuality, not a possibility. And given the fact that there are no real-life risks in virtual racing, accidents in gaming are a definite. In some games, in fact, they're an instrumental part of the play mechanics. But in a simracing situation, for instance (in fact, even in less serious instances), they're not desirable. It's necessary to have complex damage models like those found in *Race Driver: GRID* – one of the leaders in this area – to appreciate the dramatic undercurrent that accidents bring to the racing experience (there's little point taking Eau Rouge at Spa-Francorchamps flat out without an element of danger involved, after all) – but unless you're involved in a destruction derby-style event with like-minded players online, there's considerable more enjoyment to be had from a race that has been hard-fought but won cleanly and fairly.

Pic 1: In some games, like *FlatOut Ultimate Carnage*, much of the game dynamic revolves around crashing and consequence-free jostling. And the action is most enjoyable, while also a good way to showcase modern damage modelling. *(Empire)*

Pic 2: Crashes during online races, particularly during closely fought events, will happen – as in real-life. *(Race Driver: GRID, Codemasters)*

Pic 3: Expectedly, simracing titles take damage seriously. *(GTR2, 10tacle Studios)*

Pic 4: *Pole Position II* shows off the best in early crash dynamics. *(Namco)*

Pic 5: Terminal damage in recent games is a crucial factor in increasing a player's level of involvement. *(TOCA Race Driver 3, Codemasters)*

That said, you obviously can't control the actions of those around you – human or AI – and so you go into each virtual race expecting on-track altercations to occur. You should therefore enter events with the right attitude in order to help you minimise your involvement in them.

Avoidance

The majority of racing accidents normally come down to a car going for a gap that doesn't exist, or trying to squeeze out a passing vehicle, refusing to accept that they've been overtaken and stubbornly claiming a corner that is no longer theirs (normally a human rather than AI trait – although the behaviour of computer-controlled rivals in some games can be worryingly aggressive), taking out the car in front as a result of outbraking themselves into a corner or spinning under braking and collecting the following drivers.

Being caught up in any of these will cost you precious time and potentially the race, depending on how realistic you like your digital racing. You won't be able to always avoid them all, naturally, but it nevertheless pays to try and minimise the risks.

So, when overtaking don't go for a gap that's overambitious. If there's a chance of the car in front turning in on you, it's better to retain your position and focus on setting yourself up for a run up the inside at the next opportunity.

If you're being overtaken, by all means fight your corner but realise and accept when the battle is over. Better to tuck in behind them and look for another chance to regain your position than get involved in fisticuffs that will see you off the track and end up further down the running order.

If you do end up off the black stuff, don't just rush back onto the track and into the path of a competitor who will definitely take you out of the race through the resulting unavoidable shunt – so try to rejoin safely.

Most important, perhaps, is that when a collision in front of you occurs you should immediately look for a gap. If you're looking ahead, as you should, you then have more time to react and find a way through the carnage. A real-life trick that tends to work is to aim for the spot of any car that's still moving, as the likelihood that it will still be in that position when you get there is low. Remember also that cars losing control in corners will almost always spin towards the outside of the bend, so directing yourself towards the inside should prove a wise move.

The golden rule is to look at the gap rather than the wrecks. Do the latter and, because human nature dictates that you go where your eyes are looking, you'll inevitably collide as well or suffer a 'sympathy' spin off.

Driver Technique

The Driving Games Manual

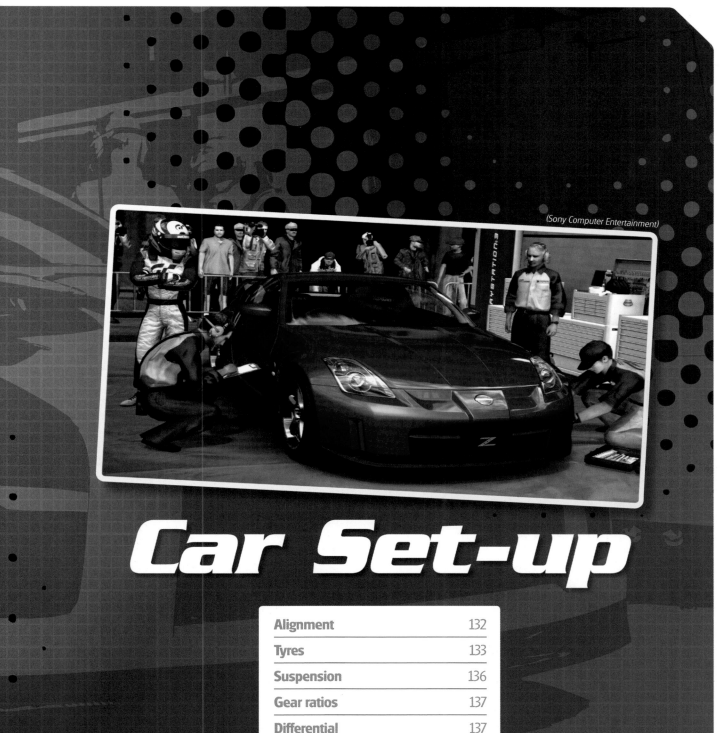

(Sony Computer Entertainment)

Car Set-up

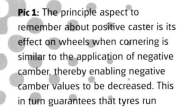

Pic 1: The principle aspect to remember about positive caster is its effect on wheels when cornering is similar to the application of negative camber, thereby enabling negative camber values to be decreased. This in turn guarantees that tyres run flatter on straights, which obviously enables a vehicle to speed up and slow down more efficiently – the disadvantage of negative camber is its effect on the tyre contact patch when on straights. *(The arrow in the diagram represents the direction of travel.)*

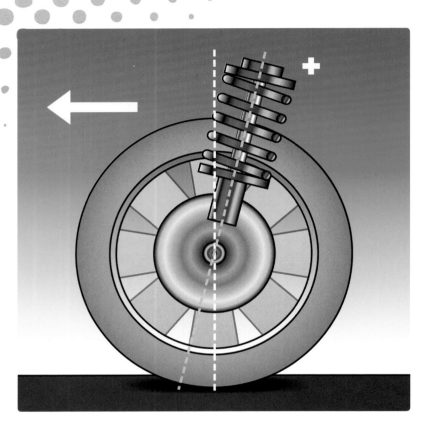

Introduction

While countless books exist detailing most of the elements in this chapter in far more comprehensive fashion than space allows here, it's nevertheless worth getting a fundamental understanding of the most obvious elements affecting a car's set-up. If you're the kind of virtual racer that enjoys tinkering with a vehicle's handling dynamics so as to best match them to a track's characteristics and therefore maximise your in-car performance, the following should get you going.

Before launching into this, however, it's worth remembering that set-up changes should ideally be made one at time, with a timed practice run establishing whether the tinkering has helped or hindered the vehicle's abilities. If you make three changes and you suddenly knock a second off your lap time, you'll be hard pushed to determine which had the biggest effect and which should perhaps be further explored.

Alignment

Chances are you've previously come across the Holy Trinity of vehicle dynamics: caster, camber and toe. They pop up in some fairly mainstream driving titles and in the majority of cases players haven't dared go near them. It's understandable – mess around with any of these three without knowing what you're doing and the results can be catastrophic. However, if you're serious about your virtual racing you're going to have to get to grips with their function. Read on and don't be afraid to touch next time they show up in the options menu.

Caster

Caster relates to the angle of the steering axis, in other words the angular difference between the pivot line – an imaginary line running through the centre of the spindle or ball joint (depends on the vehicle, but essentially it's the part of the steering assembly that attaches to the wheels) – and the vertical. If the pivot line tilts 'backwards' (the top ball joint is positioned further back from the bottom ball joint) the caster is said to be positive. In other words the pivot line intersects the track ahead of the tyre's contact patch (see p134).

Positive caster is used to increase straight-line stability, but in racing its significant advantage is the way it increases the negative camber of the steering wheels when turning, improving cornering. So by increasing positive caster you can decrease negative camber settings, enabling the tyres to run flatter when in straight lines (helping with acceleration and braking). The greater the caster angle, however, the harder the steering (not necessarily much of a concern in a game situation, to be fair).

Camber

The vertical inclination of a wheel when viewed from the front or rear is the camber angle. If the top of a wheel is further away from the chassis than its bottom, it's said to have positive camber. Negative camber, then, relates to a situation where the top of a wheel is seen to be leaning towards the chassis.

In racing, camber mostly comes into effect during cornering, where negative camber enables the outside tyre to maintain a larger contact patch than if the same turn was attempted with zero camber (where the load on the outside tyre would force it to roll on itself,

Pic 1: Viewed from the front, camber is said to be negative when the top of the tyre is closer to the chassis – here on the left, though not illustrated – than the bottom. Conversely, positive camber results in the bottom of the tyre being closer than the top.

Pic 2: Viewed here from above, toe is measured in the way the wheel aligns in relation to the chassis – here on the left, not illustrated. Toe values are used minimally due to their effect on tyre performance. *(The arrow in the diagram represents the direction of travel.)*

resulting in the inside edge of the tyre lifting and thereby reducing the contact patch and affecting the level of traction). In other words, camber enables tyres to run flat (or flatter) during cornering. This also facilitates a more even heat distribution in the tyre.

Bear in mind that camber obviously has an effect on the straights, when the tyres would theoretically run flat (or with zero camber), so it's a delicate balance (although when combined with caster, as previously mentioned, this effect can be reduced).

Toe

This relates to the difference in distance between the front and rear sections of the directional wheels: in other words, whether the front wheels are parallel, or point towards or away from each other. Toe is normally used minimally, as the resulting increase in tyre scrubbing affects top-end speed. Toe-in (positive toe) is usually applied to rear-wheel-drive cars, as the fact that the front wheels are turned slightly towards each other helps straight-line stability. It does, however, affect turn-in.

Toe-out (negative toe) does the opposite, improving turn-in at the cost of stability. It's often used in some categories of racing to exaggerate the turn-in characteristics of a car in, for instance, wet-weather conditions (as well as to help maintain tyre operating temperature as a result of the increased scrubbing).

Whether in or out, excessive toe obviously wears out tyres more quickly.

Tyres

They may look like four rings of rubber, but tyres are arguably the most important aspect of a car. That's because everything you do at the wheel, everything the car does on track, and all the handling feedback you experience, goes through the tyres. Nothing else is connecting you to the tarmac, after all.

So tyres are a fundamental component when setting up a car properly and learning their characteristics is crucial because they will have a massive effect on your performance. True, in most games you simply get to race what you're given, but in simracing and sim-flavoured console titles like *Forza Motorsport 2* you're allowed to tinker with tyres to a considerable extent. But before we get to the obvious parameters you can toy with – such as pressure and compound – it's worth quickly going through some of the core dynamics of tyres.

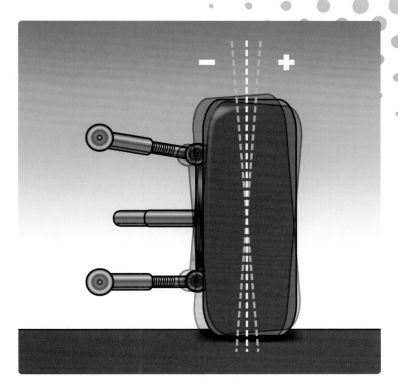

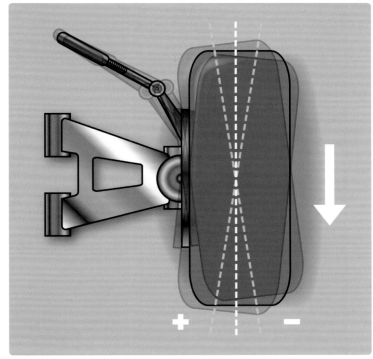

ability to corner quickly and therefore reduce your lap times. With enough practice, this eventually becomes second nature.

Slip angle

Simply put, this is the difference between the direction a tyre is pointing in and the actual trajectory it is following. At slow speeds there will obviously be no difference – a tyre happily follows the direction in which it's pointing. The slip angle in this case is therefore said to be zero. But as speed increases, so does the slip angle.

A certain amount of slip angle is actually desirable when cornering, as it suggests you're on the limit – that is, given the current set-up of the car, this is as fast as it will negotiate the bend in question. The ideal slip angle represents the point at which the tyres offer their most grip. Getting a feel for what constitutes the right slip angle takes practice – too much angle, for instance, and you'll drift wide and lose speed.

Load

The force or weight being placed on a tyre is called load. In a car in motion, the load value is directly affected by the weight transfers that occur. When you brake, for instance, the weight distribution of the car transfers forwards, at which point the front tyres will have the most load. When you accelerate the reverse happens, while during cornering the majority of the load will transfer to the outside tyres. An awareness of the load on the tyres helps when determining set-ups.

Contact patch

Also known as its footprint, the concept of a tyre's contact patch becomes logical once you understand load. It depends on the size of the tyre and the amount of load being placed on it, but essentially the contact patch is the area of the tyre that connects with the track and which therefore provides the vehicle's traction. Load affects the footprint in the same way that pressing your hand down on a foam ball would squash it down and increase the amount of its surface area in contact with the surface beneath it.

With a tyre, if you increase the surface area – the contact patch – you increase the level of traction; so if you reduce the load, you reduce the amount of grip. When racing, this manifests itself through a car's steering and cornering characteristics (such as oversteer or understeer – see Chapter 7).

Traction

Think of traction as the amount of grip a tyre generates. This value will be affected by the hardness of the rubber being used, its temperature, the amount of load (see below) acting upon it and the coefficient of the friction of the track surface and the tyre (ie how easy the two slide against each other, also referred to as the level of abrasion between them).

Unless you're drifting, most forms of track-based motorsport require you to be at the limit of traction and not over – exceeding the limit results in a loss of grip and therefore a skid.

When racing, a tyre is required to handle a driver's braking, steering and accelerating requests. A tyre can meet any of those demands to the maximum of its traction threshold, but it can only do them at that maximum one at a time. It cannot, for instance, be at 100 per cent of its traction threshold while braking and then be asked to turn as well – it simply has no grip level left to be able to accommodate a direction change. It can, however, handle any two (such as steering and braking during trail-braking, or steering and accelerating when exiting corners – see Chapter 7), or even all three (should a situation ever require it), for as long as the overall demands on its traction levels are balanced and do not exceed the tyre's overall traction limit.

Understanding traction and learning to push tyres to their limit without overstepping it determines your

Compounds and wear

Not all tyres are created equal. Just as they vary in size, racing tyres also come in different levels of rubber hardness. Generally, a harder compound provides less grip and also requires a higher operating temperature, but in its favour it keeps its properties (ie lasts) longer than a soft tyre. The latter heat up more quickly, and the softer they are, the more traction you can expect, but they'll also wear out proportionally. And as a tyre wears out, so does the level of grip. The choice of tyre will depend on the type of event, category of car, the nature of the track, pit strategy and your driving style.

Pressure

Perhaps the most complex element when dealing with tyres, pressure values are nevertheless crucial because of how they affect a vehicle's handling. There is no one-size-fits-all answer here and the best way to get familiar with the effects of tyre pressure is to go out on the track, gradually increasing or decreasing and noting how this changes a car's behaviour.

In terms of handling, a rough guide is that if you're planning to counter oversteer, you should increase rear tyre pressure (this also helps smooth the steering). Increasing front pressure, meanwhile, reduces understeer and improves turn-in ability.

Often the consideration is rarely that simple, however. Track temperature also comes into the mix – if it's high you run the risk of overheating the tyres so it's wise to lower the pressure, whereas if it's too low you should increase the pressure to ensure the tyres generate more heat (as a result of higher load values) and keep their operating temperature and therefore grip level. Generally a lower pressure tyre will heat up more quickly but run at lower temperature and offer less responsiveness. At higher pressures there's more responsiveness and speed, but the tyre can overheat, resulting in loss of overall grip.

The type of compound being used also plays a part – remember that harder compounds can handle higher pressures because they don't generate heat as easily as their softer counterparts.

Lastly, the thing to remember is that whichever pressure you start off with it will inevitably go up once the car is running. That's because as tyres warm up, the heat build-up increases the pressure inside them. So this must also be taken into account when playing around with pressure settings.

Temperature

Tyres need heat to provide traction and it may take several laps before they reach operating temperature (high downforce cars will normally heat their tyres up quicker). So until that happens (and in games that model tyre temperature, clearly) be aware that you're unlikely to have the necessary grip to follow the racing line at the usual racing speed; so think about extending your braking distances and reducing cornering velocity.

Just as you can have a lack of traction with too low a tyre temperature, the same is true of tyres that overheat (as a result of too high a pressure setting, for instance). In games, excessive tyre heat is a relatively rare occurrence, however.

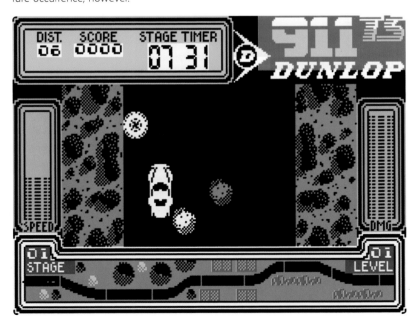

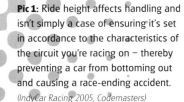

Pic 1: Ride height affects handling and isn't simply a case of ensuring it's set in accordance to the characteristics of the circuit you're racing on – thereby preventing a car from bottoming out and causing a race-ending accident.
(IndyCar Racing 2005, Codemasters)

Pic 2: Sim-flavoured console titles such as *Gran Turismo 5 Prologue* tend to include several aspects of set-up but try to present these in a manner that won't alienate the wide-ranging audience that plays them.
(Sony Computer Entertainment)

Suspension

Without suspension, you wouldn't be able to negotiate a circuit at the speeds racing cars – virtual or otherwise – allow. You'd simply skit your way off the track. Not to mention the fact that your osteopath would be kept busy. Remove shock absorbers (sprung, hydraulic devices that resist chassis behaviour by forcing fluid through valved passages), and you just wouldn't have anything resembling handling.

So suspension plays a vital role in getting a car around a track, particularly around bends and during direction changes because of the way it manages the weight transfer forces involved, while keeping you on the black stuff and away from gravel traps or, worse, the Armco.

Spring rate

This, in a sense, is the 'strength' of the springs used in the suspension assembly so as to control a car's weight transfer during cornering, acceleration and braking. Too soft and the resistance won't be enough to prevent the vehicle from bottoming out, resulting in loss of control. Too hard and it will be tantamount to having no suspension. In a racing car driver comfort isn't much of a consideration, so the tendency is to operate within the harder side of the equation, though there are still great effect differences to be felt within this limited range and both car category and track conditions obviously come into play.

As such, only general guidelines can be given: softening the front spring rate increases grip and reduces understeer, while stiffening the rear values increases oversteer.

Damping

Damping controls the travel speed and resistance of a car's suspension by altering the resistance to fluid flow in the shock absorber. A properly set up car, with appropriate damping levels, will quickly settle once its suspension has been 'disturbed' – a crucial aspect for a racing car travelling at absurd speed – and will therefore affect grip levels.

Bump stiffness and rebound stiffness relate to a shock absorber's resistance to being compressed and extended respectively. Both affect a car's behaviour when turning, so that increasing either at the front increases understeer, while doing the same at the rear increases oversteer. For maximum efficiency the two values should be set not too far from each other.

Ride height

This refers to the distance between the lowest part of the vehicle and the (flat) track beneath it, in other words the ground clearance. Altering the ride height has significant effects on a car's handling – a high ride height means the centre of gravity will be higher, thus increasing body roll and affecting cornering ability, as well as interfering with aerodynamics (although a higher rear ride height can help with weight transfer during acceleration). A lower ride height cures these problems, but care must be taken to consider the bumpiness and profile of the track in ensuring a safe minimum setting or the car will bottom out and you'll lose control.

Anti-roll bars

An anti-roll bar is used to control body lean when cornering. It's essentially a piece of steel that connects to the top of the right and left suspension assemblies, resisting the tendency of a car's sides to roll at different rates in turns.

That balance of the stiffness of front and rear anti-roll bars determines the car's under- and oversteering

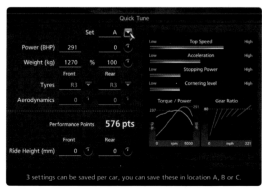

characteristics. Decreasing stiffness at the front reduces understeer, whereas doing the same at the rear decreases oversteer.

There are also advantages in setting the bar to force the inside wheels in certain cars to lift during hard cornering. In racing applications the bar is usually adjustable so as to set the tension level in accordance to the demands of the track. On rougher surfaces, for instance, it's worth remembering that any bumps affecting a wheel are transferred to the opposing wheel 'through' the bar, affecting the handling.

Gear ratios

Don't worry, this isn't about the equations needed to work out gear ratios. However, it's important to have even a rudimentary understanding of how gearing affects a car's acceleration and speed in order to tweak the settings to suit a circuit's characteristics.

Some games occasionally only give you the choice between low (or short), normal and high (long) gearing. A lower gear set-up offers better acceleration through the gears but a slower top speed – it's therefore suited to a circuit made predominantly of short straights and tight corners – something like the Monaco Grand Prix track, for instance. Comparatively, a high gear set-up suffers in the acceleration department but is able to reach a higher top speed in each gear. This setting is suitable with circuits with long straights and fast, open corners – Monza is a perfect example.

In simracing and some of the more advanced console driving titles you're given the ability to tweak the settings for each individual gear, meaning you can tailor the gear ratios to ensure your engine's characteristics suit a circuit perfectly. It may be that you need a slightly longer fourth gear just to be able take advantage of the last few metres of a medium-length straight in an otherwise slow-speed, corner-heavy track, for example. Whatever it may be, working out the individual gearing requirements for a track can only be done by getting out in the car and driving, making a note of where you're changing up needlessly, not accelerating quickly enough or lacking top speed, and adjusting accordingly.

Differential

If you imagine a car going round a corner, think about how the inner wheel has to travel on a shorter radius than the outer wheel. The outer wheel covers a wider radius, and therefore has a longer journey than its inner counterpart. If cars had a solid axle, you can see how this would cause conflict – the inner driven wheel would be fighting to keep to its shorter trajectory but would inevitably spin as a result of the outer wheel having no choice but to cover the longer distance (though clearly the outer wheel can also drag when the inner wheel gets its way – usually both effects occur during cornering).

As an example, this is what a kart has to deal with, and in order for it to be able to turn (and minimise time lost to wheels spinning or dragging) the idea is to lift the inside wheel when rounding a bend.

In a car that's less practical, and so a differential comes into play. Its function is to drive two wheels with the same torque, but allow those wheels to spin at different speeds when necessary. However, a standard production car differential won't do in a race application where you need to maximise drive while still trying to incorporate the difference in rotational speed between the driven wheels. So the use of a limited slip differential (LSD) effectively 'locks' at a predetermined point to limit that difference in speed between the driven wheels and increase traction under acceleration and deceleration.

Braking

Brakes, apart from ensuring your car doesn't end up a crumpled mess at the end of every long straight, are a fundamental element of racing because, more often

Pic 1: Braking may have been recreated in increasingly realistic aesthetic fashion in recent years, but in-game it remains one area that varies greatly in its ability to convince from one game to another. *(Gran Turismo 4, Sony Computer Entertainment)*

Pic 2: If leading simracing titles like *Live for Speed* bother themselves with going as far as modelling tyre dynamics, real-world elements like tweaking brake balance and dealing with fuel aspects are obvious and expected inclusions. *(Live for Speed)*

Pic 3: Set-up options have traditionally been considerably more limited on console titles than PC sims. But the essence of brakes, suspension, gear ratios and tyres is often covered, as shown in the first *Colin McRae Rally*. *(Codemasters, courtesy of Edge magazine)*

than not, they're the key to setting a great lap. There is arguably more time to be gained from getting the braking component of a corner right than the accelerating segment that leads out of it. As such, ensuring the brakes work for the car and your driving style becomes paramount.

Brake pressure

This refers to the amount of pedal travel needed to lock the wheels under braking. If you reduce the pressure, you increase the pedal travel, which is often necessary in force feedback wheel and pedal set-ups in order to enable a more progressive 'feel' of the brakes. But it can also come into play with joypads.

Brake balance

Brake balance determines the braking force being applied to the front and rear brakes of the car. In doing so, it affects a car's weight transfer behaviour, which in turn determines under- and oversteer characteristics. Increasing the front bias results in better stability but with additional understeering tendencies. Moving the balance over to the rear, meanwhile, increases oversteer but you also lose stability. Either way, the settings are delicate and never hover too far from a perfect 50/50 balance.

Aerodynamics

An extraordinarily complicated field – notice how much of a Formula 1 team's budget is spent on research in this area alone – but one that will be dealt with here in

Pic 1: While aerodynamics is a hugely intricate affair, thankfully games only concern themselves with wing settings. One of the early and very basic examples can be found in *REVS* but in reality it's not a world away from what is required today. *(Acornsoft)*

Pic 2: The nature of certain console games requires them to include fuel level as part of the fun – this is 1996's *Formula 1* for PlayStation. *(Psygnosis)*

Pic 3: Fuel concerns in simracing titles is almost a given, but for added realism examples now model fuel load as well as level. *(F1GP2, MicroProse)*

Pic 4: Production car-based games like *Forza Motorsport 2* often include driving aids such as STM – stability management. *(Microsoft Game Studios)*

absolutely basic terms for the purposes of a very generalised assessment.

In short, when a car moves through air it disturbs it in a way that creates 'lift' underneath it. Clearly this has considerable repercussions for handling. One way to combat this is to create downforce, which pushes the car into the track, thereby increasing grip and handling but increasing drag – which slows the car down – and tyre wear.

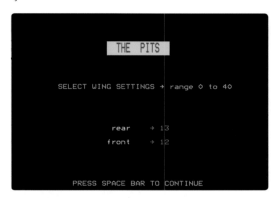

Driving aids

Now commonplace in nearly every car manufactured, driving aids also show up in driving games with increasing regularity. Their terminology tends to make them generally self-explanatory and so they're mentioned here briefly, and primarily to suggest how much fun you could have by switching them off (at which point a steering wheel and pedal set-up is recommended).

Anti-lock braking system (ABS)

A safety system designed to prevent a car's wheels from locking up during heavy braking and therefore enable road users to maintain control of their vehicle and even steer themselves out of trouble. There's no denying its effectiveness, although in a racing game situation there is arguably more reward to be had from learning to judge a car's braking limits without relying on ABS.

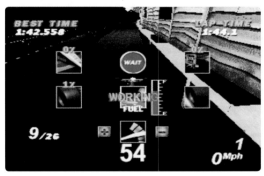

Fuel

Relatively few games bother with fuel load and fuel consumption. But for those that do, remember that a car set up for a qualifying lap with minimal fuel in the tank won't handle the same way when it's filled up for the race, so you'll need to tweak the settings accordingly. A heavier car will also eat its tyres up more quickly, so that's another consideration when planning pit/refuelling stops.

Fuel economy is partly governed by driving style, but remember that it's also affected by downforce (the more you have, the more drag you create and therefore the harder the engine has to work) and gear ratios (a lower ratio burns more petrol over the course of a race).

Traction control system (TCS or ASR)

Initially designed to 'smooth out' abrupt driver input in high-performance road cars by automatically regulating the power going to any driven wheel and therefore preventing the loss of traction, TCS is now found in a wide range of vehicles. Its advantage in racing car applications is obvious in the way TCS maximises traction under acceleration, without allowing wheel spin.

Electronic stability control (ESC)

A more intrusive system than those above, ESC monitors a driver's intended trajectory with the car's actual movement and automatically steps in to correct any detected loss of control by applying braking to individual wheels until tyres have regained traction. While undoubtedly useful for everyday drivers, it should really have no place in a racing game.

(Virtual-E Corporation)

Player Set-up

Pic 1: For years it's been unrealistic to expect driving peripherals within the domestic setting to be able to replicate the industrial-strength build of the set-ups of arcades, which have been designed to withstand years of heavy handed abuse. Yet for those prepared to invest in their hobby there now exist numerous wheels and simulators that in the right combination deliver an experience that will eclipse that offered by a purpose-built yet generic arcade driving game cabinet. *(Author)*

Introduction

In all likelihood, simracing fans will already possess a driving simulator environment conducive to great lap times and able to recreate a convincing driving experience – you wouldn't be able to play the likes of *Live for Speed* or *iRacing* using the keyboard or a joystick, after all.

So the primary purpose of this chapter is to communicate to console owners the transformation to be found in playing your favourite racing game with a force feedback wheel and pedal set-up, to name the most immediate 'upgrade'. Because while some joypads can do an impressive job in communicating the essence of driving a car (particularly if they include rumble function to provide a morsel of 'feedback') – and in fact they remain preferable over wheels for a handful of games – there is little that beats the experience of getting to grips with your digital racing

Pic 1: A force feedback wheel can make all the difference. *(Microsoft)*

Pic 2: Now lagging technologically next to the home consoles, arcade experiences rely on extravagant set-ups to tempt players. *(Author)*

Pic 3: The introduction of analogue control in joypads – in this case the PlayStation's DualShock – has played an integral part in the evolution of the console driving game by enabling the implementation of better handling dynamics. *(Sony Computer Entertainment)*

Pic 4: Over the years several attempts at novel analogue control for driving titles such as Namco's intriguing NeGcon have emerged. *(Namco)*

Pic 5: Driving Force GT is the latest in official *Gran Turismo* wheels. *(Logitech)*

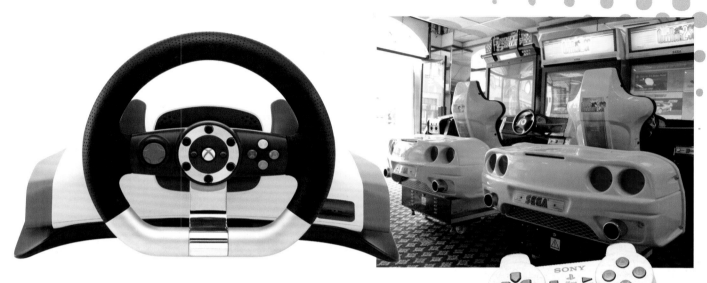

machine via the control method that best approximates its real-world equivalent.

For those that are really serious, the next step is arguably a home racing simulator. For clarity, it's worth mentioning that 'racing simulator' in this chapter refers not to the style of driving game but the seating structures specifically designed to accommodate wheels and pedals in order to replicate the position and experience of driving a car. They range as much in complexity as they do price and practicality, but again their contribution with regards to increasing a player's level of involvement far outweighs the expense and effort required.

That said, there are smaller additions to your virtual racing experience that will also vastly increase its enjoyment, and these are dealt with here too.

Force feedback steering wheels

Today's generation can walk into a game shop and select from a relatively wide variety of force feedback wheels – where motors work against your steering input and react to the surface of the road to increase the level of handling feedback – and pedal set-ups. It wasn't so long ago, however, that gamers faced no such abundance of choice.

It's no exaggeration to say that the first home steering wheel and pedal set-ups to appear were abysmal. Anyone coming home from their PC specialist store in the mid-'90s, excitedly hoping to recreate what they'd experienced at their local arcade in *Ridge Racer* or *Sega Rally Championship* – two examples with

memorable force feedback wheels – would invariably end up bitterly disappointed. Home units back then were simply and poorly made, broke easily and regularly, proved to be of limited use and were extremely expensive.

Because of the success of simulations such as *IndyCar Racing* and *Formula One Grand Prix*, the first 'serious' wheels appeared for the PC and from there things developed relatively quickly, so that the simracing community didn't have to wait too long before decent sim-like models worthy of the rapidly evolving subgenre became available.

On console, the story was similar in that the first models – that is, the first models attempting to move on from the highly simplistic such peripherals that had previously appeared on early consoles and computers of the '70s and '80s (few who experienced it are ever likely to forget the 'steering wheel' that came bundled with 1984's *Formula 1 Simulator* on the Spectrum) – were also dreadful. But then so were those that followed for

Player Set-up

Pic 1: The *Gran Turismo* series has been instrumental in driving console wheel technology forward. *(Sony Computer Entertainment)*

Pic 2: The preferred choice of most simracers, Logitech's G25 is a high-end force feedback wheel and pedal set-up that distinguishes itself through the quality of its build – which features, amongst others, dual motors and different pedal resistance levels – as well as a seven-speed gearstick add-on. *(Logitech)*

the remainder of the 1990s – just as console driving experiences lagged behind those on PC with regards to handling, so did the peripherals available.

It took the release of *Gran Turismo 3: A-spec* on PlayStation 2 in 2001 to see the arrival of the first genuine force feedback analogue wheel for console that proved rewarding to use. (Although they were more than happy to label it as such on the box of their products, few manufacturers at the time offered true force feedback and instead simply included a 'rumble' feature similar to that found on some consoles' joypads – hardly a convincing compromise).

By this point, PC owners were enjoying a considerable choice of peripherals, with leading manufacturers occasionally offering licensed versions from renowned real-world motorsport specialists, which might have included leather bound wheels and metal pedals, for instance. Consoles again followed suit (though stuck stubbornly with plastic), yet the majority of these branded wheels – just like nearly all console wheels – proved

disappointing in terms of feedback and driving precision.

Again it was left to the console racing's biggest brand, *Gran Turismo*, to push things forward with the series' fourth instalment (*GT4 Prologue*). Another Logitech-developed official wheel, this time with 900-degree rotation, stronger feedback and incorporating a sequential gearstick, appeared in 2003, offering the kind of quality and precision only otherwise available on PC at the time.

These days the balance of choice still swings towards the PC user, but even official wheel and pedal set-ups for current consoles (such as Microsoft's Xbox 360 Wireless Steering Wheel) provide a very decent experience. At the higher end of the market for console (specifically PlayStation 3) you can expect models with metal and hand-stitched leather wheel, fully adjustable metal pedals, a six-speed gate (plus reverse) and sequential gearstick, alternative paddle shift option, simulation-grade force feedback and separate programmable button console. Beyond the

Pic 1: If you haven't tried the multi-screen version of *Forza Motorsport 2*, you haven't lived. *(Microsoft)*

Pic 2: Given enough money, it is possible to enjoy hydraulic-powered simulators at home. But why bother when the VRX Mach 4, with its triple 37-inch LCD, rearview 'mirror', four Xbox Elites, 5.1 surround sound, integrated 1,500W transducer, and even wind-generating devices is likely to provide all the fun you'll ever need? *(VRX Industries)*

'ready-made' wheel and pedal set-ups, on PC things get considerably more hardcore, with companies specialising in commercial grade standalone pedal, wheel or gearstick units for the simracing community that appear in look and build indistinguishable from their real-life equivalents.

Admittedly, only the more serious driving game players will consider investing in a wheel and pedals, but the universal response by anyone who first experiences force feedback steering either on console or PC is highly positive. It genuinely makes an enormous difference in terms of enhancing virtual driving, with the force feedback element conveying every nuance a driver may face (anything from the engine start to backfire, contact, loss of traction, blown tyre, ice-covered surfaces, gravel, mud, rumble strips, chassis damage and much, much more). That a wheel and pedal set-up is indispensable for simracing is a given, but it's worth realising console simulation-style titles will benefit immeasurably. (From experience, strictly arcade affairs such as *Burnout* still tend to work considerably better on joypad, so a wheel isn't to be considered a one-size-fits-all solution). For anyone wanting to extract the best experience from realism-based games, it is a highly recommended control solution.

Home racing simulators

In the same way that home racing games have surpassed arcade games technically, there are now solutions in terms of creating your own personal virtual racing simulator that would shame many arcade cabinets. Granted, few homes in the world will ever boast anything that will beat an eight-player *Daytona USA* commercial set-up, but that's not to say there aren't some exceptionally advanced racing simulators for those with the room – and the budget – to own such things.

At the top of the range for the domestic market expect to find full hydraulic, multi-directional cabinets designed to replicate the g-forces felt in racing, complete with mounted projector and screen. But even before you go down the hydraulic road, a high-end fixed driving simulator can include multiple screens (for games that support them), full surround sound (complete with separate bass/vibration unit), genuine race seat and even front-mounted wind machines to simulate movement.

Naturally these commercially available, ready-to-build (or ready-built) set-ups come at a price and remain beyond the reach of many. But the really determined will find a way – it's not unusual to come across simracing aficionados who've managed to transform the front end of a scrapped single-seater into a personal virtual racing module, housing their monitor, PC, wheel and pedals, gearstick and so on.

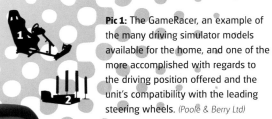

Pic 1: The GameRacer, an example of the many driving simulator models available for the home, and one of the more accomplished with regards to the driving position offered and the unit's compatibility with the leading steering wheels. *(Poole & Berry Ltd)*

Pic 2: Surround sound in driving games makes all the difference, so make sure you're not missing out on the significant level of involvement a decent set-up can deliver. And if you can't feel the engine vibrations in your chest, it's not loud enough. *(Sony)*

instance), to get an idea of how a particular simulator model rates amongst users, is advisable.

Other elements to watch out for are the sturdiness of the wheel and pedal support – there's little worse than a wobbly wheel and loose pedal assembly – as well as, preferably, a universal mounting plate to enable the attachment of other wheels (should you upgrade or change console – and therefore wheel).

Sound

It's very common for people to play video games – any genre, not just driving titles – with the sound far lower than they ought to. Clearly there are considerations to be taken into account with regard to other members of the household, neighbours and so on, but only when you realise that the aural part of a game (as in a film) is as important as the visuals do you get an idea of what you're potentially missing out on.

If you are indeed in a situation where it's simply impossible to turn up the volume without feeling intimidated every time you blip the throttle of your virtual 1966 GT40 MkII (which is roughly the level you ideally want the sound to be at), then one immediate compromise is to invest in a decent pair of (surround sound) headphones.

If that still sounds like the kind of dedication you lack, but the appeal of such a driving simulator lingers, then consider the lower-end solutions. These are no frills, simple metal structures that normally consist of a seat and wheel and pedal assembly plates on which to mount your favoured control choice. But don't let their basic, functional appearance fool you – the effect can be every bit as convincing. Besides, they compensate in practicality for some of what they may lack in luxury – many models pack relatively neatly away when not in use. Try doing that with your three-37in screen, four-Xbox 360 *Forza Motorsport 2* fully loaded set-up.

The choice in this sector is wider than you might expect and while it is difficult to try before you buy, one consideration is that not all of the units available offer a good sitting position – and bear in mind that you could be spending relatively long stints in the simulator if you're doing a few laps of the Nordschleife. So a little research online (through game forums, for

Pic 1: If you have the space, larger and high-end home driving simulators such as the stylish Virtual GT are just waiting to fill it. Assuming you can justify such a purchase to your partner or parents, of course. *(Virtual-E Corporation)*

Pic 2: The aptly named ButtKicker LFE is one example of a powerful low frequency effects transducer – meaning you feel the bass, rather than hear it – designed for home cinema use that has also found itself part of simracing rigs. *(The Guitammer Company)*

If, however, your street loves the sweet melody of a finely tuned race engine as much as you do, then the next step is to ensure that you're playing your games loudly and, crucially, in surround sound. Again, the difference in the quality of the game experience, regardless of genre, increases exponentially with a 5.1-channel set-up. But it's not just the atmosphere levels that rev up – being in the thick of the sonic action brings with it gameplay implications, in that you're able to determine the position of opponents about to put a move on you, or even get additional feedback on what your car is up to from the sound coming from each individual tyre.

Additional elements

Aside from the aspects already mentioned in this chapter and the suggestion that you play with a generously sized monitor or television to enhance the level of immersion, there are other elements that can add to your domestic virtual racing experience.

Perhaps the most basic, yet surprisingly convincing, is the addition of a low frequency speaker (a subwoofer or transducer) unit to provide the vibrations normally associated with a racing car. Some products are specifically designed for gaming applications and will usually attach to your racing simulator rig or sit underneath it, and activate with engine revs and any other aspect that will trigger its use (such as riding kerbs and contact with opponents or circuit barriers).

At the other end of the technological spectrum, consider a chair incorporating G-seat technology. Powered by electric motors, the chair's various pressure pads react to in-game events to give the illusion of the g-forces a driver would experience in real life.

Another item that attempts to increase player engagement is a head tracking device. Available for PC simracing applications, these units attach to a headset or hat and will transfer your real-life head movements into real-time in-game head motion, so that wherever you look while in cockpit view, the game display will move accordingly. Want to see if there's anyone on the inside as you turn-in? Just turn your head and take a look.

These are three examples of how companies strive to increase the home virtual racing experience. As racing games develop – both in scope and community – expect products to develop alongside them designed purely to enhance the level of immersion, particularly as new technology advancements are made.

The day when you no longer need to visit your local track to get your racing kicks will come.

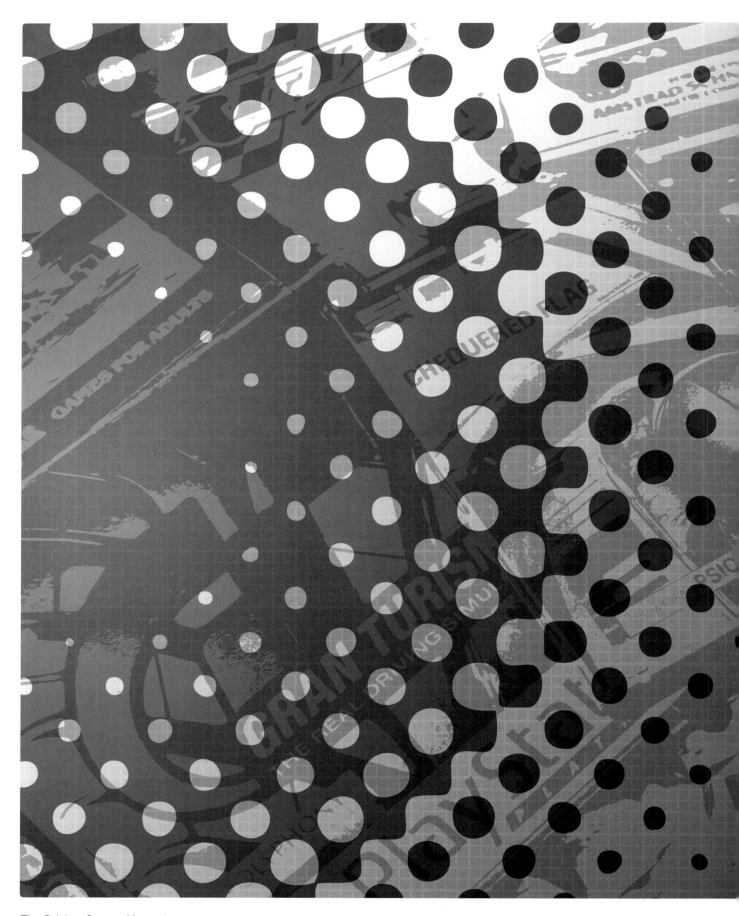

The Driving Games Manual

The Driving Games List

Introduction

The selection criteria for the games researched for this book are detailed in Chapter 1. So what you find here is by no means an exhaustive listing of every racing game ever created and published – that would run into a few thousand – but in its carefully selected form it does represent as comprehensive a selection of car-related titles to have been released in the West as research has allowed.

Aside from arcade titles, the games listed in this chapter relate to official releases for the most prominent commercially available consoles in European and North American territories. In total, that selection represents around 700 games across 44 formats.

For reference, the games have been listed according to the following structure:

Game Name (Year)
Format
Developer
Publisher

Where possible the dates are those of European release, with the exception of arcade games, where the distribution model works a little differently from that of console and computer titles and so release dates can be nebulous. Therefore, for arcade titles the original territory release date applies.

Lastly, as a result of space constraints some of the formats have been abbreviated. You'll find their full names in the list below:

32X – Sega Mega Drive 32X
360 – Microsoft Xbox 360
400/800 – Atari 400, Atari 800
2600 – Atari 2600
5200 – Atari 5200
7800 – Atari 7800
3DO
Amiga – Commodore Amiga
Apple II
Arcade
BBC Micro
C128 – Commodore 128
C64 – Commodore 64
CD-i – Philips CD-i
CD32 – Commodore CD32

ColecoVision – CBS ColecoVision
CPC – Amstrad CPC
DC – Sega Dreamcast
GC – Nintendo GameCube
Intellivision – Mattel Intellivision
Jaguar – Atari Jaguar
Mac – Apple Macintosh
MD – Sega Mega Drive
MS – Sega Master System
MSX
Neo Geo – SNK Neo Geo AES
N64 – Nintendo 64
NES – Nintendo Entertainment System
Odyssey – Magnavox Odyssey2
PC – DOS & Windows

PS – Sony PlayStation
PS2 – Sony PlayStation 2
PS3 – Sony PlayStation 3
Sat – Sega Saturn
Sega CD
SNES – Super Nintendo Entertainment System
ST – Atari ST
TG-16 – NEC TurboGrafx-16
TI-99/4A – Texas Instruments TI-99/4A
VIC-20 – Commodore VIC-20
Vectrex
Wii – Nintendo Wii
Xb – Microsoft Xbox
ZX – Sinclair ZX Spectrum

---

007 Car Chase (1985)
C64
N. Coplin
Coplin Software

1000 Miglia (1991)
Amiga; C64, PC (1992)
Simulmondo
Simulmondo

280-ZZZAP (1976)
Arcade
Midway
Midway

3D Stock Car Championship (1988)
ZX
Ace Software
Firebird

4 Wheel Thunder (2000)
DC
Kalisto
Midway

4x4 Evolution (2000)
Mac, PC; DC, PS2 (2001)
Terminal Reality
2K Games

4x4 Evolution 2 (2002)
GC, PC, Xb; Mac, PS2 (2003)
Terminal Reality
2K Games (PC, Xb), Universal Interactive (GC), BAM! (Mac, PS2)

4x4 Off-Road Racing (1988)
Amiga, C64, CPC, MSX, PC, ZX; ST (1989)
MicroDesign (CPC), **Epyx** (C64)
Epyx, US Gold (CPC, MSX, ST, ZX)

911 TS (1985)
ZX
Elite Systems
Elite Systems

A history of Driving Games

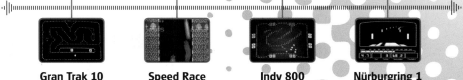

1974

Gran Trak 10
Atari

1974
Speed Race
Taito

1975

Indy 800
Kee Games

1975

Nürburgring 1
Trakus

Ace Driver (1994)
Arcade
Namco
Namco

African Raiders-01 (1988)
ST; Amiga, PC (1989)
Coktel Vision
Tomahawk

Aguri Suzuki F-1 Super Driving (aka Redline: F1 Racer) (1993)
SNES
Absolute Entertainment
Absolute Entertainment

Al Unsen Jr Arcade Racing (1995)
Mac, PC
Mindscape
Mindscape

Alley Rally (1976)
Arcade
Exidy
Exidy

Andretti Racing (1996)
PS; PC, Saturn (1997)
Stormfront Studios, High Score Entertainment (PC), **Press Start** (Saturn)
Electronic Arts

APB (1987)
Arcade; Amiga, C64, CPC, PC, ZX, ST (1989)
Atari
Atari (Arcade), Domark

ARCA Sim Racing (2008)
PC
The Sim Factory
The Sim Factory

ATR: All Terrain Racing (1995)
Amiga, CD32
Team 17 Software
Team 17 Software

Auto Modellista (2002)
PS2, GC (2003), Xb (2004)
Capcom Production Studio 1
Capcom

Auto Racing (1979)
Intellivision
APh Tech Consulting
Mattel Electronics

Automobili Lamborghini (aka Lamborghini 64) (1997)
Nintendo 64
Titus Software
Titus Software

Autotest (1990)
C64
Daisy Soft
Byte Back

Ayrton Senna's Super Monaco GP II (1992)
MD, MS
Sega
Sega

BAJA: Edge of Control (2008)
360, PS3
2XL Games
THQ

Baja Buggies (1982)
400/800
Gamestar
Gamestar

Battle Gear (1999)
Arcade
Taito
Taito

Battle Gear 3 (2004)
Arcade
Taito
Taito

Battle Gear 4 (2005)
Arcade
Taito
Taito

Battle Gear 4 Tuned (2006)
Arcade
Taito
Taito

Battle OutRun (1989)
MS
Sega
Sega

Beetle Adventure Racing! (1999)
N64
Paradigm Entertainment
Electronic Arts

Beetle Crazy Cup (2000)
PC
Xpiral
Infogrames

Bigfoot (1990)
NES
Beam Software
Acclaim

Bikini Beach: Stunt Racer (2003)
PC, PS2
Davilex
Davilex

Bill Elliott's NASCAR Challenge (1990)
PC; Amiga, Mac, NES (1991)
Distinctive Software
Konami

Buggy (1998)
PC, PS, Saturn
Gremlin Interactive
Gremlin Interactive

Buggy Boy (aka Speed Buggy) (1985)
Arcade; C64, CPC (1987), Amiga, ST, ZX (1988)
Tatsumi Electronics; Maz Spork, Paul Walker, Mark Cooksey (ZX); **Dave & Bob Thomas** (C64)
Taito; Elite Systems (C64/ZX)

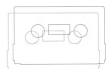

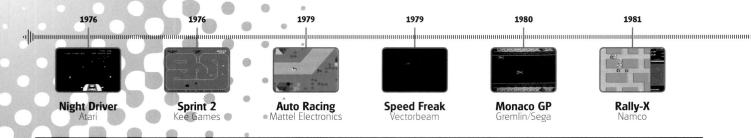

1976	1976	1979	1979	1980	1981
Night Driver Atari	**Sprint 2** Kee Games	**Auto Racing** Mattel Electronics	**Speed Freak** Vectorbeam	**Monaco GP** Gremlin/Sega	**Rally-X** Namco

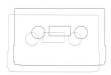

Buggy Challenge (1984)
Arcade
Taito
Taito

Buggy Heat (aka TNN
Motorsports Hardcore Heat) (1999)
DC
CRI
Sega

Buggy Run (1993)
MS
SIMS
Sega

Bump'n Jump
(aka Burnin' Rubber) (1982)
Arcade; 2600, C64, Intellivision
(1983); ColecoVision (1984), NES (1988)
Bally Midway
Bally Midway, Mattel Electronics
(2600, Intellivision), **Coleco**
(ColecoVision), **Vic Tokai** (NES)

Bumping Buggies (1984)
C64
Bubble Bus Software
Bubble Bus Software

Burning Rubber (1993)
Amiga, ST
Harlequin
Ocean Software

Burnout (2001)
PS2; GC, Xb (2002)
Criterion Games
Acclaim

Burnout 2:
Point of Impact (2002)
PS2; GC, Xb (2003)
Criterion Games
Acclaim

Burnout 3: Takedown (2004)
PS2, Xb
Criterion Games
Electronic Arts

Burnout Dominator (2007)
PS2
Criterion Games/EA UK
Electronic Arts

Burnout Paradise (2008)
360, PC, PS3
Criterion Games
Electronic Arts

Burnout Revenge (2005)
PS2, Xb, 360 (2006)
Criterion Games
Electronic Arts

California Speed (1998)
Arcade, N64 (1999)
Atari Games
Atari Games, Midway (N64)

Carlos Sainz (1990)
CPC, MSX, PC, ZX
Zigurat
Zigurat

Carmageddon (1997)
PC
Stainless Software
Interplay

Cars (2006)
360, GC, Mac, PC, PS2, Xb, Wii
Rainbow Studios
THQ

CART Fury: Championship
Racing (2000)
Arcade, PS2 (2001)
Midway Games
Midway Games

CART Precision Racing:
IndyCar Simulator (1997)
PC
TRI
Microsoft

CART Racing (1997)
PC
Papyrus Design Group
Sierra

CART World Series (1997)
PS
**Sony Computer
Entertainment America**
Sony Computer Entertainment

Champion Driver (1991)
Amiga
Idea Software
Idea Software

Championship Run (1991)
Amiga, ST, ZX
Impulze
Impulze

Championship Sprint (1986)
Arcade; C64 (1987), ZX
(1988), PS3 (2007)
Atari
Atari, Electric Dreams Software (C64,
ZX), Sony Online Entertainment (PS3)

Change Lanes (1983)
Arcade
Taito
Taito

Chase HQ (1988)
Arcade; Amiga, C64, CPC, MSX,
NES, SNES, ST, ZX (1989), MS
(1991), TG-16 (1992), Saturn (1996)
Taito
Taito (Arcade, MS, NES), **Ocean** (others)

Chase HQ II (1992)
MD
Taito
Taito

Chase HQ 2 (2006)
Arcade
Taito
Taito

Chequered Flag (1983)
ZX
Psion
Sinclair Research

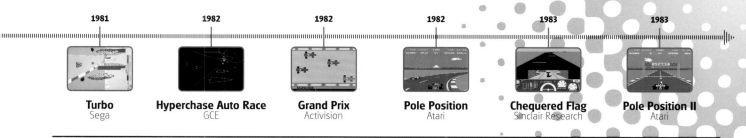

1981	1982	1982	1982	1983	1983
Turbo Sega	**Hyperchase Auto Race** GCE	**Grand Prix** Activision	**Pole Position** Atari	**Chequered Flag** Sinclair Research	**Pole Position II** Atari

Chequered Flag (1994)
Jaguar
Rebellion
Atari

Chevy Chase (1991)
C64
P.A.L Developments
HiTec Software

Chicago 90 (1989)
Amiga, CPC, PC, ST
Microïds
Microïds

Choro Q (1984)
MSX
Taito
Taito

ChoroQ (2004)
PS2
Barnhouse Effect
Atlus

Cisco Heat: All American Police Car Chase (1990)
Arcade; Amiga, C64, CPC, PC, ZX, ST (1991)
Jaleco, Ice Software (C64)
Jaleco, Imageworks (C64)

City Connection (1985)
Arcade, MSX (1986), NES (1988), Wii (2008)
Jaleco, Hect/NMK (MSX)
Jaleco

The Classic Lotus Trilogy (1994)
CD32
Magnetic Fields
Gremlin Graphics

Club Drive (1994)
Jaguar
Atari
Atari

Club Kart (2000)
Arcade
Sega
Sega

Coaster Race (1986)
MSX
Sony Corporation
Sony Corporation

Colin McRae: DiRT (2007)
360, PC, PS3
Codemasters
Codemasters

Colin McRae Rally (1998)
PC, PS
Codemasters
Codemasters

Colin McRae Rally 04 (2003)
PS2, Xb, PC (2004)
Codemasters
Codemasters

Colin McRae Rally 2.0 (2000)
DC, PC, PS
Codemasters
Codemasters

Colin McRae Rally 3 (2002)
PS2, Xb, PC (2003)
Codemasters
Codemasters

Colin McRae Rally 2005 (2004)
PC, PS2, Xb; Mac (2007)
Codemasters
Codemasters, Feral Interactive (Mac)

Continental Circus (aka Continental Circuit) (1987)
Arcade; Amiga, C64, CPC, MSX, ZX, ST (1989)
Taito, Teque (ZX)
Taito (Arcade), Virgin Mastertronic (others)

Corvette GT Evolution (2006)
PC, PS2
Milestone
Valcon Games

Corvette: Zero To Gone (aka Corvette) (2003)
PC, Xb, PS2 (2004)
Steel Monkeys
2K Games

Crash (1979)
Arcade
Exidy
Exidy

Crash 'n' Burn (2004)
PS2, Xb
Climax
Eidos Interactive

Crash 'n Score (1975)
Arcade
Atari
Atari

Crashed (aka Totaled!) (2002)
PS2, Xb
Rage Sheffield
Rage

Crashing Race (1976)
Arcade
Taito
Taito

Crazy Cars (1988)
Amiga, C64, CPC, MSX, PC, ST, ZX
Titus
Titus

Crazy Cars 2 (1989)
Amiga, C64, CPC, MSX, PC, ST, ZX; Mac (1990)
Titus
Titus

Crazy Cars III (1992)
Amiga, C64, CPC, PC, ST; SNES (1993); CD32 (1994)
Titus
Titus, Paragon (CD32)

1984 GP World — Sega
1984 Pitstop II — Epyx
1984 Revs — Acornsoft
1984 Championship Sprint — Atari
1985 Buggy Boy — Taito
1986 WEC Le Mans — Konami

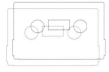

Crazy Streets Thrill Drive (2007)
Arcade
Konami
Konami

Crazy Taxi (1999)
Arcade, DC (2000); GC, PS2 (2001)
AM3 (Arcade)**, Hitmaker**
Sega, Acclaim (GC, PS2)

Crazy Taxi High Roller (2002)
Arcade
Hitmaker
Sega

Crazy Taxi 3: High Roller (2002)
Xb, PC (2004)
Hitmaker
Sega

Cross Racing Championship 2005 (2005)
PC
Invictus Games
Project 3

Cruis'n (2008)
Wii
Midway
Midway

Cruis'n Exotica (1999)
Arcade, N64 (2000)
Midway
Midway

Cruis'n USA (1994)
Arcade, N64 (1996)
Midway
Midway, Nintendo (N64)

Cruis'n World (1996)
Arcade, N64 (1997)
Midway
Midway, Nintendo (N64)

D1GP Professional Drift Game Arcade (2007)
Arcade
Taito
Taito

Dakar 2: The World's Ultimate Rally (2003)
GC, PS2, Xb
Acclaim Studios Cheltenham
Acclaim

Days of Thunder (1990)
Amiga, C64, NES, PC, ZX, ST
Argonaut (PC, ST)**, Creative Materials** (Amiga)**, Tiertex Design Studios** (C64, ZX)**, Beam Software** (NES)
Mindscape

Daytona USA (1994)
Arcade, Saturn (1995), PC (1996)
AM2
Sega

Daytona USA: Championship Edition (1997)
Saturn, PC (as Daytona USA Deluxe)
AM3
Sega

Daytona USA 2: Battle on the Edge (1998)
Arcade
AM2
Sega

Daytona USA 2: Power Edition (1999)
Arcade
AM2
Sega

Daytona USA 2001 (2001)
DC
Amusement Vision
Sega

Death Race (1976)
Arcade
Exidy
Exidy

Death Race 64 (1987)
C64
Atlantis Software
Atlantis Software

Demolition Derby (1977)
Arcade
Chicago Coin
Chicago Coin

Demolition Derby (1985)
Arcade
Bally Midway
Bally Midway

Demolition Racer (1999)
PC, PS
Pitbull Syndicate
Infogrames

Demolition Racer: No Exit (2000)
DC
Pitbull Syndicate
Infogrames

Destruction Derby (1976)
Arcade
Exidy
Exidy

Destruction Derby (1995)
PS; PC, Saturn (1996)
Reflections
Psygnosis

Destruction Derby 2 (1996)
PS, PC
Reflections
Psygnosis

Destruction Derby 64 (1999)
N64
Looking Glass Studios
THQ

Destruction Derby Arenas (2004)
PS2
Studio 33
Gathering

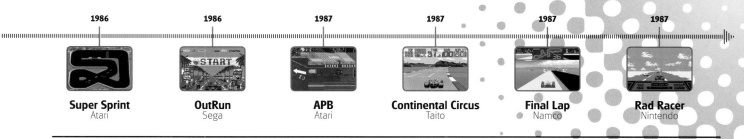

1986
Super Sprint
Atari

1986
OutRun
Sega

1987
APB
Atari

1987
Continental Circus
Taito

1987
Final Lap
Namco

1987
Rad Racer
Nintendo

Destruction Derby Raw
(2000)
PS
Studio 33
Midway Games

Dirt Dash (1995)
Arcade
Namco
Namco

Dirt Devils (1998)
Arcade
AM3
Sega

Dirt Track Racing: Sprint Cars (2000)
PC
Ratbag
Atari

Dodge 'Em (1980)
2600
Atari
Atari

Drag Race (1977)
Arcade
Kee Games
Kee Games

Drag Race Eliminator (1986)
C64
Bob Kodadek
Family Software

Dragster (1980)
2600
Activision
Activision

Dragster 64 (1984)
C64
Beam Software
Melbourne House

Drift Out (1991)
Arcade
Visco
Visco

Driven (2002)
N64, PS2
BAM! Studios Europe
BAM! Entertainment

Driver (1999)
PC, PS; Mac (2000)
Reflections
GT Interactive, MacSoft (Mac)

Driver 2 (2000)
PS
Reflections
Infogrames

Driver: Parallel Lines (2006)
PS2, Xb; PC, Wii (2007)
Reflections
Ubisoft

Driver's Edge (1993)
Arcade
Incredible Technologies
Strata Group

Driver's Eyes (1991)
Arcade
Namco
Namco

Driven to Destruction (aka
Test Drive: Eve of Destruction) (2004)
PS2, Xb
Monster Games
Atari

Drivin' Force (1990)
Amiga, ST
Digital Magic Software
Digital Magic Software

Driving Emotion Type-S
(2001)
PS2
Escape
Electronic Arts

Driving Party: Racing in Italy (2000)
Arcade
Konami
Konami

The Duel: Test Drive II (1989)
Amiga, Apple II, C64, CPC, Mac, MSX,
PC, ZX; ST (1990); MD, SNES (1992)
Distinctive Software
Accolade, Dro Soft (MSX)

The Dukes of Hazzard (1984)
ColecoVision
Coleco
Coleco

Dukes of Hazzard: Racing for Home (1999)
PS, PC (2000)
Sinister Games
SouthPeak Interactive

Dukes of Hazzard II: Daisy Dukes It Out (2000)
PS
Sinister Games
SouthPeak Interactive

The Dukes of Hazzard: Return of the General Lee
(2004)
PS2, Xb
Ratbag Pty
Ubisoft

EA Sports NASCAR Racing
(2007)
Arcade
EA Sports
Global VR

Emergency Heroes (2008)
Wii
Ubisoft Reflections/Barcelona
Ubisoft

Enduro (1983)
2600, ZX (1984)
Activision
Activision

Enthusia Professional Racing (2004)
PS2
Konami
Konami

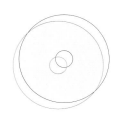

Test Drive
Accolade

Chase HQ
Taito

Hard Drivin'
Atari

Hot Rod
Sega

Power Drift
Sega

**Indianapolis 500:
The Simulation**
Electronic Arts

Excite Truck (2006)
Wii
Monster Games
Nintendo

F-1 Dream (1988)
Arcade
Capcom
Capcom

F-1 Grand Prix (1991)
Arcade
Video System
Video System

F-1 Spirit: 3D Special (1988)
MSX
Konami
Konami

F-1 Spirit: The Way to
Formula 1 (1987)
MSX
Konami
Konami

F-1 Super Battle (1994)
Arcade
Jaleco
Jaleco

F-1 World Grand Prix (1998)
N64
Paradigm Entertainment
Video System

F-1 World Grand Prix II
(1999)
N64
Paradigm Entertainment
Video System

F1 (aka Formula One) (1993)
Amiga, MD, MS, PC (1994)
Lankhor
Domark

F1 2001 (2001)
PC, PS2
Visual Science
Electronic Arts

F1 2002 (2002)
GC, PC, PS2, Xb
Visual Science
Electronic Arts

F1 Career Challenge (2003)
GC, PS2, Xb
Visual Science
Electronic Arts

F1 Challenge '99–'02 (2003)
PC
Image Space Incorporated
Electronic Arts

F1 Championship
Season 2000 (2000)
PC, PS, PS2; Mac (2002)
Visual Science, Image Space (Mac)
Electronic Arts, Feral
Interactive (Mac)

F1 Exhaust Note (1991)
Arcade
Sega
Sega

F1 GP Circuits (1991)
C64
Magnetica
Idea Software

F1 Grand Prix Nakajima
Satoru (1991)
MD
Varie
Varie

F1 Grand Prix Star II (1993)
Arcade
Jaleco
Jaleco

F1 Hero MD (1992)
MD
Aisystem Tokyo
Varie

F1 Pole Position 64 (1997)
N64
Human Entertainment
Ubisoft

F1 Racing (2002)
Arcade
Simaction
Simaction

F1 Racing Championship
(2000)
N64, PS; DC, PC, PS2 (2001)
Ubisoft
Ubisoft

F1 Racing Championship 2
(2002)
PC, PS, PS2
Ubisoft
Ubisoft

F1 Racing Simulation (1997)
PC
Ubisoft
Ubisoft

F1 Super Lap (1993)
Arcade
Sega
Sega

F1 World Championship
Edition (1994)
Amiga, MD
Lankhor
Domark

F1 World Grand Prix (1999)
DC
Video System
Video System

F1 World Grand Prix 2
(2000)
DC
Konami
Konami

F1 World Grand Prix 2000
(2001)
PC, PS
Eutechnyx
Eidos

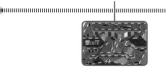
1989
Ivan 'Ironman' Stewart's
Super Off Road
Leland

1989
Turbo OutRun
Sega

1989
Stunt Car Racer
MicroProse Software

1989
Super Monaco GP
Sega

1989
Winning Run
Namco

1990
Lotus Esprit Turbo Challenge
Gremlin Graphics

F1ROC: Race of Champions (1992)
SNES
SETA
SETA

F17 Challenge (1993)
Amiga
Holodream Software
Team 17 Software

F40 Pursuit (1989)
C64
Titus
Titus

F355 Challenge (1999)
Arcade, DC (2000), PS2 (2002)
AM2
Sega

F355 Challenge 2: International Course Edition (2000)
Arcade
AM2
Sega

The Fast and the Furious (2004)
Arcade, PS2, Xb
Namco Bandai, Genki (PS2, Xb)
Namco Bandai, Sierra (PS2, Xb)

The Fast and the Furious (aka The Fast and the Furious: Tokyo Drift) (2006)
PS2
Eutechnyx
Electronic Arts

The Fast and the Furious Drift (2007)
Arcade
Namco Bandai
Namco Bandai

Fast Tracks (1985)
C64
M. Turmell
Activision

Faster Than Speed (2000)
Arcade
Sammy
Sammy

Ferrari Challenge Trofeo Pirelli (2008)
PS2, PS3, Wii
Eutechnyx
System 3

Ferrari Formula One (1988)
Amiga; PC, ST (1989), C64 (1990)
Electronic Arts
Electronic Arts

Final Lap (1987)
Arcade
Namco
Namco

Final Lap 2 (1990)
Arcade
Namco
Namco

Final Lap 3 (1992)
Arcade
Namco
Namco

Final Lap R (1993)
Arcade
Namco
Namco

Final Lap Twin (1990)
TG-16
Namco
NEC

Fisco 400 (1977)
Arcade
Taito
Taito

FlatOut (2004)
PC, PS2, Xb
Bugbear Entertainment
Empire

FlatOut 2 (2006)
PC, PS2, Xb
Bugbear Entertainment
Empire Interactive

FlatOut: Ultimate Carnage (2007)
360, PC (2008)
Bugbear Entertainment
Empire Interactive

Ford Mustang (2005)
PS2, Xb
Eutechnyx
2K Games

Ford Racing 2 (2003)
PC, PS2, Xb; Mac (2004)
Razorworks
Empire, Feral Interactive (Mac)

Ford Racing 3 (2004)
PC, Xb; PS2 (2005)
Razorworks
Empire

Ford Racing Full Blown (2006)
Arcade
Razorworks
Sega

Ford Racing Off Road (2006)
PC, PS2, Wii
Razorworks
Xplosiv (PC), Crave

Ford Street Racing (aka Ford Bold Moves Street Racing) (2006)
PC, PS2, Xb
Razorworks
Xplosive, Empire (Xb)

Ford vs Chevy (2005)
PS2, Xb
Eutechnyx
Global Star Software

Formula 1 (1996)
PS, PC (1997)
Bizarre Creations
Psygnosis

1991	1991	1991	1991	1991	1992

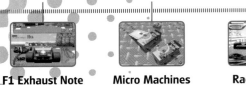

Driver's Eyes
Namco

F1 Exhaust Note
Sega

Micro Machines
Codemasters

Rad Mobile
Sega

Vroom!
Lankhor

Formula One Grand Prix
MicroProse Software

Formula 1 04 (2004)
PS2
Sony Studio Liverpool
Sony Computer Entertainment

Formula 1 05 (2005)
PS2
Sony Studio Liverpool
Sony Computer Entertainment

Formula 1 06 (2006)
PS2
Sony Studio Liverpool
Sony Computer Entertainment

Formula 1 97 (1997)
PS, PC (1998)
Bizarre Creations
Psygnosis

Formula 1 98 (1998)
PS
Visual Science
Psygnosis

Formula 1 Championship Edition (2007)
PS3
Sony Studio Liverpool
Sony Computer Entertainment

Formula 1 Sensation (1993)
NES
Konami
Konami

Formula 1 Simulator (1984)
ZX; C64, CPC, MSX (1985)
Spirit Software, Mr Chip (C64)
Mastertronic

Formula K (1974)
Arcade
Kee Games
Kee Games

Formula Karts: Special Edition (1997)
PS, Saturn
Manic Media Productions
Telstar Electronic Studios

Formula One 99 (1999)
PC, PS
Studio 33
Psygnosis

Formula One 2000 (2000)
PS
Studio 33
Sony Computer Entertainment

Formula One 2001 (2001)
PS, PS2
Studio 33 (PS), **Sony Studio Liverpool** (PS2)
Sony Computer Entertainment

Formula One 2002 (2002)
PS2
Sony Studio Liverpool
Sony Computer Entertainment

Formula One 2003 (2003)
PS2
Sony Studio Liverpool
Sony Computer Entertainment

Formula One Arcade (2002)
PS
Studio 33
Sony Computer Entertainment

Formula One: Built to Win (1990)
NES
Winky Soft
SETA

Formula One Grand Prix
(aka World Circuit) (1992)
PC, Amiga, ST
MicroProse Software
MicroProse Software

Formula One Grand Prix 2 (1996)
PC
Geoff Crammond (P. Cooke, D. Surplus, N. Surplus)
MicroProse

Formula One World Championship: Beyond the Limit (1994)
Sega CD
Sega/Fuji
Sega

Forza Motorsport (2005)
Xb
Turn 10
Microsoft Game Studios

Forza Motorsport 2 (2007)
360
Turn 10 Studios
Microsoft Game Studios

Fuel (2008)
360, PC, PS3
Asobo Studio
Codemasters

Furious Karting (2003)
Xb
Babylon Software
Atari

Gale Racer (1994)
Saturn
Sega
Sega

Get A Way (1979)
Arcade
Universal
Universal

Go-Kart Simulator (1989)
C64
Zeppelin Games
Zeppelin Games

GP World (1984)
Arcade
Sega
Sega

Gran Trak 10 (1974)
Arcade
Grass Valley Think Tank/Atari
Atari

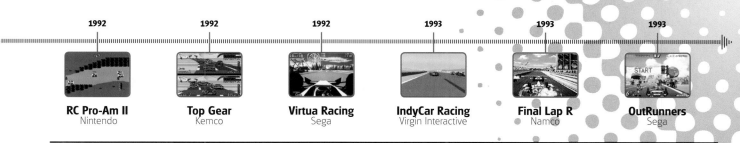

1992	1992	1992	1993	1993	1993
RC Pro-Am II Nintendo	**Top Gear** Kemco	**Virtua Racing** Sega	**IndyCar Racing** Virgin Interactive	**Final Lap R** Namco	**OutRunners** Sega

Gran Trak 20 (1974)
Arcade
Atari
Atari

Gran Turismo (1998)
PS
Polyphony
Sony Computer Entertainment

Gran Turismo 2 (1999)
PS
Polyphony Digital
Sony Computer Entertainment

Gran Turismo 3 A-Spec
(2001)
PS2
Polyphony Digital
Sony Computer Entertainment

Gran Turismo 4 (2005)
PS2
Polyphony Digital
Sony Computer Entertainment

Gran Turismo 4 Prologue
(2004)
PS2
Polyphony Digital
Sony Computer Entertainment

Gran Turismo 5 Prologue
(2008)
PS3
Polyphony Digital Inc
Sony Computer Entertainment

Gran Turismo Concept
2002 Tokyo-Geneva (2002)
PS2
Polyphony Digital
Sony Computer Entertainment

Gran Turismo HD (2007)
PS3
Polyphony Digital
Sony Computer Entertainment

Grand Champion (1980)
Arcade
Taito
Taito

Grand Prix (1982)
2600
Activision
Activision

Grand Prix 3 (2000)
PC
MicroProse Software
Hasbro Interactive

Grand Prix 4 (2002)
PC
MicroProse Software
Infogrames

Grand Prix Challenge (1991)
ZX
Vincent City, Graham Shaw
Challenge Software

Grand Prix Challenge (2003)
PS2
Melbourne House
Infogrames

Grand Prix Circuit (1988)
PC, C64; Amiga, Apple II
(1989); CPC, ZX (1990)
Distinctive Software
Accolade

Grand Prix Legends (1998)
PC
Papyrus Design Group
Sierra

Grand Prix Simulator (1987)
400/800, C64, CPC, ZX
Codemasters
Codemasters

Grand Prix Simulator 2
(1989)
C64, CPC, ZX
Codemasters
Codemasters

Grand Prix Star (1992)
Arcade
Jaleco
Jaleco

Grand Prix Unlimited (1992)
PC
Accolade
Accolade

Great 1000 Mile Rally (1994)
Arcade
Kaneko
Kaneko

Great 1000 Mile Rally 2
(1995)
Arcade
Kaneko
Kaneko

The Great American Cross-
Country Road Race (1985)
Apple II, 400/800, C64
Activision (K. Kalkut, A. DeMeo)
Activision

GripShift (2007)
360
Sidhe Interactive
Sidhe Interactive

Grooverider: Slot Car
Racing (aka Grooverider: Slot Car Thunder) (2003)
GC, PS2, Xb
King of the Jungle
Play It

Ground Effects (1992)
Arcade
Taito
Taito

GT 64 (aka GT Racing) (1998)
N64
Imagineer
Ocean

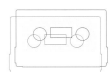

Ridge Racer
Namco

Ace Driver
Namco

Cruis'n USA
Midway

Daytona USA
Sega

Micro Machines 2: Turbo Tournament
Codemasters

Stunt Race FX
Nintendo

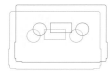

GT Legends (2005)
PC
SimBin Development Team
10tacle Studios

GT Pro Series (2006)
Wii
MTO
Ubisoft (Wii)

GT Roadster (1979)
Arcade
Ramtek
Ramtek

GT World Tour (1999?)
N64
Boss Game Studios
Midway

GTI Club Rally Côte D'Azur (1996)
Arcade
Konami
Konami

GTR – FIA GT Racing Game (2005)
PC
SimBin Development Team
Atari

GTR 2 – FIA GT Racing Game (2006)
PC
SimBin Development Team
10tacle Studios

GTR Evolution (2008)
PC
SimBin Development Team
Viva Media

Gumball 3000 (2002)
PS2
Climax Studios
SCi

Hard Drivin' (1988)
Arcade; Amiga, C64, CPC, ST, ZX (1989); MD, PC (1990)
Tengen/Atari; Binary Design (ZX)
Atari (Arcade), Domark (others)

Hard Drivin' II (1991)
Amiga, ST, PC (1992)
Tengen
Domark

Hardcore 4x4 (1996)
PS; PC, Sat (1997)
Gremlin Interactive
Gremlin Interactive

Head On (1979)
Arcade
Sega
Gremlin

Head On 2 (1979)
Arcade
Sega
Gremlin

High Velocity: Mountain Racing Challenge (1995)
Saturn
CAVE
Atlus Software

High Way Star (1983)
MSX
Way Limit
ASCII Corporation

Highway (aka Hi-Way) (1975)
Arcade
Atari
Atari

Highway Patrol II (1990)
Amiga, PC, ST
Microïds
Titus

Hold Up (1984)
CPC
ERE Informatique
ERE Informatique

Hot Rod (1988)
Arcade; C64, CPC, ST, ZX (1990)
Sega, Software Studios (C64)
Sega (Arcade), Activision (others)

Hot Wheels (1985)
C64
A. Eddy Goldfarb & Associates
Epyx

Hot Wheels: Stunt Track Challenge (2004)
PC, PS2, Xb
Climax Brighton
THQ

Hot Wheels: Turbo Racing (1999)
N64, PS
Stormfront Studios
Electronic Arts

Human Grand Prix (aka F1 Pole Position) (1992)
SNES
Human Entertainment
Ubisoft

Hummer: Badlands (2006)
PS2, Xb
Eutechnyx
Global Star Software

Hyper Rally (1985)
MSX
Konami
Konami

Hyperchase Auto Race (1982)
Vectrex
GCE
GCE

IHRA Motorsports Drag Racing (2000)
PC, PS (2001)
Digital Dialect
Bethesda Softworks

1994 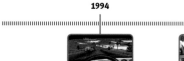 1994 1994 1995  1996 1996

The Need for Speed
Electronic Arts

Virtua Racing Deluxe
Sega

Indycar Racing II
Sierra

**Sega Rally
Championship**
Sega

Destruction Derby 2
Psygnosis

Formula 1
Psygnosis

Ignition (1997)
PC
Unique Development Studios
Virgin Interactive Entertainment

Import Tuner Challenge
(2006)
360
Genki
Ubisoft

Indianapolis 500: The
Simulation (1989)
PC, Amiga (1991)
Papyrus Design Group
Electronic Arts

Indy 4 (1976)
Arcade
Atari
Atari

Indy 500 (1977)
2600
Atari
Atari

Indy 500 (1995)
Arcade
AM1
Sega

Indy 800 (1975)
Arcade
Kee Games
Kee Games

Indy Heat (aka Danny Sullivan's
Indy Heat) (1991)
NES; Amiga, C64, ST (1992)
Leland Corporation
Storm

Indy Racing 2000 (2000)
N64
Paradigm Entertainment
Infogrames

IndyCar Racing (1993)
PC
Papyrus Design Group
Virgin Interactive

IndyCar Racing II (1995)
PC; Mac (1996)
Papyrus Design Group
Sierra

IndyCar Series (2003)
PC, PS2, Xb
Brain in a Jar
Codemasters

Initial D 4 (2006)
Arcade
Sega Rosso
Sega

Initial D Arcade Stage (aka
Initial D) (2001)
Arcade
Sega Rosso
Sega

Initial D Special Stage (2003)
PS2
Sega Rosso
Sega

Initial D Ver.2 (2003)
Arcade
Sega Rosso
Sega

Initial D Version 3 (2004)
Arcade
Sega Rosso
Sega

International Rally
Championship (1997)
PC
Magnetic Fields
Europress Software

iRacing Simulation (2008)
PC
**iRacing.com Motorsport
Simulations**
iRacing.com Motorsport Simulations

The Italian Job (2001)
PS, PC (2002)
Pixelogic
Eidos, Sold Out (PC)

The Italian Job: LA Heist
(2003)
GC, PS2, Xb
Climax
Eidos Interactive

Ivan 'Ironman' Stewart's
Super Off Road (1989)
Arcade, NES; Amiga, C64,
CPC, MS, PC, ST, ZX (1990);
SNES (1992), MD (1994)
**Leland, Graftgold Creative
Software** (ZX, C64), **Software
Creations** (SNES)
Leland (Arcade), Virgin
Mastertronic (others)

Jaguar XJ220 (1992)
Amiga, Sega CD, ST
Core Design
Core Design

Jaleco Rally Big Run: The
Supreme 4WD Challenge
(1989)
Arcade; Amiga, ST (1992)
Jaleco
Jaleco, Storm (Amiga, ST)

John Anderson's Rally
Speedway (1983)
400/800, C64 (1985)
Adventure International
Adventure International,
Commodore (C64)

Juiced (2005)
PC, PS2, Xb
Juice Games
THQ

Juiced 2: Hot Import
Nights (2007)
360, PC, PS2, PS3
Juice Games
THQ

Kart Champions (2008)
PC
SE Games
SE Games

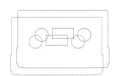

Formula One Grand Prix 2
MicroProse

GTI Club Rally Côte D'Azur
Konami

San Francisco Rush: Extreme Racing
Atari

Screamer 2
Virgin Interactive Entertainment

Scud Race
Sega

Le Mans 24
Sega

Kart Duel (2000)
Arcade
Namco
Namco

Karting Grand Prix (1988)
Amiga, ST
Anco Software
Anco Software

Knight Rider: The Game (2002)
PS2, PC (2003)
Davilex Games
Davilex Games

Konami GT (1985)
Arcade
Konami
Konami

Kyle Petty's No Fear Racing (1996)
SNES
Leland Interactive Media
Williams/Virgin Interactive

LA Rush (2005)
PS2, Xb, PC (2006)
Midway Studios Newcastle
Midway Home Entertainment

Laguna Racer (1977)
Arcade
Midway
Midway

The Last V8 (1985)
C64; 400/800, C128, CPC (1986)
D. Darling, R. Darling
Mastertronic

Le Mans (1976)
Arcade
Atari
Atari

Le Mans (1982)
C64
HAL Laboratory
Commodore Electronics

Le Mans 24 (1997)
Arcade
AM3
Sega

Le Mans 24 Hours (2000)
DC, PS2 (2001), PC (2002)
Melbourne House
Infogrames

LED Storm (1988)
Arcade; Amiga, C64, ST, ZX (1989)
Capcom, Software Creations (others)
Capcom

Lego Stunt Rally (2000)
PC, PS
Intelligent Games
Lego Media

Live for Speed (2003)
PC
Live for Speed
Live for Speed

Lombard RAC Rally (1988)
Amiga, PC, ST
Red Rat Software
Mandarin Software

London Racer (aka M25 Racer) (2000)
PC, PS
Davilex Games
Koch

London Racer II (2002)
PC, PS, PS2
Davilex Games
Koch

London Racer: World Challenge (2003)
PC, PS2
Davilex Games
Davilex Games

Lotus III: The Ultimate Challenge (1992)
Amiga, ST; MD (as Lotus II RECS), PC (1993)
Magnetic Fields
Gremlin Graphics

Lotus Challenge (2001)
PS2; GC, PC, Xb (2003)
Kuju Entertainment
Avalon (PS2), Xicat

Lotus Esprit Turbo Challenge (1990)
Amiga, C64, CPC, ST, ZX
Magnetic Fields
Gremlin Graphics

Lotus Turbo Challenge 2 (1991)
Amiga, PC, ST; MD (1992)
Magnetic Fields
Gremlin Graphics, Electronic Arts (MD)

m&m's Kart Racing (2007)
Wii
Frontline Studios
Destination Software

Mario Andretti Racing (1994)
MD
Stormfront Studios
Electronic Arts

Master Rallye (2002)
PC, PS2
Steel Monkeys
Microïds

Max Power Racing (1999)
PS
Eutechnyx
Infogrames

Maximum Speed (2003)
Arcade
Sammy
Sammy

1997
Porsche Challenge
Sony Computer
Entertainment

1997
Rage Racer
Namco

1997
Felony 11-79
ASCII Entertainment

1997
Screamer Rally
Virgin Interactive
Entertainment

1997
TOCA Touring Car
Championship
Codemasters

1997
V-Rally
Ocean

Metropolis Street Racer
(2000)
DC
Bizarre Creations
Sega

Miami Chase (1991)
C64
Codemasters (check)
Codemasters

Michael Andretti's World GP (1990)
NES
Sammy
Sammy

Michael Schumacher Racing World Kart 2002
(2002)
PC
TerraTools
JoWood

Micro Machines (1991)
NES; Amiga, MD, MS (1993),
SNES, PC (1994), CD-i (1995)
Codemasters, Merit Studios (SNES)
Codemasters, Ocean (SNES),
Philips Interactive Media (CD-i)

Micro Machines 2: Turbo Tournament (1994)
MD; PC, SNES (1995)
Codemasters, Supersonic Software (PC)
Codemasters, Ocean (SNES)

Micro Machines: Turbo Tournament 96 (1995)
MD
Supersonic Software
Codemasters

Midnight Club (2002)
PS2
Angel Studios
Rockstar Games

Midnight Club II (2003)
PC, PS2, Xb
Rockstar San Diego
Rockstar Games

Midnight Club 3: DUB Edition (2005)
PS2, Xb
Rockstar San Diego
Rockstar Games

Midnight Club: Los Angeles (2008)
360, PS3
Rockstar San Diego
Rockstar Games

Midnight Club: Street Racing (2000)
PS2
Angel Studios
Rockstar

Midnight Run: Road Fighter 2 (1996)
Arcade, PS (1997)
Konami
Konami

Midnite Racer (1976)
Arcade
Midway
Midway

Midtown Madness (1999)
PC
Angel Studios
Microsoft

Midtown Madness 2 (2000)
PC
Angel Studios
Microsoft Game Studios

Midtown Madness 3 (2003)
Xb
Digital Illusions
Microsoft Game Studios

Mille Miglia (2000)
PS
Kung Fu Games
SCi Games

Monaco GP (1980)
Arcade
Sega
Gremlin

Monaco Grand Prix Racing Simulation 2 (1998)
PC; DC, PS (1999)
Ubisoft
Ubisoft

Monster 4x4: Masters of Metal (2003)
GC, PS2
Ubisoft
Ubisoft

Monster 4x4: World Circuit (2006)
Xb, Wii
Ubisoft Montreal
Ubisoft

Monster Jam: Maximum Destruction (2002)
GC, PC, PS2
Inland Productions
Ubisoft

Monster Truck Madness (1996)
PC
Terminal Reality
Microsoft

Monster Truck Rally (1990)
SNES, NES (1991)
Realtime Associates
INTV Corporation

Monster Trucks (1997)
PS
Reflections
Psygnosis

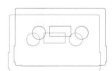

1998
Colin McRae Rally
Codemasters

1998
Daytona USA 2:
Battle on the Edge
Sega

1998
F-1 World Grand Prix
Video System

1998
Gran Turismo
Sony Computer
Entertainment

1998
Grand Prix
Legends
Sierra

1998
Monaco Grand Prix
Racing Simulation 2
Ubisoft

Monte Carlo (1980)
Arcade
Atari
Atari

Moonshine Racers (1991)
Amiga, PC, ST
Peakstar Software
Millennium Interactive

Motor Mania (1982)
C64
J.A. Fitzpatrick
UMI

Motorhead (1998)
PC, PS; Arcade (2000)
Digital Illusions
Gremlin, Cybermind (Arcade)

MotorStorm (2007)
PS3
Evolution Studios
Sony Computer Entertainment

MotorStorm Pacific Rift
(2008)
PS3
Evolution Studios
Sony Computer Entertainment

Multi-Racing
Championship (1997)
N64
Ocean
Imagineer

MX vs ATV Unleashed (2005)
PS2, Xb, PC (2006)
Rainbow Studios
THQ

MX vs ATV Untamed (2007)
360, PS2, PS3, Wii (2008)
Rainbow Studios
THQ

NASCAR 06: Total Team
Control (2005)
PS2, Xb
EA Tiburon
EA Sports

NASCAR 07 (2006)
PS2, Xb
EA Tiburon
EA Sports

NASCAR 08 (2007)
360, PS2, PS3
EA Tiburon
EA Sports

NASCAR 09 (2008)
360, PS2, PS3
EA Tiburon
EA Sports

NASCAR 98 (1997)
PS, Sat
EA Sports
EA Sports

NASCAR 99 (1998)
N64, PS
Stormfront Studios
EA Sports

NASCAR 2000 (1999)
N64, PS; PC (2000)
EA Sports/Stormfront Studios
EA Sports

NASCAR 2001 (2000)
PS, PS2
EA Sports
EA Sports

NASCAR 2005: Chase for
the Cup (2004)
GC, PS2, Xb
EA Tiburon
Electronic Arts

NASCAR Arcade (2000)
Arcade
Sega AM3
Sega

NASCAR: Dirt to Daytona
(2002)
GC, PS2
Monster Games
Infogrames

NASCAR Heat (2000)
PC, PS
Monster Games, Digital
Illusions (PS)
Hasbro Interactive

NASCAR Heat 2002 (2001)
PS2, Xb
Monster Games
Infogrames

NASCAR Legends (1999)
PC
Papyrus Design Group
Sierra

NASCAR Racing (1994)
PC
Papyrus Design Group
Sierra

NASCAR Racing 2 (1996)
PC
Papyrus Design Group
Sierra

NASCAR Racing 3 (1999)
PC
Papyrus Design Group
Sierra

NASCAR Racing 4 (2001)
PC
Papyrus Design Group
Sierra

NASCAR Racing 2002
Season (2002)
PC
Papyrus Design Group
Sierra

NASCAR Racing 2003
Season (2003)
PC
Papyrus Design Group
Sierra

NASCAR Rumble (2000)
PS
EA Sports
EA Sports

1998

Motorhead
Gremlin

1998

**Need for Speed III:
Hot Pursuit**
Electronic Arts

1998

Racing Jam
Konami

1998

Sega Rally 2
Sega

1998

Thrill Drive
Konami

1998

TOCA 2 Touring Cars
Codemasters

NASCAR SimRacing (2005)
PC
EA Tiburon
EA Sports

NASCAR Thunder 2002
(2001)
PS, PS2, Xb
EA Tiburon
EA Sports

NASCAR Thunder 2003
(2002)
GC, PC, PS, PS2, Xb
EA Sports, Budcat Creations (PS)
EA Sports

NASCAR Thunder 2004
(2003)
PC, PS, PS2, Xb
EA Tiburon, Budcat Creations (PS)
EA Sports

The Need for Speed (1994)
3DO, PC (1995); PS, Saturn (1996)
Pioneer Productions, EA Canada
Electronic Arts

Need for Speed (2003)
Arcade
EA Games
Global VR

Need for Speed 2 (1997)
PC, PS
EA Canada
Electronic Arts

Need for Speed 2 Special
Edition (1997)
PC
EA Canada
Electronic Arts

Need for Speed III: Hot
Pursuit (1998)
PS
EA Canada
Electronic Arts

Need for Speed Carbon
(2006)
360, GC, PC, PS2, PS3, Xb,
Wii; Arcade, Mac (2008)
EA Black Box
Electronic Arts, Global VR (Arcade)

Need for Speed GT (2004)
Arcade
EA Games
Global VR

Need for Speed Hot
Pursuit 2 (2002)
GC, PC, PS2, Xb
EA Black Box
Electronic Arts

Need for Speed Most
Wanted (2005)
360, GC, PC, PS2, Xb
EA Canada
Electronic Arts

Need for Speed ProStreet
(2007)
360, PC, PS2, PS3, Wii
EA Black Box
Electronic Arts

Need for Speed: Road
Challenge (aka Need for Speed:
High Stakes) (1999)
PC, PS
Electronic Arts
Electronic Arts

Need for Speed
Undercover (2008)
360, PC, PS3
EA Canada
Electronic Arts

Need for Speed
Underground (2003)
GC, PC, PS2, Xb; Arcade (2004)
EA Black Box
Electronic Arts, Global VR (Arcade)

Need for Speed
Underground 2 (2004)
GC, PC, PS2, Xb
EA Black Box
Electronic Arts

NetKar Pro (2006)
PC
Kunos Simulazioni
Kunos Simulazioni

Newman Haas Indy Car
(1994)
MD, SNES
Gremlin Graphics
Acclaim Entertainment

Newman Haas Racing
(1998)
PC, PS
Studio 3
Psygnosis

NHRA Championship Drag
Racing (2005)
PS2
Lucky Chicken Games
ValuSoft

Nigel Mansell's Grand Prix
(1988)
Amiga, CPC, ST, ZX
DJL Software
Martech

Nigel Mansell's World
Championship (1992)
Amiga, C64, CPC, ST, ZX; CD32,
MD, NES, PC, SNES (1993)
Gremlin Graphics
Gremlin Graphics

Night Driver (1976)
Arcade, 2600 (1980), C64 (1982)
Atari, HAL Laboratory (C64)
Atari, Commodore (C64)

Night Racer (1975)
Arcade
Micronetics
Micronetics

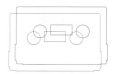

The Driving Games List

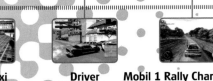

1999
Crazy Taxi
Sega

 1999
Driver
GT Interactive

 1999
Mobil 1 Rally Championship
Europress Software

 **1999**
F355 Challenge
Sega

1999
Gran Turismo 2
Sony Computer
Entertainment

1999
Ridge Racer Type 4
Namco

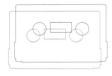

Night Racer (1988)
C64
K.T. Green
Mastertronic

Nürburgring 1 (1975)
Arcade
Dr-Ing R. Foerst
Trakus

Nürburgring 3 (1980)
Arcade
Dr-Ing R. Foerst
Trakus

Off Road Challenge (1997)
Arcade, N64 (1998)
Midway, Avalanche Software (N64)
Midway

Official F1 Racing (1999)
PC
Video System
Eidos

Offroad Thunder (1999)
Arcade
Midway Games
Midway Games

OutRun (1986)
Arcade; C64 CPC, MS, MSX, ZX
(1987); Amiga, PC, ST (1989), TG-16
(1990), MD (1991), Saturn (1996),
DC (2001, as *Game Works Vol 1*),
PS2 (2006, as *Sega Ages Vol 13*)
AM2 (Arcade, MS), **Amazing
Products/US Gold** (C64), **Probe
Software** (CPC, MSX, ZX, Amiga, ST),
Unlimited Software (PC), **NEC**
(PC Engine), **AM2/Sanritsu** (MD),
AM2/Rutubo Games (Saturn)
Sega (Arcade, MD, Saturn, PS2), US
Gold (C64, ZX), Pony Canyon (MSX)

OutRun 3-D (1989)
MS
Sega
Sega

OutRun 2006: Coast to
Coast (2006)
PC, PS2, Xb
Sumo Digital
Sega

OutRun 2019 (1993)
MD
Sims Co
Sega

OutRun2 (2003)
Arcade, Xb (2004)
AM2, Sumo Digital (Xb)
Sega

OutRun2 SP (2004)
Arcade
AM2
Sega

OutRun Europa (1991)
Amiga, C64, CPC, MS, ST ZX
Probe
US Gold

OutRunners (1993)
Arcade, MD (1994)
AM2, Data East (MD)
Sega

Over Drive (1990)
Arcade
Konami
Konami

Overdrive (1984)
BBC Micro
Peter Johnson
Superior Software

Overdrive (1993)
Amiga, PC (1995)
Psionic Systems
Team 17 Software

Over Rev (1997)
Arcade
Jaleco
Jaleco

Pace Car Pro (1975)
Arcade
Electra Games
Electra Games

Paris-Dakar (1988)
Amiga, C64, CPC, MSX, PC, ZX
Zigurat
Zigurat

Paris-Dakar Rally (2001)
PC, PS2
Broadsword Interactive
Acclaim

Paris-Marseille Racing (2000)
PC, PS
Davilex Games
Davilex Games

Pit & Run F-1 Race (1984)
Arcade
Taito
Taito

Pitstop (1983)
400/800, C64, ColecoVision
Epyx
Epyx

Pitstop II (1984)
Apple II, 400/800, C64
Epyx (S.H. Landrum, D. Caswell),
Synergistic Software
(Apple II, 400/800)
Epyx

Pole Position (1982)
Arcade; 2600, 5200, 400/800, C64,
Vectrex, VIC-20, ZX (1983); TI-99/4A
(1984), PC (1986), Intellivision (1987)
Namco
Atari, GCE (Vectrex), US Gold
(C64, ZX), INTV (Intellivision),
Thunder Mountain (PC)

Pole Position II (1983)
Arcade; 7800 (1987); C64, PC (1988)
Namco
Atari, Mindscape (C64, PC)

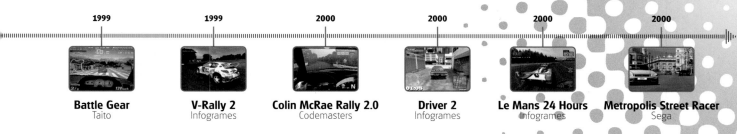

1999	1999	2000	2000	2000	2000
Battle Gear Taito	**V-Rally 2** Infogrames	**Colin McRae Rally 2.0** Codemasters	**Driver 2** Infogrames	**Le Mans 24 Hours** Infogrames	**Metropolis Street Racer** Sega

Porsche Challenge (1997)
PS
Sony Computer Entertainment Europe
Sony Computer Entertainment

Power Drift (1988)
Arcade; Amiga, C64, CPC, MSX, ST, ZX (1989); PC, TG-16 (1990), Saturn (1998)
AM2; Sega (others)**, C. Butler, D. Lowe** (C64)
Sega (Arcade, Saturn), Activision (others)

Power Drive (1986)
Arcade
Bally Midway
Bally Midway

Power Drive (1994)
Amiga, CD32, MD, PC
Rage Software
US Gold

Power Drive Rally (1995)
Jaguar
Rage Software
Time Warner Interactive

Power F1 (1997)
PC
Teque London
Eidos

Pro Rally (2002)
GC, PS2
Ubisoft
Ubisoft

Project Gotham Racing (2002)
Xb
Bizarre Creations
Microsoft

Project Gotham Racing 2 (2003)
Xb
Bizarre Creations
Microsoft

Project Gotham Racing 3 (2005)
360
Bizarre Creations
Microsoft

Project Gotham Racing 4 (2007)
360
Bizarre Creations
Microsoft

R: Racing (aka R: Racing Evolution) (2004)
GC, PS2, Xb
Namco Bandai
EA

R4 – Ridge Racer Type 4 (1999)
PS
Namco
Namco

Race! (1976)
Arcade
Fun Games
Fun Games

RACE – The WTCC Game (2006)
PC
SimBin Development Team
Eidos

RACE 07 – The WTCC Game (2007)
PC
SimBin Development Team
SimBin Studios

Race America (1992)
NES
Imagineering
Absolute Entertainment

Race Driver: GRID (2008)
360, PC, PS3
Codemasters
Codemasters

Race Drivin' (1990)
Arcade; Amiga, PC, ST (1992), MD (1993)
Atari
Atari/Tengen (Arcade), Domark (others)

Race On (1998?)
Arcade
Namco
Namco

RACE Pro (2008)
360
SimBin Development Team
Atari

Racin' Force (1994)
Arcade
Konami
Konami

Racing Beat (1991)
Arcade
Taito
Taito

Racing Destruction Set (1985)
400/800, C64
R. König, D. Warhol, C. Goldman
Electronic Arts

Racing Evoluzione (2003)
Xb
Milestone
Atari

Racing Jam (1998)
Arcade
Konami
Konami

Racing Pak (1982)
2600
Atari
Atari

Rad Mobile (1991)
Arcade
Sega
Sega

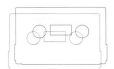

2000
2001
2001
2001
2001
2001

TOCA World Touring Cars
Codemasters

Burnout
Acclaim

Daytona USA 2001
Sega

Gran Turismo 3 A-Spec
Sony Computer Entertainment

Initial D Arcade Stage
Sega

World Rally Championship
Sony Computer Entertainment

Rad Racer (1987)
NES
Square
Nintendo

Rad Racer II (1990)
NES
Square
Nintendo

Rad Rally (1991)
Arcade
Sega
Sega

Radio Controlled Racer (1991)
Amiga, ST
Cloud Nine Developments
Byte Back

Rage Racer (1997)
PS
Namco
Namco

RalliSport Challenge (2002)
PC, Xb
Digital Illusions
Microsoft Game Studios

RalliSport Challenge 2 (2004)
Xb
Digital Illusions
Microsoft Game Studios

Rally Championship (1996)
PC
Magnetic Fields
Europress Software

Rally Championship (aka Mobil 1 Rally Championship) (1999)
PC, PS (2000)
Magnetic Fields
Europress Software

Rally Championship (2002)
PS2, GC (2003)
Warthog
SCi Games

Rally Championships (1994)
Amiga, ST
InSide Team
Flair Publishing

Rally Cross (1997)
PS
989 Studios
Sony Computer Entertainment

Rally Cross 2 (1998)
PS
989 Studios/Idol Minds
Sony Computer Entertainment

Rally Cross Challenge (1989)
Amiga, C64, CPC, PC, ST, ZX
Ultra Graphix (Amiga, PC, ST),
Enigma Variations (others)
Anco Software

Rally Driver (1984)
ZX, CPC (1986), C64 (1988)
Five Ways Software
Hill MacGibbon

Rally Fusion: Race of Champions (2002)
GC, PS2, Xb
Climax
Activision

Rally Masters: Race of Champions (2000)
N64, PC, PS
Digital Illusions
Gremlin

Rally Shift (2004)
Mac
Codeblender Software
Codeblender Software

Rallycross Simulator (1989)
C64
Codemasters
Codemasters

Rave Racer (1995)
Arcade
Namco
Namco

RC Cars (aka Smash Cars) (2003)
PC, PS2
Creat Studio
1C Company, Metro3D (PS2)

RC de Go! (1999)
Arcade, PS
Taito
Taito

RC Grand Prix (1989)
MS
Absolute Entertainment
Seismic Software

RC Pro-Am (1987)
NES
Rare
Nintendo

RC Pro-Am II (1992)
NES
Rare
Nintendo

Re-Volt (1999)
DC, N64, PC, PS; Arcade (2004)
Probe
Acclaim, Tsunami (Arcade)

Redline Racer (1986)
Arcade
Leland Corporation
Leland Corporation

REVS (1984)
BBC Micro, C64 (1986)
Geoff Crammond
Acornsoft, Firebird (C64)

REVS+ (1987)
C64
Firebird Software
Firebird Software

rFactor (2005)
PC
Image Space Incorporated
Image Space Incorporated

2002

Auto Modellista
Capcom

2002

Burnout 2: Point of Impact
Acclaim

2002
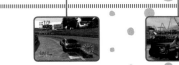
Grand Prix 4
Infogrames

2002

Sega GT 2002
Sega

2002

Grand Prix Challenge
Atari

2003
IndyCar Series
Codemasters

Richard Burns Rally (2004)
PC, PS2, Xb
Warthog
SCi

Richard Petty's Talladega (1984)
400/800, C64 (1985)
Cosmi (R.T. Bonifacio)
Cosmi, Electronic Arts (C64)

Ridge Racer (1993)
Arcade, PS (1995)
Namco
Namco

Ridge Racer 2 (1994)
Arcade
Namco
Namco

Ridge Racer V (2000)
PS2
Namco
Namco

Ridge Racer V: Arcade Battle (2000)
Arcade
Namco
Namco

Ridge Racer 6 (2006)
360
Namco Hometek
Electronic Arts

Ridge Racer 7 (2006)
PS3
Namco Bandai
Namco Bandai

Ridge Racer 64 (2000)
N64
Namco
Nintendo

Road Avenger (1992)
Sega CD
Wolf Team
Sega

Road Champion (1977)
Arcade
Taito
Taito

Road Race (1976)
Arcade
Sega
Sega

Road Riot (1991)
Arcade
Atari
Atari

Road Trip (2004)
GC
Hudson Soft
Takara

Roads Edge (aka Round Trip RV) (1997)
Arcade
SNK
SNK

Rough Racer (1990)
Arcade
Sega
Sega

RPM Tuning (aka Top Gear: RPM Tuning) (2004)
PS2; PC, Xb (2005)
Babylon Software
MC2

RS3: Racing Simulation Three (2002)
GC, PC, PS2
Ubisoft
Ubisoft

Felony 11-79 (1997)
PS
Climax Entertainment
ASCII Entertainment

Rush 2: Extreme Racing USA (1998)
N64
Midway
Midway

San Francisco Rush: Extreme Racing (1996)
Arcade, PS (1997), N64 (1998)
Atari, Midway (N64, PS)
Atari, Midway (N64, PS)

San Francisco Rush: The Rock – Alcatraz Edition (1997)
Arcade
Atari Games
Atari Games

San Francisco Rush 2049 (1999)
Arcade; DC, N64 (2000)
Atari
Atari, Midway (DC, N64)

San Francisco Rush 2049: Special Edition (2003)
Arcade
Atari
Atari

Scalextric (1985)
C64
Andrew Bradley
Leisure Genius

SCAR: Squadra Corse Alfa Romeo (2005)
PC, PS2, Xb
Milestone
Pulsar

SCI – Special Criminal Investigation (aka Chase HQ 2) (1989)
Arcade; Amiga, C64, CPC PC, ZX, ST (1990), TG-16 (1991), MS (1992)
Taito, Probe (C64, ZX), **ICE Software** (Amiga, PC, ST)
Taito (arcade, MS), Ocean (others)

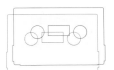

2003
2003
2003
2003
2003
2003

Live for Speed
Live for Speed

Midtown Madness 3
Microsoft Game
Studios

**NASCAR Racing
2003 Season**
Sierra

**Need for Speed
Underground**
Electronic Arts

OutRun2
Sega

**Project Gotham
Racing 2**
Microsoft

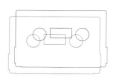

SCORE International Baja
1000 (2008)
360, PC, PS2, PS3, Wii
Left Field Productions
Activision

Screamer (1995)
PC
Milestone
Virgin

Screamer 2 (1996)
PC
Milestone
Virgin Interactive Entertainment

Screamer Rally (1997)
PC
Milestone
Virgin Interactive Entertainment

Scud Race (aka Sega Super GT)
(1996)
Arcade
AM2
Sega

Scud Race Plus (1997)
Arcade
AM2
Sega

Sega GT (2000)
DC, PC (2001)
Wow Entertainment
Sega

Sega GT 2002 (2002)
Xb
Wow Entertainment
Sega

Sega GT Online (2004)
Xb
Wow Entertainment
Sega

Sega Race TV (2008)
Arcade
Sega
Sega

Sega Rally (2007)
360, PC, PS3
Sega Racing Studio
Sega

Sega Rally 2 (1998)
Arcade; DC, PC (1999)
AM Annex (Arcade), AM9
Sega

Sega Rally Championship
(1995)
Arcade, Saturn
AM3
Sega

Sega Touring Car
Championship (1996)
Arcade, Saturn (1997), PC (1998)
AM Annex, AM9 (PC, Saturn)
Sega

Shirley Muldowney's Top
Fuel Challenge (1987)
C64
R.T. Bonifacio, P. Norman
Cosmi

Side by Side (1996)
Arcade
Taito
Taito

Side by Side 2 Evoluzione
(1997)
Arcade
Taito
Taito

The Simpsons: Road Rage
(2001)
PS2; GC, Xb (2002)
Radical Entertainment
Electronic Arts

Slicks (1992)
C64
Digital Design
Codemasters

Smuggler's Run (2000)
PS2
Angel Studios
Rockstar

SODA Off-Road Racing
(1997)
PC
Papyrus Design Group
Sierra

Speed Busters (1998)
DC, PC
Ubisoft
Ubisoft

Speed Challenge: Jacques
Villeneuve's Racing Vision
(2002)
PC, PS2, GC (2003)
Ubisoft
Ubisoft

Speed Devils (1999)
DC
Ubisoft
Ubisoft

Speed Freak (1979)
Arcade
Vectorbeam
Vectorbeam

Speed Race (1974)
Arcade
Taito
Taito

Speed Race GP-5 (1980)
Arcade
Taito
Taito

Speed Race Twin (1976)
Arcade
Taito
Taito

Speed Up (1996)
Arcade
Gaelco
Gaelco

2003
2004
2004
2004
2004
2005

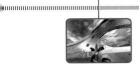

TrackMania
Digital Jesters

Burnout 3: Takedown
Electronic Arts

RalliSport Challenge 2
Microsoft Game Studios

Richard Burns Rally
SCi

TOCA Race Driver 2
Codemasters

Forza Motorsport
Microsoft Game Studios

Speedster (aka Rush Hour) (1997)
PS, PC
Clockwork Games
Psygnosis

Speedway! Spin-Out! (1978)
Odyssey
Magnavox
Magnavox

Spirit of Speed 1937 (1999)
PC, DC (2000)
Broadsword Interactive
MicroProse, Acclaim (DC)

Sports Car GT (1999)
PC, PS
Image Space Incorporated
Electronic Arts

Sprint 1 (1978)
Arcade
Kee Games
Kee Games

Sprint 2 (1976)
Arcade
Kee Games
Kee Games

Sprint 4 (1977)
Arcade
Kee Games
Kee Games

Sprint 8 (1977)
Arcade
Kee Games
Kee Games

Sprint Car Challenge (2005)
PS2
Brain in a Jar
Liquid Games

Sprint Cars: Road to Knoxville (2006)
PC, PS2
Big Ant Studios
THQ

Sprint Master (1988)
2600
Atari
Atari

SRS: Street Racing Syndicate (2005)
GC, PC, PS2, Xb
Eutechnyx
Namco Bandai (GC), Hip Interactive (PC), Codemasters (PS2, Xb)

Street Burners (1975)
Arcade
Allied Leisure Industries
Allied Leisure Industries

Street Racer (1978)
2600
Atari
Atari

Street Rod (1989)
C64, PC, ST; Amiga (1990)
Magic Partners
California Dreams

Street Rod 2: The Next Generation (1991)
Amiga, PC
PZ Karen Co
California Dreams

Stunt Car Racer
(aka Stunt Track Racer) (1989)
Amiga, C64, ST, PC, ZX; CPC (1990)
Geoff Crammond/MicroStyle
MicroProse Software

Stunt GP (2001)
DC, PC, PS2
Team 17
Titus, Eon (PC)

Stunt Race FX (1994)
SNES
Nintendo
Nintendo

Stuntman (2002)
PS2
Reflections
Infogrames

Stuntman: Ignition (2007)
360, PS2, PS3
Paradigm Entertainment
THQ

Stunts (aka 4D Sports Driving) (1990)
PC, Amiga (1992)
Distinctive Software
Mindscape

Super 1 Karting Simulation (2000)
PC
Interactive Entertainment
Midas

Super Bug (1977)
Arcade
Atari
Atari

Super Cars (1990)
Amiga, CPC, MSX, ST, ZX; C64, NES (1991)
Magnetic Fields
Gremlin Graphics

Super Cars II (1991)
Amiga, C64, PC, ST
Magnetic Fields
Gremlin Graphics

Super Cars International (1996)
PC
Magnetic Fields
The Hit Squad

Super Chase: Criminal Termination (1992)
Arcade
Taito
Taito

Super Chase HQ (1993)
SNES
Taito
Taito

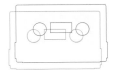

The Driving Games List

Gran Turismo 4
Sony Computer
Entertainment

GT Legends
10tacle Studios

**Need for Speed
Most Wanted**
Electronic Arts

**Project Gotham
Racing 3**
Microsoft

rFactor
Image Space
Incorporated

**TrackMania
Sunrise**
Digital Jesters

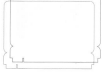

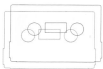

Super Formula (1989)
Arcade
Video System
Video System

Super Ground Effects (1992)
Arcade
Taito
Taito

Super GT 24h (1996)
Arcade
Jaleco
Jaleco

Super Highway (1977)
Arcade
Taito
Taito

Super Monaco GP (1989)
Arcade; MD, MS (1990), Amiga,
C64, CPC, ZX, ST (1991)
Sega, Probe (C64, ZX)
Sega (Arcade, MS, MD), US Gold (others)

Super Road Champions
(1978)
Arcade
Model Racing
Model Racing

Super Runabout (2000)
DC
Climax Entertainment
Virgin Interactive Entertainment

Super Skidmarks (1995)
Amiga, CD32, MD
Acid Software
Guildhall Leisure Services,
Codemasters (MD)

Super Speed Race GP V
(1980)
Arcade
Taito
Taito

Super Speed Race Jr (1985)
Arcade
Taito
Taito

Super Speed Race V (1978)
Arcade
Taito
Taito

Super Speed Racing (aka
CART: Flag to Flag) (1999)
DC
Zoom/Sega
Sega

Super Sprint (1986)
Arcade; C64, CPC, ZX, ST
(1987), NES (1989)
Atari
Atari (Arcade), Electric Dreams (others)

Super Stock Car (1990)
C64
Virgin Games
Virgin Games

Supercar Street Challenge
(2001)
PC, PS2
Exakt Entertainment
Activision

SuperKarts (1995)
PC
Manic Media
Virgin Interactive Entertainment

Techno Drive (1998)
Arcade
Namco
Namco

Test Drive (1987)
C64, PC, ST; Amiga, Apple II (1988)
Distinctive Software
Accolade

Test Drive (2002)
PC, PS2, Xb
Pitbull Syndicate
Infogrames

Test Drive II: The Collection
(1990)
Amiga, C64, PC
Distinctive Software
Accolade

Test Drive III: The Passion
(1990)
PC
Accolade
Accolade

Test Drive 4 (1997)
PS
Pitbull Syndicate
Electronic Arts

Test Drive 5 (1998)
PC
Pitbull Syndicate
Accolade

Test Drive 6 (1999)
DC, PC
Pitbull Syndicate
Infogrames

Test Drive Off-Road (1997)
PC, PS
Accolade, Infogrames (PS)
Infogrames

Test Drive Off-Road 3 (1999)
P1C, PS
Elite Systems
Accolade, Eidos (PS)

Test Drive Off Road: Wide
Open (2001)
PS2, Xb (2002)
Angel Studios
Atari

Test Drive Unlimited (2006)
360; PC, PS2 (2007)
Eden Games
Atari

Thrash Rally (1991)
Arcade, Neo Geo
Alpha Denshi
SNK

Thrill Drive (1998)
Arcade
Konami
Konami

2005

WRC: Rally Evolved
Sony Computer
Entertainment

2006

**GTR 2 – FIA GT
Racing Game**
10tacle Studios

2006

TOCA Race Driver 3
Codemasters

2006

**Test Drive
Unlimited**
Atari

2007

MotorStorm
Sony Computer
Entertainment

2007

Colin McRae: DiRT
Codemasters

Thrill Drive 2 (2001)
Arcade
Konami
Konami

Thrill Drive 3 (2004)
Arcade
Konami
Konami

TOCA 2 Touring Cars (1998)
PC, PS
Codemasters
Codemasters

TOCA Race Driver (2002)
PS2; PC, Xb (2003)
Codemasters
Codemasters

TOCA Race Driver 2 (2004)
PC, PS2, Xb
Codemasters
Codemasters

TOCA Race Driver 3 (2006)
PC, PS2, Xb
Codemasters
Codemasters

TOCA Touring Car
Championship (1997)
PC, PS
Codemasters
Codemasters

TOCA World Touring Cars
(aka Jarrett and Labonte Stock Car
Racing) (2000)
PS
Codemasters
Codemasters

Tokyo Cop (2003)
Arcade
Gaelco
Gaelco

Tokyo Xtreme Racer (aka
Tokyo Highway Challenge) (1999)
DC
Genki
Crave

Tokyo Xtreme Racer 2 (aka
Tokyo Highway Challenge 2) (2000)
DC
Genki
Crave

Tokyo Xtreme Racer 3 (2003)
PS2
Genki
Crave

Tokyo Xtreme Racer Zero
(aka Tokyo Xtreme Racer) (2001)
PS2
Genki
Crave

Tommi Mäkinen Rally (1998)
PS
Strange Productions
Europress

Top Fuel Eliminator (1987)
C64
H. Seeley, R. Lieblich
Activision

Top Gear (1984)
Arcade
Universal
Universal

Top Gear (1992)
SNES
Gremlin
Kemco

Top Gear 2 (1985)
Arcade
Universal
Universal

Top Gear 2 (1993)
SNES; Amiga, CD32, MD (1994)
Gremlin Graphics
Kemco, Gremlin Graphics
(Amiga, CD32)

Top Gear 3000 (1994)
SNES
Gremlin
Kemco

Top Gear: Dare Devil (2000)
PS2
Papaya Studios
Kotobuki System

Top Gear Overdrive (1999)
N64
Snowblind Studios
THE

Top Gear Rally (1997)
N64
Boss Game Studios
Kemco

Top Gear Rally 2 (1999)
N64
Saffire Corporation
Kemco

Total Drivin' (1997)
PS
Eutechnyx
Ocean

Total Immersion Racing
(2002)
PC, PS2, Xb; Mac (2003)
Razorworks
Empire, Feral Interactive (Mac)

Touring Car Racer (1991)
Amiga, ST
Cloud Nine Developments
Byte Back

Toy Story Racer (2001)
PS
Traveller's Tales
Activision

Toyota Celica GT Rally (1990)
Amiga, ST; C64, CPC, ZX
(1991), PC (1992)
Gremlin
Gremlin

TrackMania (2003)
PC
Nadeo
Digital Jesters

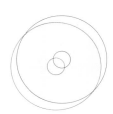

The Driving Games List

Forza Motorsport 2
Microsoft Game Studios

FlatOut: Ultimate Carnage
Empire Interactive

Project Gotham Racing 4
Microsoft

RACE 07 – The WTCC Game
SimBin Studios

Sega Rally
Sega

ARCA Sim Racing
The Sim Factory

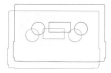

TrackMania Nations ESWC (2006)
PC
Nadeo
Nadeo

TrackMania Nations Forever (2008)
PC
Nadeo
Nadeo

TrackMania Power Up! (2004)
PC
Nadeo
Digital Jesters

TrackMania Sunrise (2005)
PC
Nadeo
Digital Jesters

Tranz Am (1983)
ZX
T. Stamper, C. Stamper
Ultimate Play The Game

Turbo (1981)
Arcade, ColecoVision (1982), Intellivision (1983)
Sega
Sega (Arcade), Coleco

Turbo Charge (1991)
C64
System 3
System 3

Turbo Cup (1988)
Amiga, CPC, PC, ST; ZX (1989)
Loriciels
Loriciels

Turbo Driver (1983)
ZX
Boss Software
Boss Software

Turbo OutRun (1989)
Arcade, C64, CPC, ZX; Amiga, PC, ST (1990), MD (1992)
Sega AM2 (Arcade, MD),
Probe Software (others)
Sega (Arcade, MD), US Gold (others)

Turbo Racing (aka Al Unser Jr Turbo Racing) (1990)
NES
Data East
Data East

Twin Racer (1974)
Arcade
Kee Games
Kee Games

Twin Turbo V8 (1988)
CPC, ZX (1989)
Codemasters
Codemasters

TX-1 (1983)
Arcade
Tatsumi
Atari

Ultim@te Race (1997)
PC
Kalisto
Kalisto

Ultim@te Race Pro (1998)
PC, Arcade (as K-Rally, 1999)
Kalisto
MicroProse

Up 'n Down (1983)
Arcade; 2600, Apple II, 400/800, C64, ColecoVision (1984)
Sega
Sega

USA Racer (2002)
PC, PS, PS2
Davilex Games
Davilex Games

V-Rally (1997)
PS
Infogrames
Ocean

V-Rally 2 (1999)
PS, DC (2000)
Eden Studios
Infogrames

V-Rally 3 (2002)
PS2; GC, PC, Xb (2003)
Eden Studios
Atari

V-Rally Edition 99 (1999)
N64
Eden Studios
Infogrames

Valve Limit R (2004)
Arcade
Avranches Automatic
Avranches Automatic

Vanishing Point (2000)
DC, PS (2001)
Clockwork Games
Acclaim Entertainment

Victory Lap (1996)
Arcade
Namco
Namco

Victory Run (1989)
TG-16, Wii (2006)
Hudson Soft
NEC

Viper Racing (1998)
PC
Monster Games
Sierra

Virtua Racing (1992)
Arcade, MD (1994), Saturn (1995)
AM2, Time Warner Interactive (Saturn)
Sega, Time Warner Interactive (Saturn)

2008	2008	2008	2008	2008	2008

Burnout Paradise
Electronic Arts

Gran Turismo 5 Prologue
Sony Computer Entertainment

Race Driver: GRID
Codemasters

GTR Evolution
Viva Media

iRacing
iRacing.com

RACE Pro
Atari

Virtua Racing Deluxe (1994)
32X
Sega
Sega

Virtual Karting (1995)
Amiga
OTM
OTM

Virtual Karts (1995)
PC
MicroProse
MicroProse

Vroom! (1991)
Amiga, ST
Lankhor
Lankhor

Wangan Midnight (2001)
Arcade
Namco
Namco

Wangan Midnight
Maximum Tune 3 (2007)
Arcade
Namco Bandai
Namco Bandai

Warm Up! (2000)
PC, PS
Lankhor
Microïds

WEC Le Mans (1986)
Arcade, CPC, MSX, ZX, C64 (1989)
Konami (Arcade), **Coreland** (others)
Konami (Arcade), **Imagine** (others)

Wheels (aka Racer) (1975)
Arcade
Midway
Midway

Wheels II (1975)
Arcade
Midway
Midway

Wild Wild Racing (2000)
PS2
Rage
Interplay

Winding Heat (1996)
Arcade
Konami
Konami

Winning Run (1989)
Arcade
Namco
Namco

Winning Run Suzuka GP
(1989)
Arcade
Namco
Namco

World Driver
Championship (1999)
N64
Boss Game Studios
Midway

World Grand Prix (1984)
MSX, MS (1986)
Sega
Sega

World of Outlaws: Sprint
Car Racing 2002 (2002)
PC, PS2
Ratbag
Infogrames

World Racing (2003)
PC, PS2, Xb, GC (2004)
Synetic
TDK Mediactive

World Racing 2 (2005)
PC, Xb, PS2 (2006)
Synetic
TDK Mediactive

World Rally (1993)
Arcade
Gaelco
Gaelco

World Rally Championship
(2001)
PS2
Evolution Studios
Sony Computer Entertainment

World Tour Racing (1996)
Jaguar (CD)
Teque Software
Atari

WRC II Extreme (2002)
PS2
Evolution Studios
Sony Computer Entertainment

WRC 3 (2003)
PS2
Evolution Studios
Sony Computer Entertainment

WRC 4 (2004)
PS2
Evolution Studios
Sony Computer Entertainment

WRC: Rally Evolved (2005)
PS2
Evolution Studios
Sony Computer Entertainment

Wreckless: The Yakuza
Missions (2002)
GC, PS2, Xb
Bunkasha
Activision

X Motor Racing (2007)
PC
Exotypos
Exotypos

XTreme Racing (1995)
Amiga
Silltunna Software
Guildhall Leisure Services

Xtreme Rally (1998)
Arcade
SNK
SNK

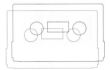

The Driving Games List

Image copyrights

Ace Driver © NAMCO BANDAI Games Inc.

Auto Modellista © Capcom Co., Ltd. 2002 All rights reserved.

BAJA: Edge of Control ©THQ. All rights reserved.

Battle Gear © TAITO Corp. 1999 All rights reserved.

Buggy Boy © TAITO Corp. 1985 All rights reserved.

Burnout © Electronic Arts Inc.

Burnout 3: Takedown © 2004 Electronic Arts Inc.

Burnout Paradise © 2008 Electronic Arts Inc.

Car Hunt © SEGA. All rights reserved.

Chase HQ © TAITO Corp. 1988 All rights reserved.

Club Kart © SEGA. All rights reserved.

Colin McRae Rally © Codemasters. All rights reserved.

Colin McRae Rally 2.0 © Codemasters. All rights reserved.

Colin McRae Rally: DiRT © Codemasters. All rights reserved.

Continental Circus © TAITO Corp. All rights reserved.

Crazy Taxi © SEGA. All rights reserved.

Daytona USA © SEGA. All rights reserved.

Daytona USA 2: Battle on the Edge © SEGA. All rights reserved.

Daytona USA 2001 © SEGA. All rights reserved.

Destruction Derby 2 © Sony Computer Entertainment Inc.

Driver's Eyes © NAMCO BANDAI Games Inc.

F355 Challenge © SEGA, Product under licence of Ferrari S.p.A.

Ferrari Challenge Trofeo Pirelli © System 3. All rights reserved.

Final Lap © NAMCO BANDAI Games Inc.

Final Lap R © NAMCO BANDAI Games Inc.

Formula 1 © Sony Computer Entertainment Inc.

Formula 1 05 © 2005 Sony Computer Entertainment Inc.

Forza Motorsport © Microsoft Corporation.

Forza Motorsport 2 © Microsoft Corporation.

GP World © SEGA. All rights reserved.

Gran Turismo © 1997 Sony Computer Entertainment Inc.

Gran Turismo 2 © 1999 Sony Computer Entertainment Inc.

Gran Turismo 3 A-spec © 2001 Sony Computer Entertainment Inc.

Gran Turismo 4 © 2004 Sony Computer Entertainment Inc.

Gran Turismo 5 Prologue © 2007 Sony Computer Entertainment Inc.

Grand Prix Legends © 1998 Sierra Games. All rights reserved.

GTI Club Rally Côte d'Azur © 1996 Konami Corporation. All rights reserved.

Indianapolis 500: The Simulation © 1989 Electronic Arts Inc.

Initial D Arcade Stage © SEGA and Shuichi Shigeno/Kodansha. All rights reserved. Manufactured and produced by SEGA under licence from Kodansha Ltd.

Initial D Ver. 2 © SEGA and Shuichi Shigeno/Kodansha. All rights reserved. Manufactured and produced by SEGA under licence from Kodansha Ltd.

iRacing © iRacing Motorsport Simulations.

Juiced 2: Hot Import Nights © THQ. All rights reserved.

Live for Speed © Scawen Roberts, Eric Bailey, and Victor van Vlaardingen. All rights reserved.

Metropolis Street Racer © SEGA. All rights reserved.

Monaco GP © SEGA. All rights reserved.

Monaco Grand Prix Racing Simulation 2 © Ubisoft Entertainment.

MotorStorm © 2007 Sony Computer Entertainment Inc.

MX vs ATV Untamed © THQ. All rights reserved.

Night Driver © Atari, Inc. All rights reserved.

Nürburgring 1 & Nürburgring 3 © Dr-Ing Reiner Foerst

OutRun2 © SEGA, Product under licence of Ferrari S.p.A.

OutRun2 SP © SEGA, Product under licence of Ferrari S.p.A.

OutRunners © SEGA. All rights reserved.

Pole Position © NAMCO BANDAI Games Inc.

Porsche Challenge © 1997 Sony Computer Entertainment Inc.

Power Drift © SEGA. All rights reserved.

Project Gotham Racing 4 © Microsoft Corporation.

R4 – Ridge Racer Type 4 © NAMCO BANDAI Games Inc.

Race Driver: GRID © Codemasters.

Racing Jam © 1998 Konami Corporation. All rights reserved.

Rad Mobile © SEGA. All rights reserved.

Rad Racer © 1987 Nintendo.

Rage Racer © NAMCO BANDAI Games Inc.

RalliSport Challenge 2 © Microsoft Corporation.

Rally-X © NAMCO BANDAI Games Inc.

RC Pro-Am II © 1992 Nintendo.

RACE Pro © 2008 Atari, Inc.

rFactor © Image Space Incorporated. All rights reserved.

Richard Burns Rally © SCi Entertainment. All rights reserved.

Ridge Racer © NAMCO BANDAI Games Inc.

San Francisco Rush: Extreme Racing © 1996 Atari, Inc.

Sega GT 2002 © SEGA. All rights reserved.

Sega Rally © SEGA. All rights reserved.

Sega Rally 2 © SEGA. All rights reserved.

Sega Rally Championship © SEGA. All rights reserved.

Speed Race © TAITO Corp. 1974 All rights reserved.

Stunt Race FX © 1994 Nintendo.

Super Mario Kart © 1992 Nintendo.

Super Monaco GP © SEGA. All rights reserved.

Test Drive Unlimited © 2006 Atari, Inc.

The Need for Speed © 1994 Electronic Arts Inc.

Thrill Drive © 1998 Konami Corporation. All rights reserved.

TOCA Touring Car Championship © Codemasters.

TOCA 2 Touring Cars © Codemasters. All rights reserved.

TOCA Race Driver © Codemasters. All rights reserved.

TOCA Race Driver 2 © Codemasters. All rights reserved.

TOCA Race Driver 3 © Codemasters. All rights reserved.

TOCA World Touring Cars © Codemasters. All rights reserved.

TrackMania United © Focus Home Interactive. All rights reserved.

Turbo © SEGA. All rights reserved.

Turbo OutRun © SEGA. All rights reserved.

V-Rally © Atari, Inc.

Virtua Racing © SEGA. All rights reserved.

WEC Le Mans © Konami Corporation. All rights reserved.

Winning Run © NAMCO BANDAI Games Inc.

WRC: Rally Evolved © 2005 Sony Computer Entertainment Inc.